HOUSE OF COMMONS   SESS1

FOREIGN AFFAIRS COMMITTEE

Second Report

EUROPE AFTER MAASTRICHT

VOLUME II

Minutes of Evidence

Ordered by The House of Commons *to be printed*
4 March 1992

LONDON: HMSO

The Foreign Affairs Committee is appointed under SO No 130 to examine the expenditure administration and policy of the Foreign and Commonwealth Office and of associated public bodies.

The Committee consists of 11 members. It has a quorum of three. Unless the House otherwise orders, all Members nominated to the Committee continue to be members of it for the remainder of the Parliament.

The Committee has power:

(a) to send for persons, papers and records, to sit notwithstanding any adjournment of the House, to adjourn from place to place, and to report from time to time;

(b) to appoint specialist advisers either to supply information which is not readily available or to elucidate matters of complexity within the Committee's order of reference;

(c) to communicate to any other such committee its evidence and any other documents relating to matters of common interest; and

(d) to meet concurrently with any such other committee for the purpose of deliberating, taking evidence, or considering draft reports.

The Committee has power to appoint one sub-committee and to report from time to time the minutes of evidence taken before it. The sub-committee has power to send for persons, papers and records, to sit notwithstanding any adjournment of the House, and to adjourn from place to place. It has a quorum of three.

The membership of the Committee since its appointment on 2 December 1987 is as follows:

Rt Hon David Howell, *Guildford* (Chairman)

Mr Dennis Canavan, *Falkirk W*
Mr Nigel Forman, *Carshalton*
 and Wallington (appointed 21.3.90)
Mr David Harris, *St Ives* (appointed 18.3.91)
Rt Hon Michael Jopling, *Westmorland*
 and Lonsdale
Mr Ivan Lawrence, *Burton*
Mr Jim Lester, *Broxtowe*
Mr William Powell, *Corby*
 (appointed 26.7.90; discharged 18.3.91)
Mr Ted Rowlands, *Merthyr Tydfil*
 and Rhymney

Rt Hon Peter Shore, *Bethnal Green*
 and Stepney
Mr Ian Taylor, *Esher*
 (discharged 21.3.90)
Mr Peter Temple-Morris, *Leominster*
 (discharged 26.7.90)
Mr Bowen Wells, *Hertford and Stortford*
Mr Michael Welsh, *Doncaster N*

The cost of printing and publishing this Volume of Evidence is estimated by HMSO at £1,641.

TABLE OF CONTENTS

LIST OF WITNESSES
Session 1991–92

LIST OF MEMORANDA INCLUDED IN
THE MINUTES OF EVIDENCE

Page

Printed in the United Kingdom for HMSO.
Dd.0508268, 5/92, C7, 3382/5B, 5673, 197580.

FOREIGN AFFAIRS COMMITTEE

EUROPE AFTER MAASTRICHT

MINUTES OF EVIDENCE

HOUSE OF COMMONS
SESSION 1991–92

FOREIGN AFFAIRS COMMITTEE

EUROPE AFTER MAASTRICHT

MINUTES OF EVIDENCE

Tuesday 4 February 1992

FOREIGN AND COMMONWEALTH OFFICE

*Rt Hon Douglas Hurd CBE MP, Rt Hon Tristan Garel-Jones MP, Mr Michael Jay
and Mr John Goulden CMG*

Ordered by The House of Commons *to be printed*
4 February 1992

LONDON: HMSO
£7.50 net

MINUTES OF EVIDENCE

TAKEN BEFORE THE FOREIGN AFFAIRS COMMITTEE

TUESDAY 4 FEBRUARY 1992

Members present:

Mr David Howell, in the Chair

Mr Dennis Canavan	Mr Jim Lester
Mr David Harris	Mr Ted Rowlands
Mr Michael Jopling	Mr Peter Shore
Mr Ivan Lawrence	Mr Bowen Wells

Memorandum submitted by The Foreign and Commonwealth Office (EC 204)

EUROPE AFTER MAASTRICHT

INTRODUCTION

1. The Government want to see the Community move forward on the lines set out at the European Council at Maastricht: stronger 3rd more efficient Community institutions to handle business which falls within the Treaty of Rome (respecting the principle of subsidiarity); and effective co-operation in interior and justice matters and on common foreign and security policy (CFSP). To ensure sound economic foundations, the Community will need to maintain a liberal internal market based on free and open competition and to base progress towards economic and monetary union on genuine convergence between national economies. The Community must forge closer relationships with other European States, welcoming as members those countries who apply and are ready for membership both politially and economically. It must give priority to helping governments in Central and Eastern Europe to consolidate political reform. The Government will want to see the development of a European defence identity compatible with NATO, and expressed through the WEU.

2. The Government intend the United Kingdom to play an energetic part in all these matters, notably during its Presidency of the Council in the second half of 1992. We shall work with the Portuguese Presidency to prepare for the new Treaty to come into effect, after ratification by all member states, in early 1993. We shall pay particular attention to the development of structures to ensure effective co-operation on Common Foreign and Security Policy and justice/home affairs. In accordance with the Conclusions of the European Council in Maastricht, we shall work during our Presidency for an early start to accession negotiations for countries which meet the criteria, so that they may join the Community by 1996. We would expect some other countries to join the Community towards the end of the century. We shall also work during our Presidency to complete the single market by the end of 1992.

MAASTRICHT: GENERAL ASSESSMENT

3. The Government welcome the draft Treaty on European Union agreed at the European Council at Maastricht. The draft incorporates a number of United Kingdom proposals. It also reflects the structure for which we argued during the Inter-Governmental Conference, formalising procedures for inter-governmental co-operation outside the Treaty of Rome on justice/home affairs and on common foreign and security policy—with defence questions to be handled in the WEU—as well as introducing changes to the policies and institutions of the European Community itself. These changes include the codification and some extension of Community competence; some extension of Qualified Majority voting; and a definition within the Treaty of subsidiarity. As regards institutional change, there has been an extension of the power of the European Parliament (EP) in the legislative as well as non-legislative area, but the final word on the content of EC legislation remains with the Council. The European Parliament will have a stronger role in monitoring the Commission, and the role of the European Court of Justice will be sensibly strengthened. Overall, the institutional balance of the Community is broadly maintained, but the UK should gain from the strengthening of the rule of law and from greater efficiency and accountability of Community institutions.

4. This Memorandum does not deal with Economic and Monetary Union in any detail.

TREATY OF ROME AMENDMENTS: EC POLICIES

New competences

5. Under the rubric "Community policies" there are new treaty texts in eleven policy areas. In varying degrees, these texts clarify, codify or extend Community competence. In every case there has already been

---

The cost of printing and publishing these Minutes of Evidence is estimated by HMSO at £4,119.

activity by the Community, or the Twelve acting inter-governmentally. While the treaty texts will facilitate new Commission proposals in due course, the texts do not in themselves change UK policy and we shall consider new proposals as they come forward.

6. The main policy areas are:

— *visa lists*: the Twelve are already working inter-governmentally on a common list of countries whose nationals should require a visa to enter member states;

— *education/youth/training*: existing Article 128 provided for Community activity in this area to lay down general principles for implementing a common vocational training policy (by simple majority); some useful activity has taken place (for example COMETT—training for technology; LINGUA—language training; ERASMUS—student mobility); this can now be extended, but the voting requirement is now Qualified Majority and harmonising measures are explicitly excluded;

— *trans-European networks*: under the Structural Funds and Transport articles, the Community was already active in this area—for example the Transport Infrastructure Fund 1990; the new Article provides explicitly for action in the area of transport, telecommunications and energy infrastructures; decisions will be taken by Qualified Majority (as previously for Transport decisions);

— *industry*: the R&D programme, numerous single market measures and EC Treaty competition articles affect industry already. The new text expressly excludes measures which may distort competition; it requires decisions by unanimity;

— *public health*: the new text aims to encourage research, information and education to help prevent disease: building, for example, on the successful awareness campaigns on AIDs and cancer. The text covers health protection, but not health care which remains a matter exclusively for the member states; harmonising measures are explicitly excluded;

— *culture*: EC Culture Ministers have met regularly in recent rears and taken action In a Community or "mixed competence" format. Activities have included development of audio-visual work, cultural training, the broadcasting Directive, and the MEDIA programme. The new text will expand activity but expressly provides that national and regional diversity be respected. Harmonising measures are excluded. Decisions will be taken by unanimity;

— *development*: the Community in co-operation with the member states, has a long history of development policy, such as the Lome Convention, numerous emergency aid actions, and other specific financial arrangements with the third world; all such Community actions have been and will continue to be exercised in parallel with national development policy and do not supplant it; decisions will be taken by Qualified Majority;

— *consumer protection*: measures to establish the Single Market are mainly based on Article 100a, which calls for a high level of consumer protection. The new article complements that provision;

— *economic and social cohesion*: the new articles replace and expand the cohesion provisions in the Single European Act, which established the Structural Funds. There is a new provision for establishing a Cohesion Fund which will provide financial aid for environment and transport projects.

— *research and development*: little change to the existing Treaty;

— *environment*: the new text specifically flags the EC role in solving world-wide problems; decisions are to be taken by Qualified Majority Voting except in certain sensitive areas, where unanimity is retained.

Financial implications

7. Several of these new policy provisions may lead, in time, to Community expenditure programmes. None does so directly without separate Council decisions, although it was agreed that the new Cohesion Fund would be established by the end of 1993. No figures have been discussed for this Fund, and there is no commitment to new resources. The size of the fund will be for discussion in the review of Community finances during 1992.

8. Details of the UK's financial contribution to the European Community budget were set out in the Chancellor's Autumn statement. Even after the Fontainebleau abatement, the UK remains one of the three significant net contributors to the budget, with a contribution for the financial year 92–93 estimated at around £2.5 billion. On the basis of available information, we understand the French net contribution to be of a similar order. Germany remains by far the biggest net contributor, with a net contribution some 2–3 times that of the UK.

9. The agreement on Economic and Monetary Union will form part of the Treaty of Rome. The agreement includes the UK protocol which allows the UK to decide for itself, at the right time, whether or not it wishes to join a move to a single currency. The Treaty also satisfactorily meets the UK's other objectives, particularly that there should be no blurring of responsibility for monetary policy in Stage 2, and that Member States retain primary responsibility for economic policy. The arrangements for Stage 3 are practical and workable. In particular, compliance with clear and quantified convergence conditions is required before any Member State can move to Stage 3.

10. The UK will join fully in Stage 2 of EMU (starting in January 1994). We shall continue to contribute constructively to all relevant decisions within the Council, or the European Monetary Institute. For example, we shall participate In the ECOFIN discussions monitoring convergence of the economies of Member States. There is no question of the Maastricht outcome having put Britain into a second tier.

Social policy

11. The existing articles of the Treaty of Rome remain in force, unamended. In a Protocol signed by all twelve member states, it was agreed that eleven of them (that is not including the UK) might have recourse to the Community institutions where they wanted to take action going beyond the provisions of the Treaty of Rome. Attached to the Protocol is the text of the Agreement which they have chosen to use for this purpose. Such acts would not be part of the Community *acquis*, nor would they be applicable to the UK. The UK would not bear any budgetary burden which resulted from such activity.

12. It is not possible at this stage to forecast how much activity in this field will take place under the existing Treaty of Rome, and how much among the eleven on the basis of the separate agreement. There remains the same scope as previously for activity among all Twelve under the existing Treaty. For example, of the 33 proposals so far tabled under the Social Action Programme, 19 have been agreed. The Government expect in addition to be able to agree a number of the remaining measures. But where the measure cannot be adopted under the Treaty of Rome, the eleven may decide to have recourse to their separate procedures.

Subsidiarity

13. The draft Treaty inserts an Article on subsidiarity for the first time in the Treaty of Rome (Article 3b, with references elsewhere too). The text is designed to prevent unnecessary new Community activity on policies best left to member states; and where the Community does act, to ensure that only the minimum necessary action takes place. The text is ultimately justiciable before the European Court of Justice. This fact alone should act as a deterrent to unnecessary and over-regulatory Commission proposals. It will be open to member states to challenge any Commission proposal, during negotiations, on grounds of subsidiarity, and to challenge in the European Court of Justice any Council or Commission acts which infringe the principle.

TREATY OF ROME AMENDMENTS: INSTITUTIONAL PROVISIONS

European Union

14. The term "European Union" embraces both the Treaty of Rome on the one hand, and the two "pillars" of inter-governmental activity—CFSP and Justice/Home Affairs—on the other. The term itself has its antecedents in the Treaty of Rome ("ever closer union of the peoples"), and more explicitly in the Stuttgart Declaration of 1983 and the Single European Act Preamble ("moved by the will... to transform relations as a whole among their States into a European Union"). The European Union will not have International legal personality. International agreements will continue to be concluded by the Community or by the member states, as appropriate.

Citizenship of the Union

15. The Maastricht treaty introduces to the Treaty of Rome for the first time the concept of citizenship of the Union. Citizenship is enjoyed automatically by nationals of member states. Member states remain responsible for determining who their nationals shall be. Citizens' rights and duties are those already provided by the Treaty of Rome and later legislation (rights of free movement and residence) subject to existing limitations, plus some new rights. Citizens resident in another member state will in due course be able to vote in local and European elections in that state, but not in national elections; and they will have the right to Consular protection in third countries where their government is not represented. They will have the right to petition the European Parliament and to make applications to the EC Ombudsman. No further rights can be granted without unanimous agreement in the Council and ratification in accordance with national procedures. In the United Kingdom, there would have to be legislation to give effect to such new rights before we could ratify.

European Parliament

16. The European Parliament's role has been strengthened in two areas: non-legislative and legislative.

17. The European Parliament has been given a greater role in scrutinising the actions of the Commission, in particular through strengthened arrangements for financial accountability. There are separate but related provisions for strengthening financial control within the Community, with new requirements set for the Commission and the European Court of Auditors. Many of these arrangements flow from UK proposals. The European Parliament now has the right to conduct enquiries into maladministration. It may establish an EC Ombudsman to hear petitions from individual citizens about maladministration in the Community institutions. The European Parliament can already dismiss the Commission in its entirety. It will now have to approve the list of proposed new Commissioners, including the President of the Commission, before the member states finally appoint a new Commission.

18. In the legislative sphere, there have been some limited extensions in the application of existing procedures, including the positive assent procedure and the co-operation procedure. In addition, a new procedure has been introduced, the negative assent procedure (set out in Article 189b). In certain areas of Community legislation, this provides for a third reading by the European Parliament, with conciliation between the Council and European Parliament where the two institutions do not agree on draft legislation. If conciliation fails, the Council decides what the legislation should be, but the European Parliament has the right to reject it, acting by an absolute majority of members within a six weeks' deadline (unless the Council agrees an extension). The European Parliament cannot propose amendments to the legislation at that stage. This procedure applies in several areas of Community activity: the Single Market, rights of establishment and free movement, and many of the new competence texts. For Research and Development and culture, the procedure is combined with a unanimity voting requirement in the Council. Otherwise, it applies to legislation requiring votes by qualified majority.

19. Flow charts are attached illustrating the existing co-operation procedure and the new negative assent procedure. Tables are also attached showing the areas of Community activity where the positive assent procedure and the co-operation procedure are now extended; and showing the areas covered by the new negative assent procedure.

European Court of Justice

20. The role of the Court of Justice has been strengthened, in particular through a provision (Article 171) that the Court may impose a fine on a member state which fails to comply with an earlier Court judgement. This reflects a UK proposal and should ensure that the rule of law is strengthened in the Community. There are also new arrangements (Article 168a) which will allow further extensions of the jurisdiction of the Court of First Instance, hereby lightening the load on the European Court of Justice itself. This too was a UK proposal.

European Commission

21. The role of the European Commission has been little changed by this treaty although, as already noted, scrutiny of its actions by the European Parliament has been strengthened. From 1995 the Commission's term of office will become co-terminous with the European Parliament, and extended from four to five years. For the intervening period (1993 and 1994) the Commission will have a two year term. No changes have been made in the size of the Commission now, but this will be reviewed by the end of 1992: during the Conference there was considerable support for reducing the size of the Commission to one Commissioner per member state.

Council of Ministers

22. The Council remains the main legislative and decision-making body of the Community. Its role and procedures have not been directly changed. The main changes which will have some impact on working methods of the Council of Ministers are:

— greater use of Qualified Majority Voting;

— the new negative assent procedure with the European Parliament, including a Conciliation Committee between the Council and the Parliament where necessary;

— the need to take account of subsidiarity when taking decisions;

— new functions (though under different procedures from those applying in the EC Treaties) in the inter-governmental "pillars" of the Union Treaty, that is Common Foreign and Security Policy (which will closely resemble existing procedures for handling Political Co-operation) and justice/home affairs.

Economic and Social Committee (ESC)

23. The draft Treaty makes only minor amendments to the present arrangements, to codify existing practice. But the ESC will have greater control over its own budget, staffing and procedures.

Committee of the Regions

24. A new Regional Committee, with a consultative role, will be established. No decisions have been taken about how the 24 UK seats should be allocated as between the UK regions, nor about how individual candidates will be chosen. The Government ill consult in the course of 1992 before these arrangements are settled.

Role of National Parliaments

25. Attached to the treaty are two important declarations. The first, a UK proposal, encourages national parliaments to co-ordinate their activity more closely with the European Parliament, and to provide time for scrutiny of Commission proposals, as happens at Westminster. The second, a French proposal, is for a Conference of Parliaments consisting of representatives of the European Parliament and of national parliaments. The declaration deliberately avoids going into further details, to avoid prejudicing the arrangements which Parliaments will want for such a conference. The House itself will no doubt wish to make its own views and suggestions known.

National Courts

26. The draft Treaty will not alter application of directly effective Community law by national Courts. The treaty has no direct consequence for national courts except insofar as it extends the range of Community policies which are justiciable before the European Court of Justice, to which national courts will continue to refer cases as necessary, in accordance with Article 177. The European Court of Justice will not have jurisdiction over CFSP or Justice/Home Affairs (unless, in the latter case, Member States choose to give it jurisdiction to interpret specific conventions which they agree).

1996 Review Conference

27. The Final Provisions provide for a Review Conference in 1996. An inter-governmental conference can be called by a simple majority of member states. The draft treaty specifies five areas where there is to be a review: Article 3s (energy, civil protection and tourism); Article 189 (hierarchy of categories of legislative act) legislative powers of the European Parliament (scope of the 189b procedure); CFSP and defence: and CFSP more generally.

28. In such a conference, we can expect a wide range of proposals to be made, including proposals put forward by member states in this Inter-Governmental Conference, but not included in the draft Treaty.

JUSTICE AND HOME AFFAIRS

29. These provisions form a self-contained pillar within the European Union. They provide a sound basis for future inter-governmental co-operation. It is right that these sensitive subjects should remain essentially outside Community competence. The European Court of Justice has no jurisdiction, unless individual conventions specifically so provide. Provision is made for the transfer of some of these policy issues into Community competence if that is so decided: but by a double decision—unanimity in the Council, and ratification by Member States, only the common visa list and common visa format fall within Community competence immediately.

30. The Government intend to take a lead in ensuring that this area of co-operation is taken forward promptly and effectively. Some of the issues are ones where the UK has traditionally taken a lead; for example the United Kingdom has chaired the Working Group on the European Drugs Intelligence Unit, which is to become the first core element of Europol. On immigration and asylum, the European Council separately approved an extensive work programme proposed by immigration Ministers.

COMMON FOREIGN AND SECURITY POLICY

31. The Government welcome the provisions for Common Foreign and Security Policy agreed at Maastricht, which will provide the basis for a stronger European Foreign and Security Policy. These provisions continue the developments which have been taking place with the Government's encouragement in European Political Co-operation. Practical development of EPC (as provided for in the Single European Act) has been particularly rapid in the last two years in response to events in the Soviet Union, Eastern Europe (especially Yugoslavia), and the Middle East.

Differences between EPC and CFSP

32. The main differences between Common Foreign and Security Policy and European Political Co-operation will be:

— strengthened commitment to common positions;

— coverage of security issues, and provision for the eventual framing of a common defence policy, which might in time lead to a common defence. All of this is to be compatible with NATO;

— strengthening of the co-operation provided for in the Single European Act, including development of the concept of joint action and a procedure for defining which issues are to be subject to Joint action.

33. Important continuities with European Political Co-operation will be:

— the process will remain Intergovernmental, that is not part of the Community and not subject to European Court of Justice jurisdiction;

— all significant decisions will continue to be taken by consensus. There is provision for the Council to decide that certain decisions under joint action may be taken by a qualified majority: but any decision to do this is subject to unanimity, as is the initial decision to make any issue subject to joint action. Issues with defence implications are not subject to joint action, and therefore cannot be subject to qualified majority voting;

— the Presidency, rather than the Commission, will represent the Union on common foreign and security policy issues.

New Commitments/effects on policy

34. European political co-operation already covers all foreign policy issues: the main area for new commitments is therefore security policy. Whereas European Political Co-operation covered only the political and economic aspects of security, the Common Foreign and Security Policy will be capable of including all aspects, though the security policies of the Union must be "compatible with the common security and defence policy established" in NATO. The Treaty differentiates between security and defence policy. It confirms that the WEU is clearly responsible tor defence questions. Issues with defence implications are not subject to joint action. A common defence policy is kept as a long term prospect, reflecting the reference in the Anglo-Italian declaration to a "longer term perspective of a common defence policy".

35. The draft Treaty does not deal with the content of policies, which will continue, as under EPC, to be developed by negotiation and consultation among the Twelve—a process in which the UK has always taken a leading role. Important UK interests in particular areas of the world or on particular issues are safeguarded by the fact that all decisions will be taken by unanimity, except in those limited cases where member states agree by unanimity to the use of decisions by qualified majority on a subject of joint action. Even in these cases Articles C6 and C7 contain important clauses providing for member states to "take the necessary measures as a matter of urgency" in cases of "imperative need arising from changes in the situation", and to refer "any major difficulties in implementing a joint action to the Council, which shall discuss them and seek appropriate solutions".

36. The United Kingdom's ability to fulfil its responsibilities as a permanent member of the UN Security Council effectively is safeguarded by Article E4, which provides that "member states which are permanent members of the Security Council will, in the execution of their functions, ensure the defence of the positions and the interests of the Union, without prejudice to their responsibilities under the provisions of the United Nations Charter".

37. A declaration annexed to the Treaty at UK insistence safeguards our right and that of other member states with dependencies to represent their interests.

Procedures

38. Article H lays down the outline of CFSP procedures. The European Council will define principles and general guidelines; the Council will take the necessary decisions for defining and implementing Common Foreign and Security Policy and ensure the unity, consistency and effectiveness of action. Any member state or the Commission may refer questions or make proposals to the Council.

39. The detailed procedures for taking decisions under the Common Foreign and Security Policy and a list of "areas open to joint action vis-a-vis particular countries or groups of countries" will be negotiated during the course of 1992. The Government will work for arrangements which build on the existing flexible and effective procedures for European Political Co-operation, including a strengthening of the existing European Political Co-operation Secretariat. The continuing role of the existing Political Committee (Political Directors of Ministries of Foreign Affairs of the Twelve) is provided for in Article H5.

Enforcement of Common Foreign and Security Policy obligations

40. As noted above, the Common Foreign and Security Policy provisions are not subject to the jurisdiction of the European Court of Justice. The CFSP obligations take effect in international, not EC, law, so any breach could in principle be the subject of action before the International Court of Justice at the Hague. As now, enforcement will be achieved primarily through political pressure from other member states.

Planned future role for WEU

41. At the Maastricht European Council, in parallel with agreeing the Treaty article on defence, WEU Foreign Ministers issued Declarations on the WEU's future links with the Union and the Alliance, and enlargement of the WEU. In 1992 the WEU's work will focus on turning these Declarations into practical action. It was agreed that the role of the WEU would be developed simultaneously as the means to strengthen the European pillar within NATO, and as the defence component of the European Union. The WEU's military operational role will be developed in a manner compatible with the Atlantic Alliance. Its primary responsibilities are therefore likely to be outside NATO competences, that is, out of area. To develop its operational role, and the necessary close liaison with NATO and with the relevant institutions of European Union, the WEU Council and Secretariat will move to Brussels. The WEU is also likely to develop its liaison relationship with the countries of central and eastern Europe.

Future Political and Military development of NATO

42. The NATO Summit in Rome (7–8 November) marked the end of another phase in NATO's transformation, with the publication of the New Strategic Concept and the Rome Declaration on Peace and Co-operation. Heads of State and Government agreed to establish a North Atlantic Co-operation Council, including the former Warsaw Pact countries and the Baltic States, as a forum for discussions of European security. The North Atlantic Co-operation Council met for the first time on 20 December in Brussels, and will meet again at Ministerial level in Oslo in June.

43. The Rome Declaration also set out the views of the Allies on the relationship between NATO and a future European security and defence identity. It notes that the development of such an identity, compatible with our common defence policy in the Alliance, would strengthen the European pillar of the Alliance. It stressed the need for transparency and complementarity between the Alliance and the European security and defence identity. The relationship between NATO and the WEU will also develop further, as a result of the Declaration on the WEU's links with the Union and Alliance issued at Maastricht on 10 December. NATO Foreign Ministers, meeting in Brussels on 19 December, welcomed the decisions taken in Maastricht by the Twelve and the WEU.

44. NATO's new strategy is an "all-weather" one, designed to respond to unpredictable risks from whatever quarter, with flexible and mobile military forces deployed accordingly. It recognises that the threat of attack from the former Soviet Union has effectively disappeared. It lays much greater emphasis on co-operation. The North Atlantic Co-operation Council and meetings between other NATO bodies and the central and eastern Europeans will give substance to this. Co-operation will concentrate on areas in which NATO has particular expertise to offer, such as defence management, or civil-military relations. Following agreement at the North Atlantic Council Foreign Ministers' meeting on 19 December, NATO will contribute more actively to CSCE meetings where its expertise is relevant. There may also be a role for NATO to play in the provision of humanitarian assistance to the former Soviet Union, perhaps in terms of logistic support or co-ordination.

Role of the Commission in Common Foreign and Security Policy

45. The Commission's role remains as under European Political Co-operation: it is "fully associated" with Common Foreign and Security Policy, as it is with European Political Co-operation. This reflects the reality that Common Foreign and Security Policy, like European Political Co-operation, will often be closely connected with the Community's external relations. The Commission's functions are not as extensive as under the EC Treaties, for example it can submit proposals, but does not have the exclusive right of initiative nor the "watchdog" role on implementation.

Joint diplomacy/joint missions

46. The draft Treaty provides for missions in third countries and at international conferences to co-operate to ensure that common positions and common measures are complied with and implemented, and to contribute to the implementation of the provisions of the citizenship chapter dealing with Consular protection. There is no reference to joint missions, but we would expect further development of the existing practical co-operation among missions in third countries.

NEGATIVE ASSENT PROCEDURE (ARTICLE 189B)

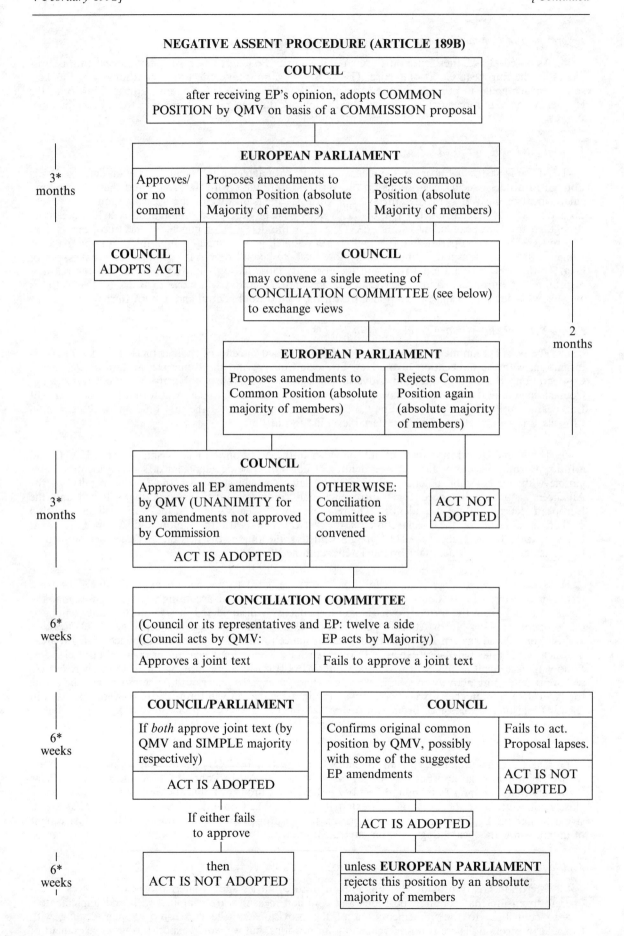

* These periods may be extended by one month or two weeks

EXISTING COOPERATION PROCEDURE

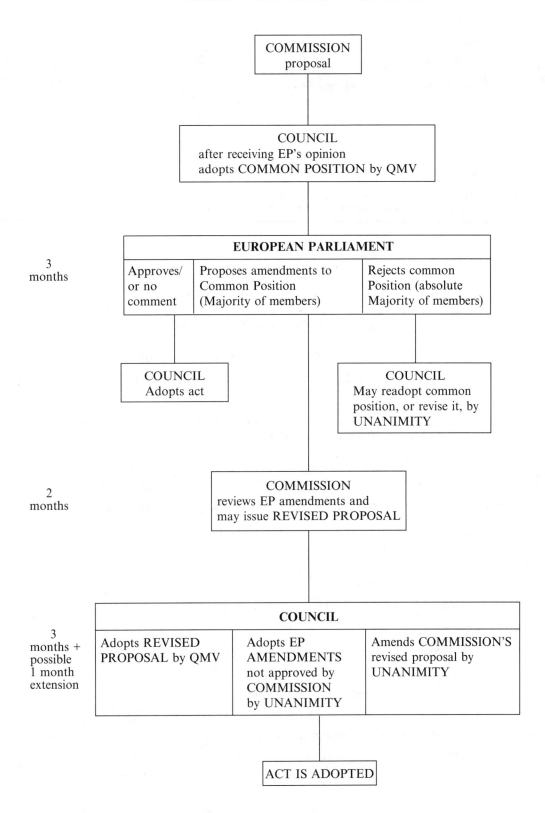

[Commission proposal LAPSES
if COUNCIL fails to act]

AREAS WHERE NEGATIVE ASSENT PROCEDURE (ARTICLE 189B) APPLIES

Article 49:	Free movement of workers
Article 54(2):	Right of establishment
Article 56(2)d:	Treatment of foreign nationals
Article 57(1):	Mutal recognition of qualifications
Article 57(2):	Right of establishment
Article 100a:	Single Market legislation
Article A (p 39):	Education Incentive measures
Article 130I:	R and D framework programmes (with *unanimity*)
Article 130S(3):	Environment multiannual action programmes
Title XIII:	Trans-European Networks
Title XV:	Public Health
Title XVI:	Culture (with *unanimity*)
Title XVIII:	Consumer Protection

EXTENSION OF (POSITIVE) ASSENT PROCEDURE (AVIS CONFORME) IN TREATY ON UNION

Article B:	citizenship—provisions to facilitate rights of free movement and residence
Article 130D:	organisation of structural funds and establishment of Cohesion Fund
Article 138:	uniform EP electoral procedure
Article 228:	for conclusion of certain additional international agreements (procedure already applies to association agreements under Article 238)
Article 106(5):	Amendments to ESCB Statutes
Article 108(4):	Prudential supervision

EXTENSION OF CO-OPERATION PROCEDURE IN TREATY ON UNION

Article 75:	Transport
Article 125:	Social Fund
Article B:	Training
Title XIII:	Trans-European Networks (measures other than guidelines)
Article 130s:	Environment (except action programmes)
Article C:	Development
Article 103(5):	Rules for multilateral surveillance
Article 104AA:	No privileged access to financial institutions
Article 104A(2):	Defining "no bail-out" rule
Article 108(3):	Regulations governing issue of coins

[N.B. Co-operation procedure has been *deleted* from the research and development specific programmes.]

Examination of witnesses

RT HON DOUGLAS HURD CBE, a Member of the House, Secretary of State for Foreign and Commonwealth Affairs, RT HON TRISTAN GAREL-JONES, a Member of the House, Minister of State for Foreign and Commonwealth Affairs, MR MICHAEL JAY, Assistant Under Secretary of State, European Community, and MR JOHN GOULDEN CMG, Assistant Under Secretary of State, Arms Control, Foreign and Commonwealth Office, were examined.

Chairman

1. Foreign Secretary, Minister, Mr Jay and Mr Goulden, welcome back to this Committee, and that word applies in all four cases because you are extremely welcome and, indeed, familiar with this Committee from many past visits. Thank you very much for sparing us time again today to share your thoughts this time on the political, constitutional, foreign policy and security implications of the Maastricht agreement now about to appear as a Treaty in due course for ratification before the parliaments of the Member States. The Committee has just returned from brief visits to Paris and Brussels as part of this inquiry, and will shortly be visiting Bonn, and we seek to produce a short report in the next few weeks. These are early days, and I think the Committee begins by recognising, Foreign Secretary, that not everything can be seen with crystal clarity in such a short space of time after the Maastricht agreement was signed. Nevertheless, we would value some thoughts on how you see the picture unfolding, and how you see the attitudes of our Community colleagues to the Maastricht agreement. Could I therefore begin with a question about your impressions about what has been agreed in principle at Maastricht, and how those principles might affect the shape of what we call the European Community. We know that there was a good deal of talk about temples and pillars beforehand, and we know that on paper there has been agreed that not only should the Community be further developed, with new competencies for the Commission, but also that new pillars should be set up outside the traditional framework of the Rome Treaty, and that all these together comprise what we would now call the European Union. We live now in a Union as well as in a European Community. Is that, Foreign Secretary, an accurate picture of what has occurred, or are we really going to see these pillars all dissolve into the familiar Community and the same pattern as before Maastricht being developed on an even more extensive scale?

(Mr Hurd) No, we clearly are going to see the pillars take shape as pillars, exactly as you described in the first part of what you said. The distinction between being in and outside the Treaty of Rome, the distinctions, are not paper distinctions they are of crucial importance. I could mention perhaps two: the absence of jurisdiction by the court, and the absence of the Commission's sole right of initiative, in these very important areas of foreign policy, foreign and security policy and interior justice. Those are the distinguishing characteristics which separate what we will do together under the Maastricht Treaty if it is ratified—in

those areas from what we will do within the former Treaty of Rome in the Community.

2. Is it correct to say that the areas falling within the Community and the competence of the Commission are the areas which will be more supranational, dare I say federal in character, and the areas falling under the Council of Ministers. and its Secretariats, including the common foreign and security policy, justice and home affairs policy and so on, will be more governmental in flavour, that is to say deriving their legitimacy direct and primarily from this House of Commons and from the nation states?

(Mr Hurd) That is right. Those of us who believe, as this Government does, that this distinction you have made is an important one must now bestir ourselves the make the inter-governmental aspect of the Union's work effective, because the argument is not over, of course; the argument will be resumed in 1996 and resumed in the light of experience between now and then. It is important from our point of view that the CFSP and, indeed, the interior/justice working together should be successful.

3. Is there not a danger that since a good proportion of foreign policy issues are, in fact, economic policy issues, and therefore within the remit of the Commission and its External Affairs Commissioner, and given that the Commission itself sits, as it were, as a 13th Minister on the European Council, that gradually all these things will fall into the ambit of the Commission and the Community?

(Mr Hurd) But we have a great deal of experience in this. This is what happens now. We had yesterday rather detailed discussions, both on how we should handle the former Soviet Union and Yugoslavia. In both of those the Commission was present, but at the lunchtime discussion on Yugoslavia, for example, the Commission was present, as you say, as a 13th member without a monopoly of initiative because, as you say, the political and economic get mixed up. It is perfectly sensible, and I do not see any reason, indeed I think it unlikely, that in that area the Commission will gain in importance beyond what it has now. It is a system which already operates.

Mr Lester

4. Is it not true, Foreign Secretary, that it may not have gained any greater competence but it will, under these arrangements, have a great deal more to do, for instance on immigration and asylum, which are not part of the competence of the Commission and not part of the Treaty of Rome;

[**Mr Lester** *Contd*]

they have been asked to produce a document and, assuming the Council of Ministers arrive at a common policy, it would I imagine perhaps confirm that the Commission will be required to carry it out?

(*Mr Hurd*) I think that would remain to be decided. I do not think that could be taken for granted. One of the decisions we took yesterday was that the personal representatives of the Ministers, who played rather a large part in the Maastricht negotiation, should continue in being in order to work out, for example, the nature of the Secretariat and how the foreign policy side of the political committee could interact and how the new Secretariat, separate from the Commission, should function. That is clearly going to be very important in keeping the pillars distinct from the Community.

Mr Wells

5. Does not the Commission provide the civil service and the research and the organisation for the meetings of the pillars? Is the Secretariat to the Foreign Affairs Committee, which was established under the Single European Act, entirely separate from the Commission? Do you envisage a similar Secretariat being established for the internal and justice affairs pillar? How will those civil servants be selected and changed?

(*Mr Hurd*) They will certainly be separate. The Commission will not provide the Secretariat for the CFSP or for the interior justice. There is, of course, already a Council Secretariat and Mr Ersboell, who may well be interviewed on the matter. That is already separate from the Commission. One of the tasks of the personal representatives will be to decide the answer to your second question, how the Secretariat will be composed. At the moment civil servants are seconded from five countries including those of the troika but that may not be a satisfactory answer for the future between now and 1996, but that is the sort of question which remains to be resolved. Certainly there is no question of the Commission becoming the civil service or the executive. There will have to be co-operation because, as you said, Mr Chairman, the political and economic sides interact but that has not proved too difficult in the past, I do not think it will prove too difficult in the future.

(*Mr Jay*) We do envisage that the European Political Co-operation—EPC—Secretariat, which is now separate from the Council Secretariat, will be folded into the Council Secretariat but we would envisage that the staff who form part of it would continue to be in good part seconded from national administrations, as they are now, and thereby you would ensure the coherence necessary between common foreign and security policy and other aspects of policy through the Council Secretariat but maintaining a certain specificity of the former EPC Secretariat which would reflect the particular character of common foreign and security policy.

6. Can I ask you about the Council of Europe meetings of Heads of State? The Commission's responsibility is, is it not, to service that very, very important—

(*Mr Hurd*) The European Council?

7. Yes, I am sorry, I get confused—the European Council and the meetings of Heads of Governments. That has to have a secretariat and that at the moment is provided by the Commission, is it not?

(*Mr Hurd*) No.

8. How is that provided?

(*Mr Hurd*) By the Council Secretariat under Mr Ersboell.

Mr Rowlands

9. Foreign Secretary, we had one detailed submission by one European guru.[1] May I just bring his conclusions to your attention? He said, first of all, on changes to Article 151, that there would be changes in the Secretariat after the Maastricht Council and "decision-making in every sphere of policy" will, in other words, be centralised in Brussels institutions, not as now dispersed physically to The Hague or wherever the president of the day might be. These changes will, in fact, lead to an enhanced Commission role which is the thirteenth highly privileged Member of the Council. He finally concludes, "Contrary to a widespread belief, Maastricht has pronounced the deathknell on 'intergovernmentalism' as preached by the British and currently practised in European Political Co-operation." I do not agree with it and I am sure you will not. Is there any danger that such a prophecy may come true—the merging of bureaucracies and secretariats, the drafting committees becoming almost the same people and our pillars, if they do not actually crumble, becoming merged, or whatever pillars do when they disappear?

(*Mr Hurd*) I read Mr Ludlow's analysis. It seemed to me a wistful piece.

10. Just wistful?

(*Mr Hurd*) That is what he would have liked to happen if the meeting on 30 September had gone the other way and Maastricht had been negotiated on the basis of the Dutch text present on that day rather than the Luxembourg text which had the pillars in it. Mr Ludlow, and many others like him, will no doubt continue to write, speak and work according to their different vocations for the end result which he prophesies and, of course, one cannot prevent that. It is part of the argument, and was part of the argument in 1960 I do not doubt. But it is not part of the Maastricht answer. Anyone who has listened in the past to the President of the European Commission and the President of the European Parliament, who share

---

[1] See evidence from Mr Peter Ludlow taken during the Committee's enquiry into Central Europe, HC21–vii for the current session.

[**Mr Rowlands** *Contd*]

Mr Ludlow's ambitions, will realise they are very far from sharing his analysis of what actually happened.

11. There is no danger of a creeping control of the kind—I am not saying anything as dramatic as a deathknell to an intergovernmental system—that would arise with the growth of a Secretariat that started to embrace both pillars or started to service both pillars?

(Mr Hurd) We have been aware of—and have dealt with the Secretariat on the idea which was obviously prevalent, that the Commission was actually going to feel its way to controlling the servicing of the pillars. That is not so. I think the answer will depend on the results and that is why I did say that I believe it is very important that the CFSP—and indeed the jurisdiction it exercises—should be successful so that they are not vulnerable to the accusation in four or five years' time, "Oh, we had better centralise that lot because it is not working well under the Maastricht arrangements". What is certain is that the Maastricht arrangement is as you read it and in these important areas of policy the Commission does not have the monopoly initiative and the ECJ does not have jurisdiction.

Mr Lawrence

12. Foreign Secretary, you always give that air of totally irresistible reassurance.

(Mr Hurd) You always try to upset it, Mr Lawrence.

13. Not at all. I am always astonished by the success that you achieve and obviously that is why John Major made you Foreign Secretary. But the fact of the matter is that we have just come back from a very short tour; we could not see everyone, but the impression some of us got was that this bureaucracy is very deeply embedded and knows exactly where it is going and what it wants. The Commission has shown itself to be exceedingly greedy in the past for power, for good. M Delors has led the way, a number of our European colleagues are federalist by nature and by inclination; it could be said that immigration policy and foreign policy are some things which are not best left to the nation states because they go their own way, they do not all pull in the same direction; if Europe is going to maintain itself as one of the greatest, if not the greatest, powers in the world, then it actually has got to pull together. Are you saying with all those forces taken together we, little Britain, will be able to resist them if, as they say, "push comes to shove" and choices have to be made. Some of us doubt whether we have got the strength to stop that kind of a juggernaut going forward.

(Mr Hurd) That point of view was powerfully expressed, particularly by the Brussels press corps before the Maastricht result. Indeed, I was told some of the Brussels press corps did not believe their correspondents with London told them what actually happened because it was so different from

what they predicted. What they predicted is what you predicted for the next round. We shall see. It is not, of course, a matter of Britain fighting for one intellectual idea and eleven fighting for the other. That is not the position at all. Look at the Danish, Dutch, Italian and Irish positions: you find all kinds of variations and nuances. The German position shows a strong struggle for subsidiarity. It is not, as is often represented, a matter of that but I do come back to that point: the next round, if I may put it that way, will depend on experience in the next few years. The next round will almost certainly not comprise 12 Members, the next round will comprise more than 12 Members and what will be one of the crucial factors when this argument is rejoined is what the experience and impressions of the enlargement are. Enlargement will be a much bigger subject and you can use that enlargement in theory to advocate a more centralised approach or, in my view, a more decentralised approach. Looking ahead—which is perhaps foolish—to the arguments that you invited me to look at, the argument in 1995 or whenever it is, I think the consequences of enlargement will be crucial.

14. We place enlargement very high in order of priorities but a number of other countries do not appear to do so; they appear to be pushing it further and further away.

(Mr Hurd) I do not think so, Mr Lawrence. I think again that would have been true a year or so ago: if you look at the pronouncements of the German Ministers, if you look at the pronouncements of M Delors, whereas a short time ago I would say they were not clearly reconciled to enlargement, now they are.

Mr Harris

15. Foreign Secretary, when we were in Paris, for example, the French Minister for European Affairs said she was very pleased with the outcome of Maastricht; give or take one or two small items, she left us with the impression that France had achieved its ambitions. No doubt in Germany next week we shall hear a similar tale and the Germans will say, yes, they are pleased with the outcome and they achieved their basic objectives. Our own Government, of course—you in particular—have said it is a great triumph for the British point of view. All those countries cannot be right. Where does the truth lie? I suppose only time will tell on this, but again, to reinforce a point made by Mr Lawrence, whichever institution we visited in Brussels last week, they all felt that basically they were the gainers. Now, all that must add up to a big increase in European powers at the expense, I would suggest, of the national states.

(Mr Hurd) You still have to judge. I think you are right in saying it is going to be best to judge in the light of experience. Maastricht was, of course, a compromise. The Prime Minister made clear to the House in advance that the only agreement on offer would be a compromise, but it was a compromise which, as I tried to show, safeguarded our

[**Mr Harris** Contd]

main objectives. The French are not, of course, federalists by instinct. We all know what we mean by "federalism" and others may dispute it, but they are not, of course they are not although they are sometimes quite skilled at how they describe their position. I simply rest on what has emerged, on the decision of September 30 to proceed on one basis, a non-federalist basis rather than federalist basis, and on what has actually emerged in the way in which these hugely important areas of policy are going to be discussed and decided inter-governmentally and, therefore, without any significant loss of power to the nation state or the national parliament. I say "significant" because you will be able to pick up detailed points which will show elements of compromise. I accept that, but the basic truth and fact remains as I think I have described it, and it explains the disappointment which was immediately felt by some of those who shared Mr Ludlow's views.

Mr Shore

16. Of course there is a substantial compromise embodied in the Maastricht Treaty, but are we not deceiving ourselves if we do not recognise the chasm in objectives that separates the United Kingdom from its partners in the European Community? Can the Foreign Secretary recall any other Member State who was anxious or indeed insistent upon the deletion of the references to a federal vocation at the beginning and the end of the draft treaties other than the United Kingdom?

(Mr Hurd) No, because there is no other nation state where this particular philosophical argument was so fervent, no other Member State where actual single words, adjectives were examined with such care; but I must remind you on September 30 a majority (not a minority) voted for the pillared structure, some because they believed in it as a matter of principle and others because they saw that it was on only that basis that there was going to be agreement. That was the crucial decision, and the rest has flowed from that.

17. My point is not necessarily that a compromise has not been reached. My point, and it is a very serious one, was there is a fundamental difference of intent. There is no point in arguing a matter of definition on the use of the word, there is a will to federalism, the will to create a federal-type state in Western Europe on the continent of Europe; a very strong will which virtually every other Government leader, other than the United Kingdom, has publicly subscribed to. I think it is foolish for us to pretend that this is not so, because we shall get some very nasty surprises in the future, and we shall not be either psychologically or practically prepared for the next major assault which will take place in 1996.

(Mr Hurd) I would question that. I would say it is a much more open argument than that, and that we, because of the nature of the public debate here, were quite rightly, in my view, compelled or volunteered to give a much more precise definition than other leaders had to give. That is clearly true.

I certainly would not accept, and I think it flies in the face of the evidence, that there is an 11:1 line-up with 11 countries solid in favour of what you call a "federal solution", by which you actually mean, I think, a heavily centralised solution, and us against. Look at the German insistence on the subsidiarity clause, for example. Look at the French insistence on the UN Security Council seat. There are all kinds of variations here. They will be accentuated by enlargement and by what happens in the Community between now and then. I would not accept your argument.

Chairman: Let us look a little more closely at that.

Mr Shore

18. Having made out that difference, can the Foreign Secretary help us by illustrating, as it were, the differences between the trunk of the tree on the one hand and the pillars on the other. Taking a practical example, the recent Association of Treaties, with Poland, Hungary and Czechoslovakia, were those treaties negotiated within the Council of Ministers, or were they treaties referred to the Political Co-operation Council?

(Mr Hurd) No, they were association agreements on Community business. They were negotiated by the Commission on the basis of mandates approved by the Council of Ministers. That, of course, has nothing to do with the Maastricht negotiations. That is the existing system.

19. This I think really helps to make the point, does it not, which was put to you earlier on, that in fact 75 per cent of the external foreign policy is in fact commercial policy and trade policy during times of peace. If, in fact, already the right to make trade treaties, the right to make aid treaties as well has already been, as it were, taken over by the Commission, and the Council under previous acts, then quite clearly the residue for foreign policy as such is in fact going to be the smaller part of external policy. The fact that the Commission has now as it were, accorded to itself the right of co-initiative on the Political Council has surely meant an extension of the powers of the Commission over external policy?

(Mr Hurd) Again, I would dissent from that analysis. Of course it is true, as I have said, but it was not the Commission which set the policy for the negotiations with Poland, Hungary and Czechoslovakia, it was the Council which approved a mandate, and Vice President Andriessen of the Commission then went away and negotiated. He brought back the results, as Mr Shore will remember. Some of the more protectionist members of the Community objected to the relative liberality and the trade access arrangements which the Commissioner negotiated, so it came back to the Council. That is the existing system. If you look at Yugoslavia the commercial and economic aspect of that is minor. If you look at the former Soviet Union, of course there is an aspect, particularly now with humanitarian aid,

[**Mr Shore** *Contd*]

but if you look at the question of recognition and how all that is to be handled that is CFSP, that is political. I would not accept that. In this foreign policy field, with which I am reasonably familiar now, we have a system which is bedded down; the Commissioner is there. The days when that was all argued about and the foreign policy meetings, the EPC meetings went about from capital to capital and so on, the days when there was a great controversy about that are really over. The Commission is there; the Commission does not have a monopoly on making proposals, but it is there, as you said, virtually as a 13th member. That actually works quite smoothly and that existing situation is, in effect, what will happen after Maastricht is ratified, if it is ratified, with a strengthened secretariat separate from the Commission and with a number of other changes you may want to come on to in detail, although I think we have discussed them before. The basic *modus operandi* will be one to which we are accustomed.

Chairman

20. I think we would like to move on in a moment to some of these more detailed questions, including how bedded-down it is all going to stay once enlargement comes. But to re-cap this section, Foreign Secretary, looking at post-Maastricht is it the continued drift of federalism, as I think some people—perhaps Mr Shore on this Committee and others—fear, or is it a European Union beginning to develop a new and, for us, more congenial direction?

(Mr Hurd) As you rightly said, Mr Chairman, there has been some extension of Community competence, extension of majority voting, extension of the powers of the European Parliament—all that is certainly true—but there has also been for the first time embodied in the Treaty of Union the concept of "intergovernmental" work in two huge areas of policy. It is because of that that we can legitimately say that the intellectual objectives we took into the negotiations have been established in the result. I cannot say the argument is over, I would not dream of saying that, but the outcome of this particular negotiation is a satisfactory one.

Mr Lawrence

21. Would you say our Community partners are less federalist than they were before or are just, as it were, keeping quiet on federation so as not to frighten the nationalist horses?

(Mr Hurd) They vary very much is the answer to that. One can see changes—but they are mostly small changes—in the attitudes on particular subjects. The attitudes vary a good deal.

Mr Rowlands

22. In one sense my question follows on from what we have just been talking about, Foreign Secretary. One thing that strikes me is that the outcome of Maastricht was a quite detailed process of progress and time-tabling towards monetary union. I know it is subject to convergence and the

British opt-out provision. Nevertheless, very striking detailed stages were established to reach a goal for a single currency with timetables etc. No such process or timetable was established for political union of the kind which the Germans particularly wanted. They see—and indeed the statements in the Bundesbank have made this clear—that there has to be almost a parallel process towards political union to accompany any agreement on monetary union or single currency. Do you think that, given this clearly defined monetary union and single currency process, in fact sooner or later the political union side of it, which was resisted and is not as well defined at Maastricht, will be pushed forward and pulled forward to keep pace with monetary union and the single currency?

(Mr Hurd) I do not myself think so because I do not believe that is the way Europe is going to go—and I think that is partly because of enlargement, partly that when we next come to discuss these matters there will be, I would guess, an Austrian, a Swede, a Finn, maybe a Swiss and Norwegian round the table alongside those already there, and partly because I just do not believe that it would be a sensible way to go for Europe to try and centralise its political institutions. I am sure it should be the aim of the British Government—certainly a Conservative Government—to decentralise, to diffuse power, to put as much weight as we can on the doctrine of subsidiarity, for example. So I think the attempt you describe would be made, Mr Rowlands—that is perfectly right—but I do not think its success is inevitable or, indeed, likely.

23. Could you see a real, significant, rapid progress to a centralised bank, monetary union and a single currency, but nothing like the equivalent in political terms?

(Mr Hurd) Yes, I think you could.

24. You have said twice now—in answer to my question a minute ago you repeated it—that enlargement would have a decided influence on the shape and character of Community institutions. Could you tell us what particular differences enlargement is going to make if you add the Visegrad countries—Poland, Hungary and Czechoslovakia? Do you think Maastricht in a sense represented the high point of centralisation in institutional terms? With future enlargement are you going to have to devise a rather different kind of arrangement, both intergovernmentally and institutionally within the Community, to meet a Community of 14 or 20 members?

(Mr Hurd) Personally I think that what you have just said is probably right, but I could not be certain. I think it would be very foolish for me to try and forecast now what the consequences of enlargement will be. We can begin to guess who the first new entrants will be, but when we come to the new democracies of Central and Eastern Europe, it is very difficult to put a timetable on that. We certainly hope they will be in the second half of this decade. I think it is not very easy to

[Mr Rowlands Contd]

imagine them as full members when one begins again before 1996. They might be. That uncertainty makes it very difficult to be at all precise.

25. To illustrate the point you are making, if we envisage a Community not only of Sweden and the EFTA countries—let us add Poland, Hungary and Czechoslovakia to the list of members—what are the institutions that emerge from Maastricht that would be fundamentally affected and could be potentially altered by an enlargement of that kind?

(Mr Hurd) I personally think it is difficult to imagine a Community of—I am not sure how many you have added up to—18 having a centralised structure going beyond, or at any rate going far beyond, what we have now. I think it would become top-heavy and unmanageable. That would be my personal view but it is very hard to predict because so much depends on the attitudes with which the new members join and the attitudes which their arrival creates among existing Members. I cannot be sure of that, it is several years away.

Chairman: I think we would like to come back later to this crucial issue on enlargement. As you indicated, Foreign Secretary, we could be talking about a change in the fundamental nature of the Community as we have known it in its first decades of existence. Perhaps we could return to that. In the meantime, could we look first of all at another area where we have set up a pattern of variation from the mainstream of agreement, that is in social policy?

Mr Jopling

26. Foreign Secretary, given the fact that 11 Member States are going to proceed on their own and may be joined by some EFTA states as well, I wonder if first of all you could tell us how you see progress in dealing with the legal problems that arise from that situation? Secondly, given the fact that those 11 States and others will be developing the social policy, do you think it is likely that what emerges will be a social policy a great deal more integrated than it would have been if we had been there to add our voice in the consultations between now and the emergence finally of that policy?

(Mr Hurd) I would like to say first, Mr Jopling, that we hope and believe that the Commission will continue to bring forward proposals in the social field for legislation by the Twelve, it is not a question, therefore, of the whole area having been taken out of the Treaty—not at all. Indeed, work is proceeding on the basis of discussion and legislation about the Twelve. What our partners have reserved to themselves, as it were, is under the protocol which they agreed: an arrangement by which they could adopt measures which would not be Community law, but they could adopt measures among the Eleven instead of the Twelve. So I do not think the legal problem you mention arises. What we cannot be sure—what they have clearly not yet decided—is what use they are going to make of that protocol. It might be heavily used or

it might be rather lightly used, for the reasons I have given.

27. Do you not think probably at the end of the day we are going to have to sign up anyway?

(Mr Hurd) Not if the kind of legislation brought forward or the kind of proposals brought forward under the protocol of the Eleven are the kind which we rejected at Maastricht. I do not see that. I do not actually see any British Government being eager to do that.

Chairman

28. Presumably, Foreign Secretary, one of our sets of reasons for going for the opt-out in this area in relation to certain specific social measures was not merely our doubts about whether they are suitable and congenial for our own policy but doubts about whether the Community should be legislating in these areas at all: is that right?

(Mr Hurd) Absolutely. We believe there is an area here for legislation. We believe on health and safety that it is perfectly reasonable that there should be Community legislation and have taken a large part in discussing that. We believe that the Commission has misused the health and safety provisions of the Treaty and brought forward legislation under that heading, under the existing treaty, which goes well beyond what can be justified on health and safety reasons. That is a discussion and an argument we are perfectly willing to have. I repeat, we are not excluding the social dimension from the work of the Community, not at all. Largely on the grounds that these are matters of industrial relations which Member States can perfectly well work out for themselves in the light of their own traditions and experience, we are saying it does not need to be harmonised as others propose.

Chairman: This raises the whole question of subsidiarity, the who does what arguments which are enshrined in a slightly vague form under Article 3b of the Maastricht drafts. We would really like to pursue this in some detail if we may, because we think the issue keeps on being raised with the Committee and we would like to get this clear.

Mr Wells

29. Foreign Secretary, we are delighted to find the British insisting upon a subsidiarity clause in the Maastricht agreement, although I notice that you gave the Germans the responsibility for insisting that it was in the Maastricht Treaty. Some of us, in trying to study the wording of it, find difficulty in understanding what it will mean in practice. For example, it seems that the principle of subsidiarity is a matter of choice. It involves subjective judgments and assessments of where action is best taken. If that is so, how can the question of subsidiarity ever become judicial? How can we force the Commission to renounce its powers to initiate legislation and enforce that it be done at national level?

[Mr Wells *Contd*]

(Mr Hurd) This is actually a much stronger Article than most people predicted. There was a very wide assumption there would not be an Article on subsidiarity, or that it would be so weak as to be meaningless. We said throughout in the face of scepticism that there should be such an Article, but it was clearly important in tactical terms that we were joined in this by the Germans, and Article 3b I think is strong. In some areas, which I could expand on, the Community has already exclusive jurisdiction on agriculture, trade and the single market; but in the third paragraph of this Article it says that any action by the Community, whether within the exclusive competence or areas of mixed competence, must not go beyond what is necessary to achieve the objectives set out in the Treaty. I may say it shows the detailed nature of these negotiations. We had at the last minute to insist that this final sentence should be detached from the paragraph before; if it had been in the paragraph before it would only have covered the areas covered by that paragraph, non-exclusive jurisdiction; it would not have covered the exclusive jurisdiction. I had to put my hand up at a certain stage and say, "Can this sentence, with which we agree, be separated out from the paragraph before". Of course it was not immediately apparent to everybody what I was going on about. I hope I have explained why it is a crucial point, and it is characteristic of the very quick moving and detailed nature of the negotiations at that last meeting. In areas outside the exclusive competence, such as the environment, health, education and social policy, the Commission will have to prove that action cannot be sufficiently achieved by the Member States acting separately. How will this be binding? It will be binding upon the institutions at all stages of the process, on the Commission as it frames its proposals, on the Parliament and on the Council. That means any Member State can object to a Commission initiative on the grounds of subsidiarity, of course only when this Treaty has been ratified, if it is. Then they will be able to say "3b". Ultimately, of course, if the Commission persists the court may be called on to adjudicate when a dispute on subsidiarity arises. So we believe it is important. One cannot, as I think I have said before in this Committee, guarantee it is going to solve every problem in this field, we do not pretend that at all, but the position which we sustain would be much easier to sustain once Article 3b is in the Treaty.

30. Do you see the Commission, when you say Article 3b, simply saying, "Yes, you're right, we'll leave it to the national jurisdiction"?

(Mr Hurd) They will have to show what they do not have to show now. They will have to show that their proposals do not go beyond Article 3(b). They will have to show the action they propose for the Community does not go beyond what is necessary to achieve the objectives of the Treaty, and where the Community does not have exclusive jurisdiction the Commission will have to show that their proposals cover an area and propose an action which cannot be sufficiently achieved by the Member States, and can therefore be better achieved by the Community. These are tests they do not have to pass now and that is why I think this is an important Article.

31. Who will adjudicate?

(Mr Hurd) The court if necessary.

32. Can we take an example of current news. We understand that the draft Directive is being proposed inevitably in the environmental area in which environmental assessments will be required by all planning authorities throughout the Community of 12 before they continue to approve or give planning permission. That seems to me to be a typical example of where you might choose, if we ratify this Treaty, to hold up your hand and say, "3b". Is that an illustration of what you have in mind?

(Mr Hurd) It might well be. This proposal that you mention, and I have read your comments in The Independent, is not of course a Commission proposal. The Commission operates in a goldfish bowl. An official hardly has an idea before it is denounced in the Daily Star or The Sun, but this proposal obviously is an idea which is going the rounds but is not yet approved by the Commission, let alone submitted to the Council. That is its non-status, as it were. Therefore, there is plenty of discussion ahead, both inside the Commission, the Council Working Groups and the Council which will finally decide. I think everybody agrees that part of the purpose of planning in the 20th Century is to take account of the environmental views, the environmental impact. I think we would need a lot of persuading that something on these lines was necessary in order to do that. We might well, once 3b is in effect, use the existence of 3b against a proposal if it were to emerge from the Commission in the sort of form you have read about.

33. Do you see therefore that the effect of your subsidiarity clause 3b will be that the Commission will repatriate power that it has previously assumed to national parliaments and national administrations?

(Mr Hurd) I think the Commission will have to be careful, probably to a greater extent than now, about the possible collision between the proposals it puts forward and this provision. That is what I think one could reasonably claim for it.

(Mr Jay) Our understanding from the discussions we have had with members of the Commission is that even before the Treaty has come into effect the concept of subsidiarity is already having an effect within the Commission, and that some senior levels in the Commission are arguing against proposals which they regard as inappropriate coming forward for possible legislation by the Council because they do offend against the principle of subsidiarity. I think one thing which we have always regarded as possible, which is that irrespective of the justiciability of the clause

[**Mr Wells** *Contd*]

it would have a deterrent effect on the Commission, is already perhaps beginning to happen.

Chairman

34. This would depend upon the commonsense of the Commission itself policing its own activities?
(Mr Jay) Indeed.

Mr Lawrence

35. Once again, put as you put it nobody could possibly disagree but that it is a good thing. The problem is that I am not sure everybody else in Europe would put it as you put it. When we first went round doing our Single European Act inquiry and we asked people in all of the other countries, the Prime Ministers and the leaders, "How do you differentiate between that which ought to be national and that which ought to be European?", they all said, "Ah, we apply the principle of subsidiarity". When we said "What is the principle of subsidiarity? What does it mean?", everybody laughed and everybody had a different explanation of what subsidiarity meant. Now, what has happened is that we have enshrined the principle of subsidiarity into the Treaty but does it mean any more than is in the eye of the beholder? It means no more surely than what you want it to mean. We have this example of the Winchester Bypass and the Channel Tunnel. Here is the Community saying "We think this is a Community matter". We say, "No, this is an entirely national matter and mind your own business". I know it is a bit more complicated than that.
(Mr Hurd) A good deal more.

36. That in essence is a very good example of a distinction between the two. Who is going to make sure that the Commission does not initiate action which some nation state like ours believes is best left to the non-institutional, the governmental, authority? Who is going to make sure that does not happen?
(Mr Hurd) First of all, the Commission, as Mr Jay has pointed out, will as a result of 3(b) be more cautious, or should be more cautious, in what they actually propose. Secondly, Member States in the Council who believe that the Commission should be very chary about operating in details of national life will have a legal argument which they did not have before. Thirdly, the Parliament in the sphere where it exercises a blocking power on legislation will have the same point in mind. There were drawn to my attention at lunch today a couple of cases where the European Parliament has already blocked what one might call nook and cranny legislation—or tried to. I do not think the European Parliament always operates in that direction; it can do so occasionally and has done. Fourthly, the Court in the case of dispute on these matters can adjudicate and will have to take into account 3(b). I have not claimed impermeability for this, I have always been very careful not to do that. But we have pinned it

down. We have pinned it down partially, as I said, because of the German concern which is based on their constitution and the rights of the Laender— so they reach the same conclusion from a slightly different argument, but it is very important from their point of view, otherwise it will be struck down in their constitutional court. So they have approached the thing that way. I am not claiming impermeability for that, I am just saying it is more solid an article than most of us expected it to be possible to achieve.

37. If at the end of the day it is for the Court to decide, this is the European Court, the institutional court, it is taking away the decision from the nation state. So if we as the nation state are in dispute with the Commission about which side of the subsidiarity line a particular issue falls and the European Court decides we are the worse off, we have lost our nation state right to decide what we think is the correct solution.
(Mr Hurd) Mr Lawrence, I think, if I may respectfully say so, you are confusing two things, competence and subsidiarity. We are talking about areas of undisputed competence, are we not? We are talking about areas where legally speaking the Community has the right to enact legislation. What I am saying is, within that area, where there is no dispute about competence, there is now also an additional argument. Not only in the Community's competence must an action proposed be worthwhile—has it passed what one might call the common sense test? So that it is an additional argument, but it can only be justifiable by the European Court. I do not see any other way, since it is not arguing about the competence, in which it can be done.

Mr Harris

38. Foreign Secretary, can you direct the collective intellectual and linguistic powers of the Foreign Office to try and come up with a more meaningful word than this ghastly word "subsidiarity"? Are we absolutely lumbered with it because it is now enshrined in the Treaty?
(Mr Hurd) We are not actually. Well, it is mentioned but perhaps the Committee would like to arrange a little competition for alternatives. I would welcome sixth form contributions to this.

Mr Rowlands

39. Devolution.
(Mr Hurd) It has nothing to do with devolution, Mr Rowlands. It is actually common sense.

Chairman

40. Moving on from this to other things, summing up on subsidiarity before we go on, would you reassure us that this concept as now enshrined in the Treaty is a real prevention, a real obstacle against the sensation of constant drift and constant accumulation of the powers to the centre? Might we even see proposals for the nation states to bring forward legislation in the future to reinforce this

[**Chairman** *Contd*]

common sense we hope will keep the Commission out of certain areas by taking away the powers that might even have allowed them to act in a non-commonsensical way?

(Mr Hurd) I think the phrase you used is the right one. I think the real obstacle to the process you mention—I do not claim impregnability—as Europe develops, as the Community enlarges, is this kind of approach, the argument of common sense, and in a Community which will become more diverse in character this will be a stronger one.

Chairman: Can we move on to some of the institutional consequences of Maastricht. We do not want to put too much emphasis on institutions but they are important in a proper constitutional structure.

Mr Lawrence

41. What shifts in the balance of power between Community institutions are likely to follow from Maastricht? That is, which institutions in your view gain power and which institutions lose power and influence?

(Mr Hurd) We have covered some of those points, Mr Lawrence. The fundamental procedures for decision-taking remain the same. I think the Single European Act in some ways was a more radical change in the nature of the Community than the Maastricht Agreement. As I already described with foreign policy, the features of the new system are very familiar to those of us who work at the present time. To answer your question more completely, there is an enhanced role for the European Parliament in the non-legislative field the Committee have discussed with me before, arising largely from British proposals, and in the legislative field under 189(b) where they have a blocking power in certain types of legislation. There are certain extensions of competence, often of a declaratory kind, that is making clear areas like the environment where competence already has been creeping competence as a result of previous decisions. There are, of course, the two pillars which we have already discussed brought into the Treaty, common, foreign and security policy and interior justice. I think those are the main institutional changes.

42. Will those provisions in the Treaty which talk about co-decision between the Council and Parliament lead to any shifting of balance of power within the Community?

(Mr Hurd) I do not believe that the change in the legislative powers of the Parliament which I mentioned can be described as co-decision. I know they sometimes are, because some people believe in co-decision, but I think if one asked the layman what co-decision meant, he would assume it meant two people of roughly equal standing taking decisions jointly—co-decision. But that, of course, is not what happens or will happen under the Treaty of Maastricht. What will happen is, after a complicated procedure, at the end of the day on certain of types of legislation spelled out in 189(b) the Parliament will have a blocking power.

Mr Lawrence: Could I ask about the Committee of the Regions?

Chairman

43. We will come on to that in our next question, if we may. Perhaps just before we leave the European Parliament—and we want to ask questions in a moment about our own Parliament—I could ask if you feel completely comfortable about the democratic basis on which the European Parliament comes to be created. If it is to be given new powers, has it got the structure to sustain those powers? It is sometimes a little alarming to members of this Committee, when we talk, let us say, to German Members of Parliament, to find that they do not have any constituents and do not appear to have been elected for anywhere very specific. Can we think of better ways of making the European Parliament more democratic?

(Mr Hurd) I am not sure we shall succeed in persuading all of them to adopt the first past the post procedure. I do not think harmonisation of electoral procedures is going to be particularly easy, or necessarily particularly profitable. They are all elected, with the exception of the Germans, but with that exception they are all democratically elected by the procedures which each nation state has chosen.

Chairman: Could we then move to the regional aspect.

Mr Canavan

44. Secretary of State, could you tell us, please, how will the UK members of the Committee of the Regions be appointed or elected?

(Mr Hurd) We have not yet decided that.

45. When we discussed this last week with representatives of the Commission when we were in Brussels the possibility was raised of direct representation on the Committee of the Regions coming from Scottish and Welsh parliaments. What are your own views on this possibility, assuming that Scottish and Welsh parliaments become a reality in the near future?

(Mr Hurd) This is not an assumption you would expect me to share, Mr Canavan.

46. Supposing it does come about?

(Mr Hurd) Then I think the Government in power, which would not be mine, would have to decide. This is a consultative committee; it is not a committee which has authority. I am sure Mr Canavan knows that. It will have to be consulted on all proposals under the Treaty chapters on education, culture and health, networks and cohesion, and on other matters if appropriate, and it can submit opinions on its own initiative; but it is a consultative body and not an authoritative, executive or legislative body, therefore I would not myself expect that it would wield enormous influence, but we thought, on balance, it would be use-

[**Mr Canavan** *Contd*]

ful. We will need to decide how the British members, the UK members are to be appointed.

47. Within the terms of the framework already agreed there would still at least be open the possibility of representation from Scotland and Wales, as I previously mentioned?

(Mr Hurd) Representation from Scotland and Wales would clearly be essential, but how that is to be devised is another question.

48. Would you agree that it would be somewhat anomalous, and perhaps over-ambitious, for one of the four Welsh places to be taken up by the Secretary of State for Wales who, after all, is a representative of Central Government, rather than a region or a nation within the United Kingdom?

(Mr Hurd) He is a very good Secretary of State, Mr Canavan, otherwise I do not think that is ground I wish to tread.

Mr Harris

49. A consultative body it might be, or might prove to be and I think it will be, but when we were in Brussels last week Bruce Millan, the Commissioner, laid some importance on the establishment of the Committee of the Regions. One thing that is quite certain is that there will be quite keen competition among various local authorities for places. I am just wondering how you are going to try and reconcile these various claims. For example, in the part of the world I represent European regional policy is of vital importance. Do you envisage that an area like Devon and Cornwall will have its own place on the Committee? Will it be big enough to allow representation of that sort of level? How will you balance those regions which are acutely affected by various aspects of European policy, Community policy, particularly in the grants field, with those areas like your own perhaps which are not so affected? Will there be difficulties in this?

(Mr Hurd) I think it will be difficult to allocate 24 members in this way. I do not think the Foreign Office will be in the lead on this. It is not a matter on which any decisions have been taken; therefore it is a matter on which representations will no doubt be welcome.

Chairman

50. Will it duplicate the Economic and Social Committee?

(Mr Hurd) It will be in parallel.

51. Do you see a duplication there?

(Mr Hurd) I think it would be conceivable, yes. It would be conceivable but obviously they try to avoid it.

Chairman: Can we look at where the national parliaments after Maastricht are likely to fit in. I think we have our own ideas and our own not very satisfactory experiences of the last conference or assize of parliaments in Rome last summer.

Mr Wells

52. How will it be possible, Foreign Secretary, to hold Ministers to account for decisions taken about justice matters, or in the common foreign and security policy pillars and, indeed, for decisions taken by weighted majority voting in the Council of Ministers and, for that matter, at European Council meetings?

(Mr Hurd) Perhaps the Minister of State could take questions on that.

(Mr Garel-Jones) Jumping back to the earlier question on this matter, I think what seems to me, at any rate, is beginning to emerge as far as European legislation is concerned is that this House of Commons, through its scrutiny procedures, carries out what I suppose might be called a second reading debate on draft legislation that comes forward from the Community, and the whole process then between the Council and the European Parliament conciliation procedures and so on I suppose might be, broadly speaking, parallel to the committee stage of legislation here. What we have done in certain areas is we have now given to the European Parliament the right, as it were, to a third reading debate, at which they can reject that legislation. I think in a sense this House has complained in the past that when they have carried out their scrutiny procedures thereafter the legislation does not come back here anyway. A number of colleagues who expressed that anxiety have said that they actually regard the additional hurdle, if you like, of the European Parliament at third reading as a plus, because it has not taken away from this House, as it were, something which it did not already have. So far as the inter-governmental pillars are concerned, we are in a developing situation. I would imagine that the Foreign Office would wish to continue the way the Foreign Secretary does now. When developments of real importance, in which the House has a particular interest, arise through the common foreign and security policy the Foreign Office would either volunteer a statement on its own initiative, or the House would demand a statement. Equally, I think if decisions began to emerge in the new pillar of interior/justice—and I am not talking about legislative decisions or decisions or views taken in that pillar which warrant a statement—no doubt the Home Secretary would volunteer such a statement; and if he did not volunteer such a statement then the House has its own ways of asking for one if it wishes. I should add, that if any decision is taken jointly with other states in the interior/justice pillar and then was to prompt the need for legislation here in this House, that legislation would have to be taken through this House in the normal way. Agreements made between national states in the interior/justice pillar that necessitated legislation in this House would have to be taken through this House in the normal way.

53. The pillars legislation can only be taken through the national parliaments, is that not right?

(Mr Garel-Jones) Of course.

[**Mr Wells** *Contd*]

54. Therefore, they have that ability to call the pillars to account to make sure that is right. There will be national domestic legislation?

(Mr Garel-Jones) Absolutely.

55. You have also, I think, endorsed in the Maastricht Treaty the idea of a conference of parliaments. Does this involve the European Parliament meeting with the national parliaments or does it envisage the possibility of national parliaments meeting without the European Parliament? The experience of our national parliament anyway at the Assizes in Rome less than 18 months ago was unfortunate, in that the national parliaments were totally dissipated and dominated by the European Parliament. Does this conference of parliaments therefore envisage further meetings of this kind, and in which case what is it supposed to do, and how will it be structured? Or is there a possibility of national parliaments meeting together in order to understand and have reported to them by ministers from the Council of Ministers, and from the pillars, what they are proposing to do or what they have done?

(Mr Garel-Jones) I think the declaration referring to the Congress of National Parliaments ought to be seen together with the other declaration entitled "The Role of National Parliaments in the European Union". It is all, I think, part of a process, part of a wish to see a greater involvement of national parliaments in the activities of Union and there are other aspects of that you may want to ask about later. So far as the Assizes itself—or the Congress or whatever it comes to be called—is concerned, you will have noticed the declaration is very brief and also that it is a declaration. The reason it is a declaration is because we did not feel as a Government, and I suspect this view was shared by other Governments, that National Parliaments—our own in particular—would take very kindly to their procedures and their way of conducting their business being agreed in an inter-governmental conference, then placed into a treaty. So this is an area slightly of no man's land, but what we very much hope will happen—and it is not for the Government here to take an initiative—is that the Leader of the House as Leader of the House will carry out consultations through the usual channels with the Opposition and, indeed, with others (amongst whom I imagine this Committee would be one) to decide how this House would like to take forward the idea of the Congress, to then share those ideas with other Parliaments and, indeed, with the European Parliament. In essence one is building from scratch and I suspect that this House and, indeed, others who took part in the Assizes might wish to learn lessons from that and perhaps ensure that some of the unsatisfactory aspects of the Assizes were not repeated in these congresses which look as though they would be likely to take place twice a year, once in each Presidency. The indications are that the President of the Council would make a speech to the Congress and that perhaps then might be the subject of debate and discussion. It is really an area where I think it is more for this House and other Parliaments to start taking initiatives than for the Government to step in and try to shape it itself.

56. Could I ask the Minister to amplify that slightly but not to be too long? Does that mean that this Committee, for example, or any Committee in the House should be making proposals to the Leader of the House as to how this should be conducted and how it might be established right now?

(Mr Garel-Jones) I am sure the Leader of the House will welcome that. My guess would be that he himself (we have not signed a treaty yet, but as soon as the treaty is signed) as Leader of the House, who is the natural person, if you like, to lead on this matter, would wish to consult with the Opposition and with specialist committees to try and clarify a view from here. Then, of course, further consultations would need to take place with other Parliaments and with the European Parliament itself.

Mr Shore

57. Could I come back to what I consider to be the central issue, which is the massive transfer of power from the United Kingdom Government and people to the European institutions in the form, of course, of Economic and Monetary Union? Although I fully understand that we have declined to opt in, as it were, at the present stage, or indeed have insisted on having the right to opt out of stage 3 of Economic and Monetary Union, would not the Minister agree that the transfer of control over interest rate policy, over exchange rate policy, over the possession of your own currency, and over the actual freedom of the Chancellor of the Exchequer to decide his own borrowing requirements, represents in the aggregate the most enormous shift of economic power and responsibility from this Parliament to an alien institution that we have ever contemplated in our history?

(Mr Garel-Jones) I think, if I may say so, the Prime Minister himself answered your particular question in a remarkably straight and forthright way. I think what he said was that, if we reached the point where the objective criteria that have been set out to make a decision to move from stage 2 to stage 3 were possible, then clearly there were some economic advantages to that; but he went on to say it would involve a very considerable political sacrifice, not least by this House, and that was the reason why we had maintained this reserve because, if those objective criteria are met, then you are quite right, indeed there would be a political sacrifice that would have to be made and this House at that time would have to decide whether it wished to make that sacrifice.

Mr Wells

58. It could mean political enlargement of our competence, could it not?

[Mr Wells *Contd*]

(Mr Garel-Jones) There are many who regard it as such.

Mr Lawrence

59. Do you believe that time is unlikely to be reached before the European Community enlarges so greatly as completely to change the nature of the institution as it now is?

(Mr Hurd) We hope, as one of the aims of our Presidency, to make sure that negotiations on the first accession applications begin by the end of this year. The dates of EMU depend on convergence. The dates in the Maastricht Treaty are to some extent misleading in so much as they are all dependent upon countries all achieving convergence. So one cannot tell with any precision the relationship between enlargement and progress towards EMU. All the points made by the Committee, which are perfectly fair ones, I think, add to the wisdom of taking the stage 3 decision where we have to take it.

60. It would be immensely reassuring to people in the country who did not want us to give up national sovereignty if we thought the Government did believe that.

(Mr Hurd) One cannot be certain. I would not wish to mislead you. One does not know what the attitude of Austria would be. That is one of the matters that will come up in our enlargement negotiations. If stage 3 is reached and convergence conditions have been fulfilled, we will have to make a decision—the House of Commons, the Government and Parliament of the time. Mr Shore is right, it would be a very grave decision.

Chairman

61. It all adds up to a picture, where only a few countries will achieve the very demanding convergence position, given enlargement which will bring in new applicants with a variety of needs, given that the United Kingdom already has decided that it does not want to go along with some of the more centralised versions of the social policy, of a more variegated pattern of European development involving, if not two tiers, at least several speeds.

(Mr Hurd) I would not dispute that. It has happened already in the Schengen Agreement to which most Members of the Community belong. It has happened with the Exchange Rate Mechanism. So there is nothing particularly new in that.

Chairman: Could we turn in the remaining section of this meeting this afternoon to some detailed aspects of the common foreign and security policy and the implications that seem to follow Maastricht?

Mr Shore

62. The opening Article of the Common Foreign and Security Policy reads, as you will undoubtedly recall, "The Union and its Member States shall define and implement a common foreign and security policy..." and it goes on to say, "The Member States shall support the Union's external

and security policy actively and unreservedly in a spirit of loyalty and mutual solidarity.... The Council shall ensure that these principles are complied with." That is the kind of general declaration. But what really are we committed to in terms of a common foreign policy?

(Mr Hurd) We are committed to working together in co-operation. We are committed to the possibility of joint action. This is a novelty: joint action which would be legally binding. That is the novelty. It would only be achieved by unanimity. So there is no question of Britain or any Member State submitting its foreign policy to joint action, to accepting that it could only act jointly with others, if it did not wish to do so; nor even when it had done so would it be committed to any particular joint action of which it disapproved. In practice, as I have said before to the Committee, this is a familiar process, and its success or failure depends, not on the Treaty of Maastricht and provisions in that Treaty, but on our ability to reach agreement on particular questions. That is the position now and that will be the position after Maastricht is in force.

63. Have any areas of joint action yet to be agreed for any particular areas the subject of study in advance of the agreement?

(Mr Hurd) No areas have been agreed, but I would draw Mr Shore's attention to Annex III which is a declaration by the European Council on areas which could be the subject of joint action. It lists a number of them in the security field, and "...invites the Ministers for Foreign Affairs to begin preparatory work with a view to defining the necessary basic elements..." etc., and also "...invites the...[Foreign Ministers]...to prepare a report to the European Council in Lisbon on the likely development of the common foreign and security policy with a view to identifying areas open to joint action *vis-a-vis* particular countries" So Foreign Ministers have been set a task and we will have to report to Lisbon in June, but no decisions have been taken.

64. Whether or not particular joint actions are agreed. Nevertheless, simply taking account of the committee of common foreign policy and to the loyalty and co-operation which is demanded of the Member States in pursuing that Union foreign policy, what effect is this likely to have on other organisations of which we are a member but of which other Community countries are not members, or at least only some of them? I am thinking, first of all, about the impact of possible common foreign policy in Europe upon our role in the Commonwealth. Do you see there any possibility of conflict?

(Mr Hurd) No, because the nature of the CFSP is defined in the later Articles of the Treaty of Maastricht. For example, Article B, whenever it deems it necessary the Council should define a common position, therefore CFSP does not mean that on every conceivable issue the Community should act together and should adopt a common

[**Mr Shore** Contd]

position. As regards the Commonwealth, of course we have already found that matters under discussions of the two organisations to which we belong overlap. Take South Africa: there is a very, very long history of discussion of South Africa both in the Community and in the Commonwealth, and different sets of sanctions against South Africa were applied at the two bodies with a different kind of legal basis and that creates a complication, undoubtedly, but it is a complication with which we have lived for many years. I do not see any great change as far as that is concerned.

65. There are other international organisations, of course, and I can think of a number of them— but taken simply, with the Security Council of the United Nations we have obligations under the Charter as a permanent member of the Security Council. Would the adoption of a common foreign policy in any way affect our role in the Security Council of the United Nations, quite apart from the question which has now been raised in Europe that the European Community should itself have a veto and a permanent seat on the Security Council?

(Mr Hurd) This point attracted a good deal of work during the negotiations. The French and ourselves working together achieved, I think, a satisfactory answer. It is in Article E of the Treaty. It says that Member States which are also members of the UN Security Council were concerned to keep the other Member States fully informed. Member States which are permanent members of the Security Council will, in the execution of their functions, ensure the defence of the positions and the interests of the Union without prejudice to their responsibilities under the provisions of the Charter. We believe that safeguards the position. Again, I do not think in practice it will be different from what happens now and what happened last week where you had three EC members of the Security Council, two permanent and the Belgians, and there was no difficulty among the 12. I reported yesterday to the Council in Brussels on the outcome of the Security Council meeting. There was no difficulty, and I do not think there will be under Maastricht. We would certainly (and so would the French) oppose any suggestion that either of us should abandon our position as permanent members of the Council.

Mr Lawrence

66. Had there been a common foreign policy in place do you envisage that Germany would not have indicated that it was prepared to recognise Croatia ahead of the other European countries? Or would there have been some sanction which could have been brought to bear upon Germany to stop it doing so if it was determined? Would anything have changed what we understand to be the situation where, because it was so important for everybody to go along and show unity, everybody went along and recognised Croatia ahead of the time and that we thought was the best time to make that recognition. What would change?

(Mr Hurd) There would only be change if the Community had decided by unanimity that this was a subject of joint action, and then decided by unanimity on a particular date or process for recognition of particular republics in Yugoslavia, in that case. If both those things had happened, and on either of them any Member State could have a veto, then the Member State would be bound to follow the action to which it had agreed, that would be the difference. There is a double veto, as it were. First of all, you have to decide that a particular subject is for joint action and then you have to decide unanimously what that joint action is. Once those two things have happened you are bound by that, although there are certain let-out clauses to which we attach considerable importance about what happens if the situation drastically changes.

67. Any sanctions?

(Mr Hurd) Just a sanction against anybody who breaches their commitment under the Treaty, but of course people do not.

Mr Shore

68. I wanted to turn to the defence side now. It is really the changed role for WEU, accepting that there is a changed role: what are the implications of a common European security and defence policy for the long-term future of the Atlantic Alliance? What is the case, can you answer this one perhaps briefly, for a separate defence organisation in Western Europe, separate from the Atlantic Alliance?

(Mr Hurd) There are two answers to that, I think, and they both justify the enhanced role of the Western European Union: one is that it has for a long time been felt that the European allies ought to play a more coherent and larger part within that. As the American and Canadian presence on the continent of Europe diminishes, which it is clearly going to do, then that adds to that case. Secondly, there is a case for European organisations which can bring together and co-ordinate European efforts outside the NATO area. You have got those two justifications, but our concern which we achieved (and Mr Shore and I have discussed this before) was to make sure that the WEU was compatible with NATO and that the primacy of NATO as the security institution for the defence of Western Europe was established. That we achieved. That was the point of the Anglo-Italian paper which was very important in shaping the eventual result.

69. On that second reason you gave, that WEU would be able to act outside the NATO area, is there not a very powerful case for saying that the easiest way of tackling that problem of activity outside the NATO area is to change the terms of reference of NATO itself?

(Mr Hurd) Yes, there is a case for that. But it has never been accepted by NATO and would not be today.

24   MINUTES OF EVIDENCE TAKEN BEFORE

4 February 1992] RT HON DOUGLAS HURD CBE MP, RT HON TRISTAN GAREL-JONES MP,   *[Continued*
                          MR MICHAEL JAY and MR JOHN GOULDEN CMG

Mr Lawrence

70. There is a great role for a new defence organ to support the United Nations which could change the nature of NATO and nevertheless preserve all its constituent parts as a force for good in the world. Has any thought been given to that?

(Mr Hurd) I think that one of the tasks of all member states of the United Nations with any substantial military capability needs to be to consider how they are going to respond to the increasing calls from the United Nations for peace-keeping forces and peace-making. This loomed quite large in the Security Council debate last Friday. I am sure when the Secretary General of the United Nations produces his report on this by 1 July he will produce thoughts there to which we will all have to pay some attention. It might well be something that was then discussed in the WEU.

Mr Shore

71. One more question on foreign policy: there has, of course, been a considerable increase in the demand for diplomats following the demise of the Soviet Union and the creation of so many additional states in what was once the Soviet Union. I have seen it suggested that there should be joint representation, Community representation, in these separate independent Commonwealth states. Is this really something we are anxious to bring about or do we not prefer to maintain our independence in representations with foreign countries?

(Mr Hurd) We shall have in those countries where we can afford to be represented British representation. What I agreed, particularly with our German colleagues, that we would explore is shared facilities, that is we would have two ambassadors or two charges d'affaires, one British and one German who might well be sharing the same block of flats and sharing a good many facilities. We are exploring that particularly in Kazakhstan, one of the more important of the new Republics in the former Soviet Union, but we may experiment in other places as well. That seems entirely sensible.

Chairman: Two final questions if we may. First, on the widening Community, we touched on this earlier with enlargement but we have some final questions on what this union to which we have signed up is going to look like in a few years' time.

Mr Harris

72. Foreign Secretary, the Treaty says any European state may apply to become a member of the Union. I am just wondering whether there is any degree of understanding, albeit informally, behind the scenes between yourselves as Ministers and perhaps the Commission as to what that actually means. For example, what political conditions will need to be met? Which of the states east of East Germany are actually considered to be European? Is Turkey considered to be European? This is a pretty wide, sweeping statement—"any European nation may apply". Have you any idea

at all of how that is going to be implemented or handled?

(Mr Hurd) The Community has already accepted that for this purpose Turkey is European. The 1963 Association Agreement with Turkey recognised that she was eligible to apply for membership and, of course, she has done so; that does not mean to say she will achieve membership—that is a different question, but she could not now be ruled out on the basis that she was not technically European. I think the only problem which arises here is Russia itself which obviously straddles the traditional boundary between Europe and Asia. But we have a little time before we have to consider that problem because it is clear from practice that countries admitted to the European Community have to be politically and economically qualified, they have to be democracies and their economies have to be of a kind which can assume the responsibilities of membership and the rules of the Treaty. So this would therefore take a long time and the first wave are likely to be members of EFTA, the second wave are likely to be, I would think, the new democracies of Central and Eastern Europe, but the Community will also have to consider the applications from Southern Europe—Malta, Cyprus and Turkey. There are very big issues here. That is why the Maastricht Summit asked the Commission to prepare a strategy paper in addition to the work which the Commission will anyway have to do preparing opinions on these different applications which have come in. They have been asked to prepare a strategy paper. We want to use our Presidency to press on with this and to make sure that the Commission gets past the stages I have mentioned and actually starts to prepare mandates for negotiations with at any rate some of those who have already applied. We do believe that once the financial questions which would dominate the Portuguese Presidency are settled, perhaps in our Presidency, it will then be an urgent matter to get on with enlargement.

73. I believe you told us in one of your informal sessions as many as 29 countries could actually be considered as potential members, is that a figure you recognise or not? Certainly it looks as though the scope of enlargement is almost limitless, does it not?

(Mr Hurd) I have not done that sum, Mr Harris. It cannot be far wrong if you count all the republics in Yugoslavia and all the republics of the former Soviet Union this side of the Urals. I have not done an actual sum. They may not all want to join. Joining is not a bed of roses. Community membership does involve certain obligations and——

Mr Lawrence

74. It is a bed of thorns being left out.

(Mr Hurd) People want to weigh that up very carefully.

Chairman: Finally, peering into a slightly less distant future of the British Presidency in the second half of this year, you have already mentioned

[**Mr Lawrence** *Contd*]

one of the priorities will be the beginning of enlargement. Bowen Wells would like to ask an additional question.

Mr Wells

75. Foreign Secretary, could you simply outline the priorities of the British Presidency. One you mentioned is clearly enlargement. The second you mentioned is concluding financial arrangements begun, you think, in the Portuguese presidency. Are there others you have in mind?

(*Mr Hurd*) Yes, indeed. In a way logically what comes first is the completion of the Single Market. We have just got a year now in which to complete the Single Market—a liberal Single Market is something we pressed for, something Mrs Thatcher pressed for when she was Prime Minister, the Single European Act with a dateline. So I would put that logically first. Then there will be the completion of the latest discussions on CAP reform and the financial resources of the Community. We hope by then there will have been progress on those two matters, they are not likely to have been settled finally by the end of June. Then there will be enlargement which we have already discussed. I do see those as the priorities so it is quite a busy time.

Chairman: Foreign Secretary, I think that exhausts our questions—that is not quite true, we have many more, but it probably exhausts all of us in this first analysis of the post-Maastricht scene. There will be many more developments ahead. We are extremely grateful to you, Mr Garel-Jones and your colleagues, Mr Jay and Mr Goulden, for at least casting a first headlight into the fog and mist ahead. Thank you very much indeed.

Printed in the United Kingdom for HMSO
Dd.0508192, 2/92, C6, 3382/5B, 5673, 185752

HMSO publications are available from:

HMSO Publications Centre
(Mail, fax and telephone orders only)
PO Box 276, London, SW8 5DT
Telephone orders 071-873 9090
General enquiries 071-873 0011
(queuing system in operation for both numbers)
Fax orders 071–873 8200

HMSO Bookshops
49 High Holborn, London, WC1V 6HB   071-873 0011 (counter service only)
258 Broad Street, Birmingham, B1 2HE   021-643 3740
Southey House, 33 Wine Street, Bristol, BS1 2BQ   (0272) 264306
9-21 Princess Street, Manchester, M60 8AS   061-834 7201
80 Chichester Street, Belfast, BT1 4JY   (0232) 238451
71 Lothian Road, Edinburgh, EH3 9AZ   031-228 4181

HMSO's Accredited Agents
(see Yellow Pages)

and through good booksellers

ISBN 0-10-279092-2

FOREIGN AFFAIRS COMMITTEE

EUROPE AFTER MAASTRICHT

MINUTES OF EVIDENCE

Wednesday 5 February 1992

Dr P Taylor, Mr F Vibert and Dr H Wallace

Ordered by The House of Commons *to be printed*
5 February 1992

LONDON: HMSO
£8.75 net

WEDNESDAY 5 FEBRUARY 1992

Members present:

Mr David Howell, in the Chair

Mr Dennis Canavan	Mr Ivan Lawrence
Mr David Harris	Mr Peter Shore
Mr Michael Jopling	Mr Bowen Wells

THE INSTITUTIONAL AND CONSTITUTIONAL IMPLICATIONS OF THE
MAASTRICHT AGREEMENT.

**Memorandum submitted by Paul Taylor, Senior Lecturer in International Relations, London School of
Economics (EC 221)**

The Agreement is examined from three perspectives. First the character of the overall constitutional
relationship between Britain and the European Communities is examined. Second the specific changes
introduced by the Maastricht agreement are discussed. Thirdly the question is put of whether these
changes could be interpreted as challenging the established constitutional relationship. What do they
imply for the future development of the Communities?

A. THE OVERALL CONSTITUTIONAL RELATIONSHIP

1. The Agreement does not fundamentally alter the relationship in constitutional terms from that
established by the Single European Act. The main point is that although there have been changes in the
conditions of sovereignty, and the way in which it can be exercised, the case against the view that
sovereignty has been ceded either by the Treaty of Rome itself, or by its successive amendments,
remains very powerful. This case received little or no attention in Britain in the public debate before the
meeting of the European Council at Maastricht, and the false argument that integration and sovereignty
are necessarily opposed concepts prevailed by default.The main conclusion of the present writer is that
sovereignty has not been lost but that it is not exercised effectively.

The main arguments are as follows:

1. The Community is based upon a Treaty from which we could withdraw under international law—
the Treaty of Rome is not a constitution. Furthermore, if the British Parliament made it clear, *without
any ambiguity*, that it intended to nullify a particular decision made by the European institutions, the
British courts would follow the dictates of Parliament. The essence of the situation is that Parliament
unilaterally agreed to bind itself to a treaty. There is no legal or constitutional impediment in the way of
Parliament's changing its mind. In practice, therefore, the doctrine of the primacy of Community Law
over national law rests upon the *willingness* of Parliament to accept the current situation and its implications.

2. The doctrine of the sovereignty of Parliament in Britain is the basis of the argument that Parliament
could nullify an individual Community Act if it so wished, without contravening the British constitution.
It should be stressed that there are two key relationships in this case, that between Parliament and the
European Communities and that between Parliament and the courts in Britain. The doctrine of the primacy of Community Law requires that Courts in Britain give precedence to Community law in the event
of a clash with British law. But this applies only if Parliament has not made its intentions quite clear to
British courts.

Because each Parliament is sovereign there is no difference in Britain between acts of constitutional
amendment and ordinary acts of legislation. British courts would, therefore, regard a specific instruction
by Parliament to nullify a Community act as being at one and the same time an amendment of the constitution and an act of legislation: apart from issuing a specific instruction to the courts in Britain
Parliament would also in the same act be changing the terms of the constitutional arrangements which it
established in the European Communities Act of 1972 under which they were required to give priority to
the law of the Communities. British courts would do what they were told to do by Parliament because
Parliament had combined a specific instruction with a constitutional means. The ECJ would, of course,
complain about this, but it would be ineffectual because the Communities are not based upon a higher
constitutional order, but rather on the separate individual constitutional orders of the member states.

The cost of printing and publishing these Minutes of Evidence is estimated by HMSO at £5,196.

3. There are, however, a number of reasons why Parliament is unlikely to try to nullify a Regulation or Directive set forth by institutions of the Community.

   a. One of these is that such decisions will already have been approved by one or more British Ministers in the Council of Ministers who have, except in very unusual circumstances, the support of a majority of members of Parliament. In normal circumstances, it is unlikely that a majority could be found in Parliament to negate a decision made in Brussels. But this is a political impediment rather than a legal one.

   b. Another impediment is the fact that the procedures of the British Parliament for scrutinising European legislation, both before and after the taking of decisions in Brussels, are inadequate. Successive governments, over many years, have taken no steps to remedy this situation. Members of Parliament have, therefore, remained rather poorly informed about the nature of the Communities and the details of its business. However, the Government could, in principle, make it easier for Parliament to exercise its sovereignty by altering procedures at Westminster to enable proposed legislation to be more fully debated in Parliament and amended according to its wishes. An extreme example of this possibility would be if Ministers were to be given a mandate which tied them to a specified policy in Brussels. At least one other member—Denmark—has such arrangements. In such a situation, the claim that sovereignty had been lost would be hard to sustain, because Parliament would be effectively giving instructions to British representatives in Brussels as Community legislation was being formulated. Conversely the failure of Parliament to exercise its sovereign powers does not mean that this could not be done.

4. The difficulty with regards to Brussels is, therefore, to a great extent a consequence of the way in which the British Parliamentary system works, itself a product of the lack of any separation of powers between the legislature and the executive. There have been complaints about the loss of sovereignty on behalf of both branches of government under the heading of Parliamentary sovereignty. But the legislature has been weakened with regard to the European Community to a much lesser extent than has the executive, and for different reasons. The legislature's weakness could be corrected in Britain if the executive was determined to do this. The government remains reluctant to improve Parliament's procedures regarding European legislation because such alterations would limit its own freedom to act, and for a number of reasons Members of Parliament have not pushed as hard as they might to correct this situation.

5. Ironically, however, according to the terms of the European Communities Act of 1972, members of the executive and administration *are* legally constrained by regulations that were agreed upon by their predecessors in Brussels. That is, they have been subjected to constraints in an area of their external relations as a result of a previous act of a sovereign Parliament. Such constraints on the members of the executive and administration are occurring at a time when, according to a number of commentators, their powers with regard to the legislature have become positively tyrannical. The assertion that Britain has lost sovereignty to Europe is thus revealed as being, in part, a function of the weakness of the legislature with regards to the executive and the administration in Britain (a situation engineered by the executive itself), rather than of any change in the legal position of Parliament. The *executive* has, in a sense, pulled itself down by its own bootstraps. For political reasons, however, members of the executive who are opposed to the development of closer relations with the Communities would like it to be believed that the *legislature* is equally a victim—to conjure up a common enemy is to strengthen an alliance.

6. The dilemma of the government is a subtle, even delicious, one: it can only escape from one set of constraints (those deriving from the relationship with Europe) by subjecting itself to another set (those deriving from its relations with the legislature in Britain) and by reversing the pattern of development of legislative/executive relations which have evolved over a number of years. What is clear, however, is that the perception in the early 1990s that there is a problem concerning British sovereignty with regard to the European Community is as much a product of a problem in the way the British constitution is working as of our relationship with Europe.

7. This may be thought to ignore the possibility that the British government may be outvoted in the Council of Ministers according to the majority voting arrangements in the Treaty of Rome, in the Single European Act, and now, as discussed below, in the Maastricht agreement.

There are three arguments against this position.

   a. The first is quite simply that the British Parliament could nullify such an act if it proved objectionable, as has been pointed out above. Such a course might damage our relationship with the Community, but that a political cost might arise is irrelevant to the constitutional and legal possibilities.

b. Secondly, the government has retained, even in areas where the formal arrangement is majority voting—because it speaks for a sovereign state—a **reserve power** in the Council to veto any *proposed* legislation of which it disapproves. Although it is highly unlikely that this could be a part of the routine arrangements of the Community after the Single European Act, it nevertheless remains as a power to be used in extremes by member governments which object to a particular course of action. Mrs Thatcher argued this in the House of Commons after the agreement of the Single European Act in December 1985. Despite the acceptance of majority voting as the normal way of working in the ten areas named in that Act, even in these areas a government could invoke the 1966 Luxembourg Accords which allow the veto if it judged that its fundamental interests were being threatened. The need to promote the 1992 process means that governments are now less likely to resort to such thinking because, as sovereign states, they have accepted an over-riding goal.

c. Thirdly, governments have another kind of reserve power. Even though it may be accepted that a particular institution should have the power to act in specific areas without being subject to instructions from government, governments retain the right to negotiate a different set of powers for institutions in other areas. They are not subject to any general principle, for example, a federal principle, according to which the powers of future institutions are to be allocated. That they retain the right to pursue their own strategy in these matters means that they can seek to balance the loss of powers in one realm against the gain or retention of powers in another: supranational powers to the Euurofed may be balanced against unanimity in the area of economic co-ordination. It might be argued that, even though they might continue to seek such countervailing powers, they will be increasingly condemned to accept supranationalism: there is a federalizing process. As will be shown below there is little in the Maastricht agreement to substantiate this view, and this writer sees little evidence to support it. The availability of this strategy is another indication that they have retained their sovereignty.

The conclusion must be that neither accession to the European Communities, nor the terms of the Single European Act or the Maastricht Agreement, have altered the underlying legal and constitutional circumstances of British sovereignty. Indeed, the fear that this has happened is strikingly absent in other member states.

B. THE ADJUSTMENTS INTRODUCED IN THE MAASTRICHT AGREEMENT

i. The broad pattern of the development of the institutions proposed in the Maastricht Agreement is one of increasing the involvement of institutions other than the core institutions in the decision-making process. There was no blanket extension of new powers to institutions such as the European Parliament, but rather a careful extension of a right to participation in carefully designated areas. This adjustment was seen as the continuation of the efforts made hitherto to create a European Union, a term which was included in the preamble, and which appears at a number of other places, but which in practice appears to signify little which would not have been indicated by the term Federalism in this context. The phrase "ever closer Union" is retained in the revised Common Provisions, which seems to indicate further integration to come. Another broad direction of development was towards the inclusion of areas which were previously alongside the Communities, such as the foreign policy arrangements, more fully in the Union. The whole was to be consolidated into a single package of activities linked in systems of common management. The role of the Community in a number of new areas was also made explicit.

ii. There were two kinds of institutional adjustment, which might be termed institutional innovation, and institutional extension. It should be stressed that the Maastricht Agreement referred to here is that on European Union, and that the text used is that issued by the Presidency—Holland—on 13 December 1991 as CONF-UP 1862/91. It has the legal status of an amendment of the Treaty of Rome, with the exception of the section headed Provisions on a common foreign and security policy, and is arranged with reference to the specified articles of the Treaty.

1. *Institutional extension.*

a. This applied to the role of the European Parliament in two major respects, and one minor one. (The latter need not be discussed at length: it is that the Parliament has been given a modified right to initiate legislation, but only by being allowed to call upon the Commission to "submit any appropriate proposal . . . for implementing this Treaty.") First the major changes in the Parliament's powers introduced by the Single European Act were incorporated in Article 189c in the Maastricht Agreement. This was the procedure which was called the Co-operative procedure, which was introduced into the SEA as a modification of Article 149 of the Treaty of Rome. In the text of the Agreement it is to be followed in a number of new areas, but it should be recalled that in the SEA it applied mainly to Article 100(a) legislation which was of great importance for the achievement of the single market. It enhanced Parliament's say over Community business in this area but the Council of Ministers could overrule its decisions: if Parliament vetoed the Council's proposal for legislation, the Council could overcome that veto on the basis of unanimity, but if it took no decision for 3 months the proposal would be void. If Parliament proposed amendments to the legislation the Council could accept them on the basis of unanimity if they departed from the terms of the Commission's proposals to the Council.

b. A new form of participation by the European Parliament in the decision-making process of the Community was included in the Agreement's proposed new Article 189(b) of the Treaty. This form of decision making was required in a number of policy areas, specifically decisions on consumer affairs, on aspects of environmental questions, on cultural, and educational matters, and on questions concerning the Communities' programmes for furthering common and joint research programmes. Article 189b gave the European Parliament a right which it previously lacked: to impose an unconditional veto on the Council's proposals for legislation in the stated areas. From some points of view this might be regarded as a significant enhancement of its powers. The process was a complicated one and included resort to a new Conciliation Committee in the event of disagreement between the Council and the Parliament, to be made up of equal numbers from each. Whether or not the Conciliation Committee reached agreement, approval of the legislation depended on the agreement of both Council and Parliament, unless Parliament failed to respond within a six weeks period. Legislation approved under 189(b) was to be signed by the Presidents of both the European Parliament and the Council of Ministers. Except when approving amendments from the European Parliament which had not been supported by the Commission, in which case unanimity applied, the Council was to take decisions in these procedures on the basis of qualified majority.

The Agreement included a Declaration on the Role of National Parliaments in the European Union, which stressed the importance of "greater involvement of national Parliaments in the activities of the European Union" and an improvement of ways of exchanging information between national parliaments and the European Parliament; Commission proposals were to go to national Parliaments "in good time for information and *possible* examination". Closer relations between the European Parliament and national Parliaments were also to be encouraged by providing" appropriate reciprocal facilities and regular meetings". If the House were to respond positively to this invitation, sovereignty *viz a viz* the Community could be exercised more effectively.

c. The machinery of the member states in the area of foreign policy was also further developed, and different categories of response to the outside world were created. The European Council was to be responsible for agreeing the principles and guidelines of foreign policy, the Council, acting on the basis of unanimity, was to agree common positions, and the Council within the context of such guidelines, principles and common positions, was to agree so-called joint actions on the basis of a qualified majority which in this case had to include the positive votes of eight of the twelve states, with 54 votes in favour.

d. A major innovation with regards to the judicial arrangements of the Communities was the introduction of a system whereby member states which did not comply with Directives could be subject to a fine by the Court of Justice. The Commission could advise the Court as to the appropriate sum to be paid by way of the fine. This, it was thought, would be likely to encourage the more reluctant states to obey the law.

e. Although ideas had been discussed for streamlining the Commission by, for instance, reducing its membership to twelve, there were no specific decisions for this in the Agreement. The main concession was that the Commission was to be subject to the approval of the European Parliament after its appointment by the member governments, though what happened in the event of its being rejected was not indicated.

2. *Institutional Innovation.*

a. The Agreement included a number of new institutions. Perhaps the most interesting was the Committee of the Regions which was to be made up of representatives of the sub-regions in member states, though they were to be appointed by the governments. The Committee was given a consultative role in a number of issue areas, and could be required to produce its opinion within a period specified by the Council, but not less than one month, after which the Council was free to act.

b. A conciliation committee with regards to legislation was also established as indicated above. A further innovation was the creation of an Ombudsman to be appointed by the European Parliament to investigate complaints by individuals and groups about alleged misconduct by the institutions of the Community.

C. IMPLICATIONS FOR THE CONSTITUTIONAL PRINCIPLES OF THE COMMUNITY

1. The Agreement obviously included a number of cases of the expansion of the role of the Communities. The list of common policies in A.3 was much enlarged to include, education and culture, consumer protection, energy , civil protection and tourism, and trans European networks in transport.

There were a number of innovations with regard to the rights of individuals including the creation of citizenship of the European Union, the right to vote in municipal elections and to stand as candidates for citizens of other EC member states—details to be produced by 31 December 1994—and an equal right for all citizens of the Union to help by the consular and other representatives of other member states in third countries—details by 31 December 1993. The increase in the role of the Community with regard to external relations, and a limited use of qualified majority voting in that area, was also striking. But the commitment to the development of a common defense policy was extremely cautious, and it was possible to interpret it as being intended for the very distant future. It "might in time lead to a common defense". AD(1) This is not to deny, however, that the allowing of a role on some aspects of defence to the WEU on the part of the members of the European Communities was a significant step in that direction.

2. In the area of external relations the French and the British seemed to have made concessions to the demand to promote European positions in their capacity as permanent members of the Security Council of the United Nations. Under AE(4) "member states which are also members of the UN Security Council will concert [sic] and keep the other members fully informed... they will ensure the defence of the positions and interests of the Union, without prejudice to their responsibilities under the provisions of the UN Charter." There was a degree of movement here in allowing the other members a right to be consulted about Security Council business: previously the British and the French had insisted on a fairly rigid separation of the two areas.

3. Much depends upon the interpretation of the significance of the various uses made of articles 189(c) and 189(b). The evidence of the Agreement suggests that this was a matter of fine judgement by the negotiators at Maastricht, with broadly speaking 189(c) being preferred if the question was one of importance to the members of the Council who wished to get their way in the positive sense of getting something done, and 189(b) being preferred if the members were less enthusiastic about an issue and were prepared to put up with a veto by the European Parliament. The latter procedure also allowed for a kind of double block by states which opposed the policy proposal under consideration. If it was outvoted in the Council where qualified majority voting applied, then it could seek to mobilize opposition in the European Parliament in order to create a majority of members against its acceptance there. This would naturally tend to encourage the more hesitant governments to whip members of their party in the European Parliament into towing the party line, and would tend to weaken the development of European parties, despite the lip service paid to this in Annex 1 of the agreement. The latter is another instance of a well established doctrine about the development of the European Communities: that apparent concessions to superanationalism are more likely when intergovernmentalism has been bolstered. The paradox should be noted, that 189(b) which appears to give more powers to the European Parliament can be interpreted as helping the more cautious states.

4. The 189(b) procedure was introduced in some areas where 189(c) had previously applied in the form of A.149 of the Treaty of Rome. This was true for Title III legislation on the free movement of persons, services and capital, and also for Article 100a legislation under Title IV. Decisions on the Multiannual Framework programmes on research and technology co-operation under A.130i were to be taken under 189(b), though they were previously to be taken under the terms of the SEA by unanimity in the Council. Decisions on co-operation in public health matters, and in consumer protection, both brought in as specific Community policies under their own heading, were to be based on 189(b).

5. It was particularly interesting to note the discrimination between the use of 189 (b) and (c). On transport policy guidelines were to be on the basis of 189(b) but decisions on implementation, on establishing interoperability in transport, and on agreeing technical standards were on the basis of 189(c). Under the general heading of Social Policy, Title VIII, decisions to promote co-operation on matters of education were to be taken by the 189(b) procedure, whilst under the same heading decisions to promote vocational training to adapt to industrial change, facilitate mobility, and co-operation on training, were to be taken through 198(c). With regard to Research and Technological Development, the overall programmes, as already indicated, were through 189(b), but specific programmes were to be approved by majority vote in the Council, that is, not even by 189(c), the equivalent of which, the procedure introduced by the SEA through A.149, had previously applied. Here was a case of regression. Decisions on the tasks, primary objectives and organization of the structural funds were to be taken on the basis of unanimity—no change from the SEA—but implementing legislation with regard to the Regional Fund and the Social Fund were 189(c), whilst decisions on the guidance section of the Agricultural Fund were somewhat oddly to be taken solely by qualified majority vote in the Council of Ministers.

6. The reservation of unanimity in some questions was also interesting. Article 189(c) procedures could be used to decide the actions to be taken to implement environment policy, but unanimity was to be used for provisions under this heading of a fiscal character, for measures affecting town and country planning, except measures regarding water resource management, and for measures "...significantly affecting choice between different energy sources" in member states. On Title XIV questions regarding industry,

co-operation between undertakings to promote innovation and adjustment to structural change were on the basis of unanimity in the Council. There was also to be an extremely interesting innovation in giving the Communities a role in a common policy on entry visas, under A.100c, but decisions on this were to be on the basis of unanimity—to establish guidelines—until 1996, when qualified majority voting in the Council was to apply—not 189 b or c—with states reserving the right to act alone with regard to law and order and internal security questions. On decisions which could facilitate exercising the rights of citizenship, unanimity was to apply. With regard to the establishment of a Community role on education decisions concerning the harmonization of laws and regulations of members states were not to be subject to 189(b), but unanimity in the Council.

CONCLUSIONS

1. The above arguments suggest that the terms of the Maastricht Agreement on Political Union do not significantly alter the conclusions reached after the Single European Act. It is true that the role of the Community has been enhanced, both in the sense that the scope of integration has been broadened, and that a wider role has been allowed to institutions such as the European Parliament. There has also been institutional innovation in creating the Council of the Regions, the Ombudsman, and the new Conciliation Council. There are also some new principles, which enhance the degree of interpenetration of the member states. But what should be stressed is that the negotiations were very carefully judged, and a somewhat archane nuancing of the granting of powers and the reservation of powers was achieved, no doubt sometimes for political and electoral reasons, and sometimes for reasons of principle.

2. But in general terms no new powers were granted which could be seen as diminishing the sovereignty of states, and which provided evidence to challenge the argument presented in the first part of this evidence. Even the decision which seemed to increase the powers of the European Parliament, A.189(b), could be seen as being carefully judged to allow some encouragement to states which might wish to make it easier to resist integration. And the Committee of the Regions has no powers of its own. The main principle of concessions to the Community seemed to be to extend implementing powers within the framework of agreements about principles, purposes, and major structures, which had been approved by the Council, either in a positive vote in favour by all members, or by a unanimous overcoming of the EPs opposition through 189(c). This is not to mention the various reserve powers available to states.

EUROPE AFTER MAASTRICHT

(The main constitutional Implications)

Memorandum submitted by Frank Vibert, Institute of Economic Affairs (EC223)[1]

CONCLUSIONS AND RECOMMENDATIONS

Maastricht can be considered a success in two important respects. First, the political and constitutional aspects of European integration were brought up to the highest political level for review and, contrary to long held fears that such a discussion would only be divisive and lead to unbridgeable differences, it was in fact possible to reach an agreement. Secondly, the agreement actually reached does not prejudice the future and leaves the possibility of decentralised constitutional development still open.

The most important lesson to be learnt from the Maastricht experience is that the United Kingdom must use the time intervening before the next IGC scheduled for 1996 to be fully prepared with its own positive agenda covering all the points up for discussion and not leave the initiative to others.

The crucial areas where the United Kingdom must use the intervening time to prepare a positive agenda are the following:

— enlargement;

— restructuring the Commission and its terms of reference;

— the parliamentary base for the Community;

— the judicial framework;

— financial control in the Community and the fiscal constitution.

---

[1]The views expressed in this memorandum are those of the author, not of the IEA which has no corporate view.

A key question therefore is the procedural one of how the UK can best carry forward the agenda. There are two aspects of this question—one is the best procedure within the Community; the other concerns the best domestic procedure.

As far as Community procedures are concerned the UK should use its Presidency later this year not only to carry forward Community enlargement (and its associated issues) but also establish Community level procedures for technical level review of the issues mentioned above.

This note makes three other precise recommendations:

> First, there is a need to "unbundle" the Commission and separate out its activities so that the regulatory, administrative and political procedures in the European Union can develop on a fully transparent and equitable basis; (page 35)

> Secondly, there is a need to create an office in Whitehall, probably in the Office of the Prime Minister, to concern itself with strategic and co-ordination issues relating to the European Union; (page 37)

> Thirdly, there is a need to consider formalising the role of National Parliaments in the process of deciding what legislation is necessary at the Union level. (page 36)

THE SUCCESS OF MAASTRICHT

Ability to Reach Agreement

There has always been a political agenda behind the European Community. In the past however, governments have been reluctant to speak about it and in particular to confront the constitutional implications. Their fear has been that any such discussion would be divisive and thus risk setting back the process of European integration rather than furthering it. Maastricht can be counted a success first because it showed that constitutional and institutional questions could be discussed and negotiated at the highest political level in the Community and agreement reached. Maastricht however, is not the end of the story. On the contrary, the constitutional dimension of European integration is now firmly in the open and will be a continuing feature of discussions on Europe's future.

No Prejudice for the Future

Because Britain's own constitutional arrangements have evolved over a long period, we are less familiar than other Member States with constitutions as purposive constructions. In the case of Europe the constitutional debate is about putting in place a structure which will enable the Member States to take collective action in well defined areas where it makes sense to do so and at the same time to guard against over-centralisation and unnecessary intrusion from the centre into areas which concern only the Member State.

In simplified theoretical terms Maastricht can be seen as a clash between two contrasting views of Europe's constitutional future.

> (i) A *centralist* view stressed the need for collective action in most areas of public policy, the need for strong central bodies with overriding executive and legislative power to carry them out and with legal and financial autonomy for the central authority. Under this approach the institutions of the European Union are viewed primarily as instruments to attain given collective ends.

> (ii) The *decentralist* view emphasises the benefits from decentralised structures in the Community and in particular those which flow from maintaining diversified approaches to public policy through vigorous national and local jurisdictions in Member States. This view stresses the importance of process as much as instruments. There is a particular interest in 'non coercive' processes for collective action and in safeguarding against the institutional and policy dynamics that lead to over-centralisation over a period of time.

Neither view can be neatly classified as either "federal" or "confederal". In Britain, the term "federal" is often associated with centralist structures, partly because the centralist view has tended to abrogate for itself the "federal" label. In Germany, by contrast, "federal" is often interpreted as meaning decentralised structures.

Against this background, Maastricht was a success in a second sense in that it did not create a prejudice in favour of future centralised development. The main areas for strengthened collective action (in foreign affairs, security and Home Affairs) make sense under either view of Europe's constitutional future. Those with a centralist view of Europe's future can point to the gains for collective action; those in favour of decentralised means of handling such action are broadly content with the institutional and decision taking mechanisms decided in these areas.

The arrangements for monetary union might appear at first sight to carry Europe a long way towards central control. However, it is the case that those who favour safeguards against over-centralised government also tend to favour limits on the discretionary power of governments in general. Arguably, the monetary constitution agreed in Maastricht goes far in the direction of removing the discretionary power of governments over the value of the currency. Indeed it may not go far enough.[1]

LESSONS FROM MAASTRICHT

The Need for a Positive Agenda

Having successfully reached agreement in Maastricht and not having prejudiced the future course of constitutional development in the European Union, governments of the Member States including the British Government might well wish to take a prolonged rest from constitutional and institutional issues in the Community. There are other pressing concerns in the Community such as CAP reform, the GATT talks and reform of the Community budget quite apart from domestic priorities. It would however, be a mistake for the British Government to relax its attention to constitutional and institutional questions.

There are two main reasons why the British Government has to take a pro-active role in Europe's constitutional development:

> First the Maastricht agreement is not a stable agreement. Precisely because it leaves the main lines open for the future, it leaves none of the constitutional protagonists truly satisfied. Those favouring stronger centralisation in the Community will come back with their agenda. Equally those who are concerned to secure a decentralised structure will look to better safeguards and mechanisms than those agreed at Maastricht.

> Secondly, it would be a great mistake to underestimate the aspirations of members of the European Parliament and the agenda of the Commission for a centralised constitutional structure for the Union.

There are some who feel that Maastricht has made some important advances for a decentralised future that will be reinforced by Community enlargement and other developments (including those in Germany). This judgement is premature. In particular, there is a need to be aware of the proposals put forward by the Commission in the course of the Maastricht negotiations. These are summarised in Chart A, attached. While they were not accepted by Member Governments in the negotiations, there are specific references to this agenda in the Treaty in relation to future Treaty revisions. Nothing in the past behaviour of either the Commission or the Parliament suggests that this agenda will vanish of its own accord. On the contrary, those who stress the need for decentralised arrangements must put forward their own alternatives.

The Need to Prepare Ahead of Time

There are two additional reasons why the constitutional future of the Community should not be put in abeyance until the run up to the next Inter governmental review scheduled for 1996. First, the Maastricht process itself was a poor way to handle issues of such fundamental importance. A different preparation process must be put in train for the next review. Secondly it is apparent from the Maastricht agreement that where the British government had positive proposals to put forward (for example in relation to the scrutiny role of the European Parliament) it was quite successful in having them reflected in the final agreement.

[1.]There are three points of concern about the monetary constitution as embodied in the Treaty:

First there is a division of authority between the ECB with its responsibility for maintaining the value of the currency in terms of domestic price levels and the responsibility of the Council for the external value of the currency in the exchange markets. The targets of monetary policy cannot be divided this way.

Secondly, the surveillance mechanism envisaged relies on administrative mechanisms rather than on market discipline thus opening the possibility of political judgements playing a major role in determining what constitutes "sound policy".

Thirdly, if it turns out that only few Member States qualify for the single currency area by the deadlines envisaged , and if in the meantime transactions costs of different currencies have been substantially reduced (because of competition in exchange markets and the widespread use of the Ecu) it is not clear that revisions will not be seen to be desirable for market reasons. Alternatively there is the possibility that political judgements will influence the application of the convergence criteria.

In sum there is an ambiguity between discretionary political control and technocratic management at the heart of the key monetary provisions of the Treaty. At the least there is a case for making the mechanism for political "overrides" more transparent, for defining the price stability objective of the ECB in clearer terms and for introducing contract into the arrangements.

In addition, the convergence criteria are such that relatively few Member States may qualify for the single currency area leaving, in addition to administered approaches to monetary union, scope also for market oriented approaches to monetary union including the development of the Ecu as a common currency.

A course of inaction simply results in the agenda being set by others. Britain must therefore use the time between now and the start of the next negotiations to develop a positive agenda of its own for the institutional development of the European Union. The key items for this agenda are enlargement, the restructuring of the Commission, consolidating the parliamentary base for the Community, the judicial framework and the issue of financial control in the Community (the fiscal constitution).

ENLARGEMENT

It is possible that the next round of Community enlargement (notably the entry of Austria and Sweden) can be carried out within present Community structures and procedures. However, a Community of 25–30 Member States will be a different Community. Britain's economic, foreign policy and security interests are best secured by the building of this larger Community.

An enlarged Community will be different in three major respects—institutions will need to be adapted; the range of decision-taking rules will need to be extended and the approach to areas of collective action will need to be diversified. This does not require a complete break with the past but it does require building further on some of the features agreed at Maastricht.

"Multi Track" Co-operation

In respect of the approach to policy areas for collective action Maastricht establishes the beginnings of a "multi track" European Union where not all Member States will be participants in all areas of public policy. One example is Britain's non participation in the agreement on the Social Charter and another is the criteria for selective participation in any single currency area. The arrangements for cooperation in the security and defence fields also leave scope for this kind of development. Another example under way outside the Maastricht agreement is in respect of the reform of the CAP where reform in the direction of tariffication of agricultural protection may be accompanied by the "repatriation" of other aspects of the CAP notably the income transfers to be provided to farmers in different circumstances and the support to be given on environmental grounds.

Diversified Decision-Taking Rules

In respect of the decision-taking rules for an enlarged Community the Maastricht arrangements take a welcome step in the direction of a more diversified array of decision rules. In the Commission's view (shared by the European Parliament) qualified majority voting should become the norm within the Community. The issue is that with a larger Community, unanimity will be more difficult to obtain while majority voting will mean an unacceptably large number of countries that could be overruled. The Maastricht treaty however recognises the applicability of a greater range of procedures. The extension of majority voting is limited. More important for the future, it includes "two-tier" decision rules (unanimity for the basic decision of principle followed by majority voting for implementation); different qualifying majorities for different classes of decisions; special purpose derogations; opting in and opting out procedures; the use of the popular reserve (referenda) and the parliamentary reserve (acceptance subject to parliamentary approval) and also allows for flexibility in deciding on what should be included in areas for "common action". It is through the further development of this array of decision-taking arrangements, graduated and calibrated according to the importance of the subject matter, that cooperation in the Union can increase.

The common thread of this development towards a greater array of decision taking rules and towards "multi-track" policy co-operation is the need to extend and foster the European Union on the basis of "non coercive" techniques for joint action. Given the diversity in Europe and the need to maintain that diversity, as well as the fragility of any Union that relied on coercion, this development of non coercive techniques is vital for the future. Maastricht may be an important step on the way towards "non coercive" means of co-operation but it will require further consolidation in future revisions.

THE COMMISSION

Its Powers and Aspirations

Historically, the Treaties have conferred on the Commission an extraordinary range of political, judicial, executive and administrative functions. Its monopoly on the right to propose and initiate has been a particularly powerful instrument. It has justified this sweep of functions by reference to the need for a body to flesh out the sometimes opaque and general declarations of the Councils, and by purporting to stand for the interests of the Community as a whole and in particular those of the smaller Member States. However, it has used its powers and in particular its power to propose, to further its own agenda. Furthermore, it is important to realise that it sees its future as the Executive body for the Union in the sense that the President and cabinet in the United States provides the executive branch in the American system of government (see Chart A).

Maastricht represents only a partial check to the aspirations of the Commission. Article D of the Treaty confirms the European Council as the key body for conferring direction in the Community, the Council is given a greater capacity (Article 151) and the arrangements for foreign policy, security and Home Affairs cooperation generally restrict the Commission to the role of a right to be associated with the formulation of policy and selected areas of implementation.

In other respects however, the Commission continues to gain power and authority. It gains through the addition of new policies under the Economic Community, through a potentially important role in the surveillance mechanisms of the EMU arrangements, and through a new political role in the assent, and conciliation procedures of the European Parliament. In addition the procedure for the approval of the Commission by the European Parliament will be presented by the Commission as legitimising its political leadership aspirations.

The ambitions of the Commission are thus likely to remain undimmed by Maastricht. Indeed, the reference in Article C to a "single institutional framework" to serve the Union is a likely marker for the Commission to argue for a more assertive role in the new areas of the Treaty in future revisions.

"Unbundling" its Activities

Those who consider that bureaucratic direction in the Community is damaging and inappropriate also feel from this perspective that Maastricht has left incomplete an unfinished agenda of necessary reforms to the Commission. The unfinished agenda involves:

— a revision to Article 155 in order to limit its focus to the administrative role of the Commission.

— an unbundling of the Commission's non administrative responsibilities so that political functions are carried out by the Councils. Any political overrides in the Commission's regulatory functions should cease to be internalised within the Commission but be clearly identified as the responsibility of the Councils.

— a separation of some of its key duties (for example in respect of competition and external trade) so that there is a clear and transparent distinction between administrative, judicial,and regulatory functions.

— Commissioners would be limited in their term of office in a manner appropriate to their regulatory, judicial or administrative responsibilities.

There are two areas in particular where the "unbundling" of the Commission's current range of activities should be explored by the Member States—external commercial policy and competition policy.

The *external commercial policy* of the European Union has exhibited two extremely damaging tendencies—an inability to handle international trade negotiations effectively and a susceptibility to protectionism, particularly in the form of spurious anti-dumping measures and the imposition of non tariff barriers. The difficulty in the area of external commercial policy arises because it involves a mixture of high level political judgement, regulatory and quasi judicial action and day to day administration. Political conflicts are inevitable and need to be sorted out by the Council of Ministers or the European Council. What is avoidable is the clouding of the regulatory and quasi judicial function of the Commission by internal political trade-offs between Commissioners and the risks of regulatory and administrative distortions arising from the lobbying of special interest groups. An external trade Commission operating within clear guidelines, following quasi judicial procedures and with rulings that can only be overridden by the Councils for clearly stated political reasons, would aid both transparency and efficiency.

Much the same can be said of *competition policy* where politicking between Commissioners and lobbying by special interests risk damaging a vital area of the Single Market programme. Again, a separate Competition Commission operating on quasi judicial lines is needed. There are further areas where development away from a general purpose Commission towards a number of separate Commissions, structured in a way appropriate to their specific function may be desirable.

THE PARLIAMENTARY BASE

Gains Unclear

Maastricht made only limited progress in trying to define the respective roles of the European Parliament and National Parliaments which together form the Parliamentary base of the European Union. The issue is flagged in the two declarations attached to the Maastricht Treaty, but not resolved. Contacts between National Parliaments and the European Parliament can and should be improved and the Conference of the Parliaments may serve a limited purpose. Nevertheless the underlying issue remains.

The Maastricht Treaty recognises the ex post scrutiny role of the European Parliament in providing it with new powers of inquiry (Art.137b) and financial discharge (Art.206b). The problematic area is in respect of its new powers to influence selected areas of legislation ex ante through the three reading 'negative assent' procedure. Whether this will lead to a Parliamentary gain is unclear. That will partly depend on the ability of the Parliament to mobilise absolute majorities, and partly on the inter- institutional dynamics between Parliament, Commission and Council where traditionally the Parliament and Commission have tended to work in tandem against the Council.

There are two highly undesirable possible outcomes. One is that the Commission could become the main winner through its initiating role in legislation and its brokerage role in the conciliation procedure. A second possibility is that the blurring of responsibility between Council, Commission and Parliament inherent in the negative assent procedure will leave other interests such as pressure groups as the main winner. The dynamics of "regulatory capture" will increasingly focus on the central institutions of the EC and safeguards are needed.

The Role of National Parliaments in Implementing "Subsidiarity"

The issue of the *ex ante* legislative role of national parliaments and the European Parliament requires therefore much further attention than given at Maastricht. Community enlargement will make the European Parliament too large to be effective. Alternatively if it remains at its present size through the reduction of the number of MEPs per Member State, it may appear too distant and remote to engage the attention of the electorate. One alternative is to bring national parliaments more formally into the process of the *ex ante* review of European Community legislation either through cooperation between the business managers of national parliaments or through the establishment of a small second chamber of parliamentarians drawn from national parliaments.

One possible avenue would be for national parliaments to build on the Maastricht definition of subsidiarity (Art 3b) and have a voice in the decision as to whether legislation is necessary at the EC level. This would suggest that the Assembly of Parliaments would either have a formal responsibility in the initiation of legislation (instead of the Commission) or, alternatively (or as well), the first review of legislation introduced by the Council. After review by the Assembly the legislation would then go to the directly elected Chamber for its negative assent along Maastricht lines. Conciliation would take place between the two chambers with the Council having a veto right. This is illustrated schematically in Chart B.

For many reasons it is difficult for the House of Commons to grapple, together with other national parliaments, with the issues involved. Nevertheless, Members should be aware that the end result of Commission proposals at Maastricht would be the eventual reduction of national parliaments to performing essentially agency roles for the central authorities.

THE JUDICIAL FRAMEWORK

There are two different approaches to trying to guard against over-centralisation and unnecessary intrusion in the Community. One stresses the role of a Europe of the Regions. This received limited recognition at Maastricht in the form of the new advisory body of regional representatives. The other approach stresses the need to get the legal framework right and to build justiciable safeguards into the Treaty.

Maastricht gave partial recognition to the need for stronger legal safeguards. In particular, the inclusion of the principle of subsidiarity as defined in Article 3b might provide the Court of Justice with a principle to take into account in its judgements. The second paragraph of Article 3b, "any action by the Community shall not go beyond what is necessary to achieve the objectives of this Treaty" might also be developed in practice or in subsequent revisions of the Treaty as a principle against bodies acting beyond the express powers granted in the Treaty. Similarly, the power to fine might be developed in practice and in subsequent revisions of the Treaty into the concept of "damage to others" as a major criterion for whether action at the Community level is justified or not.

A highly undesirable feature of the Maastricht Treaty is the incorporation of the principle of the *"acquis communautaire"*. Not only does it convey the unfortunate impression of the Community as a "one way street", but if it has legal application it might provide a practical hindrance to the process of adaptation and adjustments in the European Union.

It should also be noted that Commission proposals for Maastricht (reflected in the Luxembourg draft) included a new category of Community law superior to any other. It also proposed that the Commission have the power to issue regulations directly. The intent behind the superior category of law is to establish the central institutions of the Community as bodies with primary authority in the Union and national parliaments as clearly subordinate. This proposal was not accepted by Member States. Nevertheless the

Maastricht Treaty retains reference to this proposal in stating that the "hierarchy" of Community acts needs to be reviewed in 1996 (Article 189, footnote 1). Key aspects of the judicial framework could therefore also be pointed in the direction of a centralist future for the Union.

FINANCIAL CONTROL (THE FISCAL CONSTITUTION)

In respect of the fiscal constitution of the Union, Article 201 essentially confirms the 1985 Council decision on the Communities' system of own resources and maintains the control of Council unanimity. In addition, Article 201a provides a potentially useful constraint on the Commission's power to introduce new expenditure proposals. Combined with the European Parliament's new powers of scrutiny and discharge, the Maastricht revisions suggest that a modest gain may have been made in framing constitutional restraints on expenditure at the Community level. However, the gains may be more apparent than real.

The underlying constitutional issue is the bureaucratic and political motivation that, unless checked, propels public expenditure ever upwards and which in turn leads to an ever increasing centralisation of expenditure and revenue powers and upsets decentralised constitutional arrangements.

In the context of the Community, both Commission and the European Parliament have a clear self interest in larger expenditures at the Community level. Expenditure programmes create clients and dependant relationships. However, the Maastricht Treaty also feeds the same process in the Council of Ministers. By opening up new funds such as the Cohesion Fund and new Heads of Expenditure (such as trans European networks) it enlarges the scope for bargaining between governments in the Council where outlays under one head can be offset by receipts under another. Such behaviour (logrolling) leads to bargains being struck at ever higher levels of expenditure unless constrained by other factors. Commission proposals made at Maastricht would have further aggravated this situation by giving the Commission and the Parliament additional budget powers and by proposing that the Community should be able to tax directly.

The Community budget is in urgent need of reform in any event. This reform must address not only the immediate financial issues but also look at a system of constitutional constraints that can be incorporated in future revisions to the Maastricht Treaty.

PROCEDURES

The United Kingdom should develop a positive agenda for each of the areas outlined above. There is much in Britain's own experience that can be contributed. It would be absurd in the light of Britain's parliamentary tradition if it did not play an active role in developing the Parliamentary base for the Union. It would also be unfortunate if the experience gained with regulatory structures in Britain and experience with the Next Steps initiatives in Whitehall were not brought to bear in proposals for the restructuring of the Commission.

The procedural question is how such an agenda can be developed and carried forward. One aspect is the organisation of the necessary preparation and oversight in the machinery of British government. There may be a case for a central unit (possibly in the Office of the Prime Minister) that would gather the strands and coordinate a position. The House of Commons would presumably also wish to at least keep itself fully informed and possibly contribute to the process.

New Strategic Office in Whitehall

As far as Whitehall is concerned, day to day co-ordination mechanisms in Whitehall on the EC agenda are believed to work well. However the need is to develop a greater strategic and advance planning capacity as well as a retrieval capacity in relation to the past history of topics returning to the table.

Even a well running machinery for day to day co-ordination is likely to be overwhelmed with the short term EC agenda and "fire fighting". It is unlikely to have the time to devote to strategic issues. An office solely concerned with strategy however is likely to find itself shut out from the mainstream of activities. There is therefore much to be said for having a strategic office that not only is responsible for forward issues but also for coordinating particularly difficult inter-departmental and inter-governmental issues (for example in respect of the Community budget reform or the GATT tables).

If the strategic/co-ordination office is to play this role, it may need to be headed by a specially appointed Minister for the European Union (at Deputy Prime Minister level) or by the Prime Minister. A Deputy Prime Minister might run into friction with other senior Cabinet colleagues, thus requiring Prime Ministerial adjudication in any case. If such friction is felt likely to occur, the simplest solution would be to place the strategic and co-ordination office for the European Union in the Office of the Prime Minister.

The British Presidency

The other aspect of the procedures is how to carry forward the discussions in the Community. The British government will assume the Presidency in the second half of this year. In addition to giving priority to Community enlargement, the Government should establish a working group of the Council of Ministers to prepare the ground for the next round of constitutional negotiations. In this way the next Intergovernmental review will be able to consider a full range of alternative approaches and arrive at the necessary political judgements on a properly prepared basis. The Secretariat of the Council could support this work.

CONCLUSIONS

The Maastricht Treaty is a success in strengthening the framework for cooperation in the Community without creating a prejudice in favour of centralised constitutional development for the future. It contains elements that could be built upon in ways that will ensure a decentralised future for the European Union with "non coercive" means for Member States to act in common. However, there is an agenda on the table from the Commission that goes clearly in the direction of a bureaucratic centralised destiny for the Community. Maastricht has not laid this to rest. On the contrary, unless active steps are taken to develop and advocate alternative proposals, a centralised destiny could still be in store. The United Kingdom should build on the successes it had in Maastricht and initiate procedures later this year in order to develop a positive agenda for the constitutional and institutional evolution in the Union consonant with the wishes of Westminster.

Chart A

CENTRALISING THE EUROPEAN UNION
(Commission Proposals for Maastricht)*

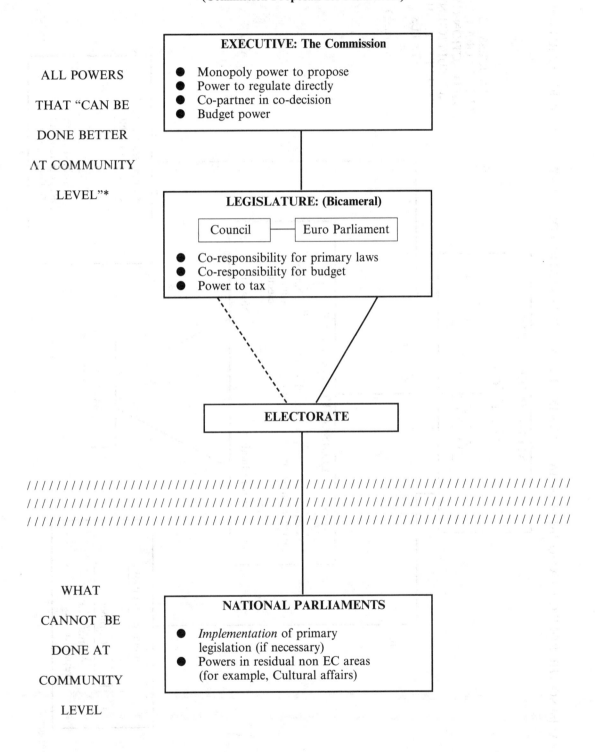

ALL POWERS

THAT "CAN BE

DONE BETTER

AT COMMUNITY

LEVEL"*

EXECUTIVE: The Commission

● Monopoly power to propose
● Power to regulate directly
● Co-partner in co-decision
● Budget power

LEGISLATURE: (Bicameral)

Council — Euro Parliament

● Co-responsibility for primary laws
● Co-responsibility for budget
● Power to tax

ELECTORATE

WHAT

CANNOT BE

DONE AT

COMMUNITY

LEVEL

NATIONAL PARLIAMENTS

● *Implementation* of primary
  legislation (if necessary)
● Powers in residual non EC areas
  (for example, Cultural affairs)

* See *"Intergovernmental Conferences: Contributions by the Commission"* Bulletin of the European Communities, Supplement 2/91, p122.

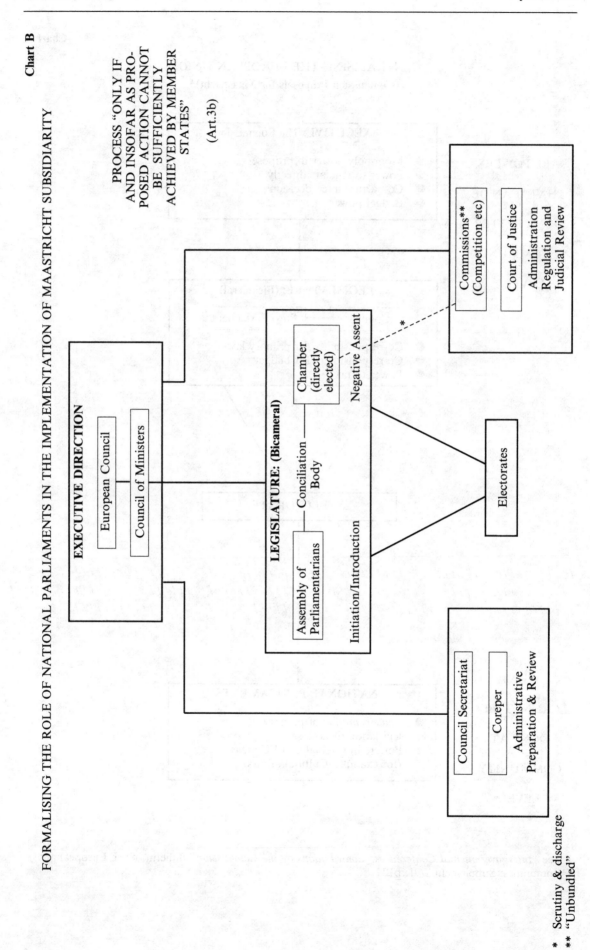

Chart B

FORMALISING THE ROLE OF NATIONAL PARLIAMENTS IN THE IMPLEMENTATION OF MAASTRICHT SUBSIDIARITY

PROCESS "ONLY IF AND INSOFAR AS PRO-POSED ACTION CANNOT BE SUFFICIENTLY ACHIEVED BY MEMBER STATES"

(Art.3b)

EXECUTIVE DIRECTION

European Council

Council of Ministers

LEGISLATURE: (Bicameral)

Assembly of Parliamentarians

Conciliation Body

Chamber (directly elected)

Initiation/Introduction

Negative Assent

Electorates

Commissions** (Competition etc)

Court of Justice

Administration Regulation and Judicial Review

*

Council Secretariat

Coreper

Administrative Preparation & Review

*   Scrutiny & discharge
** "Unbundled"

EXAMINATION OF WITNESSES

DR PAUL TAYLOR, London School of Economics, MR FRANK VIBERT, Institute of Economic Affairs, and DR HELEN WALLACE, Royal Institute of International Affairs, examined

Chairman

76. Could I begin this morning by welcoming our three witnesses, Dr Helen Wallace who of course has been with us before, Dr Taylor and Mr Vibert. Thank you all very much for coming this morning. This is the second evidence session the Committee has had on Europe after Maastricht. We are trying to put some kind of framework of thought upon the consequences of the Maastricht document. The Maastricht document is not yet, of course, presented publicly in a treaty although we understand the draft is now complete and will be circulated possibly later this week or early next week for governments and, indeed, parliaments to begin looking at. The Committee has paid some visits to other capitals of the Community, including Brussels and Paris, and will be going to Bonn early next week. What we want to concentrate on today is what might broadly be called the constitutional aspects which, of course, means to what extent the rights and sovereignty of this nation and this Parliament are likely to be further affected, or the direction of the current effects changed, by what has apparently been agreed in the Maastricht document. We are grateful for the papers that have been put in and also have read with interest the article by Dr Wallace in the Chatham House publication "International Affairs"[1]. So we have a pretty broad idea of your various views on this issue. Can I suggest as a matter of procedure that, if a question is to one of you from one of us, please would anyone else feel no hesitation about coming in. The only restraint I would urge is please do not talk over each other; that makes it absolutely impossible for the shorthand writers. Let us therefore begin with a Judgment about the Maastricht document. Perhaps I could try this first on Mr Vibert—does this Treaty as you understand it institutionalise what has already happened in terms of the growing competence of the Community (they seem to grow all the time), a stronger role for the European Parliament, and the move at least into pillar form of foreign and security policy, judicial and home affairs matters? In short, is this a further significant advance towards what we understand by federalism or does it leave open the opportunities for further decentralisation and for constitutional development to entrench that decentralisation? Would you like to try first, Mr Vibert?

(Mr Vibert) Mr Chairman, I think in my note to the Committee I did put forward the view that, in my opinion, there was underlying what has been agreed at Maastricht, a fairly fundamental clash of views, not exactly between federalism or confederalism and non-federalism, but between a view about a rather centralist destiny of the Community and a decentralised view as to how things should

be done in Europe. I think what was agreed at Maastricht does not set the Community irrevocably in the direction of centralised solutions and it leaves open the possibility of a decentralised evolution; but I think the debate is certainly not over and I think that, if the decentralised future is to be secured—if that is what the British Government wants—very active steps are going to have to be taken to secure that decentralised future, otherwise it is probably not going to happen. I think the whole history of Britain's relationship with the Community and with Europe has been rather to underestimate the power of European integration and the forces leading towards centralisation and accumulation of powers and competencies at the centre. If we want to influence the future course, then we have to get in there very actively with our view and agenda as to what that future would be.

77. Your phrase "the debate is not over" sounds a bit downbeat to me. It is the sort of thing people say when they have just lost a court case but still feel right was on their side. Would you like to put it a little more positively perhaps, that the Maastricht agreements actually open the way for a vigorous Presidency, such as the British one, to take Europe in this direction, or am I trying to draw too much out of your views?

(Mr Vibert) No, that is correct. The way is open. If the British Government wishes to take this opportunity, then there are elements in what was agreed at Maastricht which could be very helpful for the future—certain aspects of decisions taken in relation to foreign policy, the possibility of a more multi-track development, countries deciding which areas they want to co-operate in and which areas they do not want to co-operate in, doing things in common or not, and I think there are other elements in the draft framework. There are various elements which could be built upon by an active British presidency, an active British Government, and indeed by this House. But it will take an active stance.

78. Dr Taylor, how do you see the Maastricht imprint upon the unfolding scene? Do you think it gives the Community Government a particular spin in a new direction or that it is just a marker along a pre-ordained way?

(Dr Taylor) I broadly agree with the last speaker. I prefer to draw a distinction between the process of extending further competence to the Community, which I think has taken place in the Maastricht agreement, and at the same time setting up really various road blocks in that certain things I think have been in a way clawed back—the defences are in place. In fact, I see that as very much characteristic of the long-term development of the European Community, the agreement of competence. Diplomats have learned, I think, as the process has proceeded, a much greater degree

[1]Article on "The Europe that came in from the cold" International Affairs 67: 4(1991) 647-63.

[**Chairman** *Contd*]

of skill in setting up reservations. It was said about
the Single European Act, for instance, that it represented three steps forward and two steps back. I
think the same general conclusion might be made
about the Maastricht agreement—except that the
three steps forward are not quite of the same kind
as two steps back. The three steps forward are to
do with the extension of competence, a right to
manage, in slightly more areas. The two steps back
I think are to do more with finding ways of
enabling states to reserve powers. In fact, the point
of the first part of my contribution really is to
explore something that I think has been explored
insufficiently hitherto, the difference between
extending competence and extending sovereignty. I
think there is a case for saying that we need to be
more self-conscious about the ways in which
sovereignty has been protected as the Community
process has proceeded. These are complex issues. It
seems to me that there is a reservation of the parties, and that the ways in which sovereignty has
been preserved have been rather under-considered,
under-stated in the past.

79. I am just looking here to the conclusion of
an article you published in the Review of
International Studies[1] in which you say towards
the end that there is no evidence to suggest that
common arrangements could not be extended a
very long way without necessarily posing any
direct challenge to the sovereignty of states. That is
the point you are making, is it?

(*Dr Taylor*) Yes.

80. I do not want to waste the Committee's time
but you also use a word I have never set eyes on
before which is "consociationalism". Is that a way
of describing the thought you are trying to put to
us?

(*Dr Taylor*) Yes, it is. We are dealing with
something in the Community which I think is different from what we have seen hitherto. One of the
great problems is that the language we use tends to
be concerned with previous arrangements.

81. Dr Wallace, how do you see this broad
thought as to whether the Maastricht documents
change the direction of things or carry on federal-
ising?

(*Dr Wallace*) I think the history of the
Community has been more ambiguous than that.
There has always been an ambiguity between
adopting (and I would use the world "supranational" and not "centralisation") supranational
methods for dealing with some kinds of policy and
leaving other kinds of policy to be handled on a
more co-operative basis. I follow Paul Taylor's
language of consociationalism for certain areas.
Those ambiguities remain. What I think Member
States did at Maastricht was to reinforce a particular version of the supranational method for some
areas, but to leave open, particularly in new areas,

whether those were going to be pursued beyond
the immediate on more than a rather diffuse and
co-operative basis. The test of that is yet to come,
because I think Member States were not ready at
Maastricht to make a big decision about that. I
think a big decision about that will have to be
made before very long, and I share the views that
Frank Vibert put to you in his memorandum that
the big question has been ducked but will have to
be faced. My view is that that will have to be faced
in a way which would perhaps imply being tougher
in more supranational ways on a small number of
policy areas, and being more diffuse, more loosely
consociational in a number of other areas, but the
problem being which policy issues you put into
which category. I think we have rather confused
the signals from Maastricht on the whole question
of in what conditions Member States reserve powers. On the one hand one has the assertion in the
text, which I find a little puzzling, that the full
acquis communautaire has to be respected, because
that sounds very conservative in respect of the
existing powers and responsibilities of the
Community. The language of subsidiarity is introduced which perhaps implies something else,
although we do not yet know that, and that I am
sure you will want to come onto later. The protocol on the social chapter gives some very confused
signals about how areas where there are real difficulties between Member States and the political
families will be addressed in the future.

Chairman: Thank you. Could we just move on a
little to the specific position of this nation's, our
own nation's, underlying constitutional position.

Mr Jopling

82. Dr Taylor, in your paper which you kindly
sent to us on page 28 you refer to this point and I
quote what you say, "neither accession to the
European Communities, nor the terms of the
Single European Act or the Maastricht agreement,
have altered the underlying legal and constitutional
circumstances of British sovereignty". That is the
view you take, and I would be interested to know
whether the other two witnesses would subscribe to
that thought?

(*Dr Wallace*) I think it depends tremendously
on what view you take about the nature of the
Community exercise. If you take it as an exercise
in sharing powers in areas where you regard it as
important to pursue common interests then it is
attributing or sharing your sovereignty on a collective basis. I do not see it as a zero sum game at the
Member State level or at the Community level, I
think it is much more diffuse and confusing than
that. In that sense Maastricht seems to me very
much in keeping with what we have done on previous occasions in this country with the Single
European Act, at the time of accession and so on.

83. Dr Taylor is saying neither access nor the
Single European Act nor Maastricht have altered
the underlying legal and constitutional circumstances of British sovereignty. That will be a surprising statement to a lot of people?

[1]Article on The European Community and the State:
assumptions, theories and propositions. Review of
International Studies (1991), 17, 109–125.

[Mr Jopling Contd]

(Dr Wallace) I am not surprised by it.

(Mr Vibert) I think I probably, with due respect, do not take entirely the same view. I think it is correct technically in the sense that the government of the day of this House can always decide to withdraw from the Treaty of Rome and the Single European Act and any other treaty we sign. In that sense we have compromised nothing, but the fact is, as Dr Wallace says, the arrangements which are being made in Europe for co-operation on agreed objectives in Europe have a constitutional implication for us. I think it is difficult to deny that. We are well on the way to developing a constitutional framework for Europe as a whole within which we act and wish to act. Of course, we can always step out of that framework but, nevertheless, it is increasingly in place and we accept that. I think it is desirable in that sense—the circumstances in which we are operating have changed and will go on changing.

84. Dr Taylor, do you want to come back on that?

(Dr Taylor) Obviously I do not quite agree with what was just said. The important term, however, is underlying what I said there. It is a matter of what the British have a legal right to do and what we could do under our own constitutional arrangements. There is a dispute amongst the lawyers on this one as to whether there is a new kind of constitutional order in the Community, or whether the Community rests essentially upon the pillars of the constitutions of the seven states. I think that the point is often missed, that to say it rests upon the constitution of the Community is in fact a political point. It is an open question. My feeling is that as all this starts from a Treaty between sovereign states, and as there is the possibility of withdrawal under international law from the Treaty, and given the special arrangements that we have in Britain regarding our constitution, that there are a whole range of potentials there with regard to the Community that could be exercised and realised that derive from the character of our own constitution. Failure to exercise those potentials is often, not invariably, to do with the way that our internal working arrangements are worked. Had they evolved somewhat differently—and it is an "if" question—then the view that we had lost sovereignty would seem to carry far less weight, I think. But there is a political disagreement at the heart of this which has a significant legal characteristic as to what the constitutional basis of the Community is. It seems to me it is still a separate constitution of the individual Member States.

Chairman

85. There is also, is there not, legal disagreement? We are going to have some hearings later with lawyers on these matters too. Are you really saying that, because this Parliament and this nation is sovereign, in the last resort that sovereignty is ungiveable away in the sense that Parliament can always reclaim, the nation can always secede from these agreements? If that is what you are saying, how does that square with the view that the laws of the Community are superior to the laws of the nation state?

(Dr Taylor) I think there are two separate points there. One is that circumstances could arise in which it would seem to be appropriate to say that sovereignty had been transferred. Again referring to the word I used, "underlying", I would argue that the sovereignty is in a sense indivisible and that either we have it or we do not. It is a matter then of how we choose to exercise the powers that accrue to us because we have it, or how the other authority chooses to exercise those powers. As to the other part of your question, the primacy of Community law, that is something that was in the European Communities Act 1972. It is also something, of course, that has been asserted by the Court of the Community, particularly in the late 1970s in the Simmenthal case. The question then arises of where does this leave the British Parliament. Is it really the case that the European Court can negate an Act of Parliament? It can, of course, if Parliament chooses to allow that and given that in the European Communities Act that is what it has said. But we in Britain have a rather peculiar constitutional situation in that Acts of constitutional amendment are carried out by exactly the same process as ordinary legislation. So my point is that, if Parliament makes it quite clear without any ambiguity that it wishes to negate an Act from the Community, the important relationship here being with British courts, the British courts would do what the Parliament told them to do.

Mr Shore

86. With respect, I think that is very questionable. The British courts are alienated from the British Parliament as long as the European Communities Act remains on the Statute Book.

(Dr Taylor) This again I think in the literature is something that is controversial. Others apart from me have said that that is not necessarily the case and it is to do with the sovereignty of Parliament in a sense, and the sovereignty of Parliament logically means obviously——

87. The sovereignty of Parliament has been put, as it were, in pawn under the European Communities Act.

(Dr Taylor) But there are two aspects to that. One is that the sovereignty of Parliament means that no single Parliament can bind a successor. It also removes the distinction between Acts of constitutional amendment and Acts of ordinary legislation. So my point is that, if Parliament is absolutely clear about its intentions with regard to the British courts, that can be construed as involving the creation of the constitutional means, so that it is, in effect, an amendment of the European Communities Act at one and the same time. I agree there would be consequences, some of them unpleasant consequences, if we did that. But if one is talking about sovereignty, then I think it is

[**Mr Shore** Contd]

important to stress the relationship between parliament and the British courts. The European Court might complain and there may be political costs. On some occasions in the Maastricht agreement, for instance, it is agreed that, if states do not carry out their obligations under the Treaty, then there is a new provision for fining states that do not obey. Again that can be interpreted in at least two ways. One is, if you are a federalist, you will read it and say "Wonderful". Your last question was, what difference does it make in terms of the power of the community, or even the power of the court, to oblige states to do something? It goes one step further but, in a way, it is not much different from saying to a state, "You must obey this particular Directive". To say that you must pay a fine for not obeying that Directive does not take the argument much further because it is still up to the state to say if they will pay this fine or not.

Chairman

88. I am beginning to get confused, as one always does at this stage of the debate. Can I put the question in almost school-child history book terms? The Americans fought a great civil war during which the issue appeared as enunciated by Abraham Lincoln to be whether there should be the right of states to secede from the Union or whether, as was ultimately determined, secession became illegal and all those participating in secession were rebels acting against the state, the Union. Are we free of that kind of language? Are you saying everything that has happened so far—the Single European Act, any Act that comes out of the Rome Treaty itself—does not bind us in that way into this new union and we remain free to secede?

(Dr Taylor) We do remain free to secede. We have, however, extended the competencies of the Community in an increasing range of areas. There are various kinds of costs that would arise if we chose not to do what we have agreed to do when we extended those competences. After all, this is something that arises anyway in relations between states and other states in international society. If you have treaties and choose not to do what the treaties say you should, costs will arise. I am trying to make the point that our relationship with the Community is much more like that than is sometimes realised in the conventional debate between the intergovernmentalists and the federalists. So that I would say I am in favour of European integration, in favour of the creation of a region in which competences are shared, really in order to make our own arrangements more effective and more efficient; but I think that is a rather different question from talking about sovereignty and what we retain in terms of reserved rights and how we could respond, given that we have gone a long way in extending those competences. You mentioned the word "secession". As to whether we could dilute at some future stage, not secede but dilute, if you have a federal constitution that is extremely difficult; in fact, as you said, in the United States it is impossible. In the Community it is still possible.

Chairman: Could we move on from that to perhaps a less dramatic thought than secession, the question of whether we could pick or choose which bits of the union we wanted to go along with. I think Mr Shore has a point on that.

Mr Shore

89. I wanted to raise this because an essential part of the Maastricht Agreement, and one which makes it rather difficult to judge Maastricht as a whole, is the arrangements for economic and monetary union because there, as we know, there are both a process of opting in and a process of opting out, and even if the EMU does take effect in the third stage and we have a single currency about 1999, it is quite obvious, I would have thought, that a number of European Community members will not be part of that arrangement, they cannot possibly be. So in a sense this very large and important part of the Maastricht Agreement does clearly envisage the two-stage position, or whatever term one wishes to give to it. One thinks obviously also of the defence dimension if this does develop. It could well be that, for perhaps historical reasons, a number of new Member States as well as existing ones—Ireland which has never belonged to any kind of collective defence system—would opt out. Is a new pattern being established of what I think might be called Europe *à la carte?*

(Dr Wallace) I think to jump from some of those ambiguities to a doctrine of Europe *à la carte* is to jump too far and too quickly. It is not the first time in the Community that there have been arrangements envisaged in which not all Member States participate on the same basis; although it is the case that where differentiation (to use a deliberately neutral term) has been permitted it has been subject to conditions, and mostly quite careful conditions about whether there were in some sense objective reasons which would on the day preclude one Member State from joining on the same basis as others in a particular area of policy. Just to refer to the discussion that took place a little earlier, constitutional documents can provide ground rules. They can provide guidance, other things being equal, about what will happen, but they cannot prescribe in advance political realities that will be there at subsequent stages: nor can they prescribe the economic conditions that will actually be found (if you take the economic and monetary union case) at the point where a decision will have to be taken. I think it is prudent of the Community not to try and put a straitjacket on Member States in cases like economic and monetary union, because if all Member States cannot be part of a single currency, they cannot be part of a single currency for economic reasons as much as political reasons. We can all see which countries will be more fitted or less fitted and some which will depend on a mixture of political judgment and not only economic judgment. In principle I do not have a problem with what has been agreed on the economic and monetary union side. I have much more of a problem of what has been agreed on the

[**Mr Shore** *Contd*]

social policy side, because I regard social policy as an area where it is normal for there to be deep conflicts of opinion and judgment between different political families and preferences as to what the right mix of rights and legislation will be appropriate. It seems to me to be at the heart of the political debate to have arguments on issues of that sort. I think it is a mistake to try and prescribe too much in a Treaty, which is a constitutional document, what a policy should be. I think what happened at Maastricht was a confusion between framework and detail and, as it turned out, they muddled the two up even more rather than sorting them out. I would have sought for an outcome which limited the provisions in the Community really to framework, maybe to some basic rights in the employment market and of a social kind, but not have wanted to prescribe a particular policy; I think that is a matter for legislation to be made on the due date and to be changed from time to time as the policy preferences of governments change. We have muddled the two up in ways that will be very complicated from a point of view of jurisprudence and decision-making in future, because one country took a different policy view, which it was entitled to take. It seems to me it should be argued out in the course of dealing with legislation. If it is the case (and I believe it is the case) that even in the existing Community, and certainly in the enlarged Community, we are going to have to live with much wider divergences to reconcile in however the family will be defined. We are going to have to find ways of dealing with that in terms of jurisprudence in decision-making. I think that is very testing. One can envisage amongst candidate countries some that could easily be part of EMU as phrased, and others that would find it impossible. The social policy example could take us into worse and not better circumstances.

Mr Jopling

90. It was not the first time that the Treaty had gone further than the structure, because the original Treaty in the frame of the Common Agricultural Policy, as I remember very well, went into very, very great detail with regard to that.

(Dr Wallace) I think that was a mistake of the Treaty then too. I think we would have less problem in agriculture if the particular version of the policy did not have this quasi-constitutional character and was a matter of legislation, to be changed as and when the case for change was strong.

Mr Shore

91. Is it perhaps as important as the point you have just made that the Maastricht agreement has sought to deal with this matter of disagreement by creating something which seems to be outside of the machinery of the Community, that is to say, the agreement on us to go ahead with the social policy?

(Dr Wallace) I would have preferred that they had not reached that decision. It would have been

a more sensible outcome to have taken a more limited decision about the area of common action and to have left later the argument to be made or lost, as it were, about whether more legislation could be done on a collective basis. I think we shall be in real difficulties about separating, in a political sense, in a decision-making sense, in a jurisprudential sense, what is being done by 11 and what is being done by 12, and I would expect the European Court of Justice to take the Community to the cleaners on that.

(Dr Taylor) I agree with what has been said.

Chairman: If we could turn from that to another area which is the EC and national parliaments where we particularly notice Mr Vibert has some very interesting ideas which will, I think, be of great interest to this House on what sort of part national parliaments might play in a non-decentralised structure of the Community and, indeed, its associated pillars.

Mr Wells

92. The implications of Maastricht for powers and working methods of the United Kingdom Parliament should be, I think, very profound. How can Parliament render Ministers accountable for decisions taken in the Council of Ministers or influence those decisions, particularly when those decisions will be taken, of course, by weighted majority voting on occasions and some national parliaments, including this one perhaps, could be out-voted and the Minister comes back and says, "Although I wished a different solution, nonetheless, we were impotent in the light of the majority in Brussels". How then can we hold that Minister responsible for that decision?

(Mr Vibert) I think one factor there is simply, can the Minister and the Leader of the Party carry his Party? If he is continually out-voted and comes back saying, "Sorry, couldn't deliver", and we are continually losing then I suspect the parliamentary Party may have something to say, either about leadership or policies being adopted or whatever. That is a very traditional parliamentary check. After all, the House of Commons actually does not vote down legislation, because the parties resign if it is a major piece of legislation. The process is somewhat different. I look at the question slightly differently, in the sense that the point was made yesterday by the Minister of State that he saw that the case could be made, following the gist of your arguments, that a net parliamentary gain may have been made by agreeing to this final assent to the European Parliament. To my mind it is very questionable whether a net parliamentary gain has been made, because there is the danger that the net gainer in this assent procedure could be the Commission rather than the Parliament. Also the confusion of responsibilities between the parties could very well lead to pressure groups, for example, being the main winners. I notice also in yesterday's evidence that this Committee was invited to make its views known about the role of parliaments to the Leader of the House. It seems to me that there is now, post-Maastricht, a very strong

[Mr Wells Contd]

case to be made that national parliaments should have a say in what legislation is necessary at the Community levels. In other words, have a say in the determination of the subsidiarity principle. That would argue for this future Conference of Parliaments being a conference between national parliamentarians who would perhaps work in this area of what is going to be necessary in the future at Community level and what should be retained by national parliaments. That is an area presumably in which this Committee is invited to make recommendations.

93. I want to come on to the whole question of the meetings of national parliaments and the Conference of Parliaments in the second part of this question, but can we also consider the condition which is likely to arise more subtly than one where the Minster gets up at the Council of Ministers, that is, in the various pillars, the foreign affairs pillar and the home affairs pillar, and decisions there? We have seen this quite clearly, I think, in the foreign affairs pillar on the question of the recognition of Croatia. There compromises are clearly made out of sight of parliament and, indeed, of the public as a whole. It seems to me to be even more difficult therefore for a national parliament to hold responsible the minister concerned who has made that compromise. How can we tackle that problem?

(Mr Vibert) With due respect, I do not agree with that point of view. Croatia is one example where perhaps we were reluctant to go along with the Community decision, but the Minister was making a judgment, should he carry the House and his party along with that decision for the benefit of co-operation in the Community? One can envisage other decisions where he would have felt he could not have made that judgment and there would not have been common policy—for example, in relation to the Gulf where we clearly felt we needed to be up front in supporting the United States action or, for example, in the case of Libya and US intervention. There the Minister would have felt, "Well, if we did not go along with the United States in an up-front sort of way I would have difficulty with my party and with the House", and therefore Community action would not prevail. So I think these factors are very much going to play a role at the Council of Ministers level and, therefore, implicitly back to national parliaments and parties in future decision-taking.

(Dr Wallace) I agree very strongly with the point Frank Vibert has just made. At the end of the day the governors, whoever they are, have to make a judgment in some areas which (and this is perhaps not the thing to say in this Committee) cannot always be subject to detailed parliamentary decision in advance, although subject to scrutiny afterwards, particularly in areas of foreign policy where, as in the Yugoslav case, one is making decisions very fast. What has to be tested in Parliament is, as it were, the trust of Parliament in that particular set of ministers, whether they are operating at national level or at Community level.

I would draw a big distinction between that area and the judicial co-operation area where I see it as much more dangerous, from the point of view of parliamentary supervision and individual citizens' rights, to lock into a very untransparent intergovernmental and behind-closed-doors method of taking decisions about the rights of migrants and so on. In particular there I see us getting into a very difficult no man's land of intergovernmentalism behind closed doors without scrutiny powers, between the inability of our national systems to deal with these migration issues for all kinds of obvious reasons and our reluctance for some quite good reasons to put them into a Community framework where there is some kind of parallel jurisprudential control. That worries me greatly because it is an area where there is such an important case for parliamentary representation and for the legal system to be engaged. That I am worried about. May I add one other point, Chairman, on the relationship between national parliaments and Community systems. I think there is a real dilemma because there is clearly a strong interest and concern in this country to give our national parliamentary system more of a stake in the Community process, but I would have difficulty in seeing how a Community treaty could prescribe on the same basis a method of national parliamentary involvement that would apply in the same way in all Member States because our parliamentary traditions in different Member States are so very different. I find it difficult to see how far one can go beyond exhortation in a Community text, as it were providing opportunities for national parliamentarians to be involved as distinct from specific rules.

Mr Wells

94. Presumably your arguments concerning the accountability of Ministers in the pillars will also apply to the Heads of State meeting in the European Council. Do you see that that European Council can be perfectly accountable to national parliaments? I ask Mr Vibert?

(Mr Vibert) Yes. I think that it does provide a mechanism whereby national parliaments have a say, have an influence, because after all the Prime Ministers meeting in the European Council have to come back and defend their actions and explain them, and they are clearly accountable. The House can hold them to account. Ultimately the electorate will hold them to account. So that is a form of accountability we are accustomed to.

95. Do you agree with that, Dr Taylor?

(Dr Taylor) I wanted to make a point on a related matter to do with Parliament's relationship with the Community: in the Maastricht Agreement there are several references to ways in which the House can be brought closer to Community business. It seems to me there are two kinds of possible development. One is to do with increasing the level of awareness, the closeness of the relationship between the on-going business of the Community and the business of the House, locking the two

[Mr Wells *Contd]*

more closely together in terms of what is happening there. Secondly, there is quite simply more information about what is going on in the Community. I do sense that the negotiators at Maastricht at least thought they were making a contribution towards positive developments in both of those areas. One is because of the specific requirement that the Commission should inform national parliaments about its legislation—the precise wording, I think, is something like "for consideration and possible response". I think it actually uses the words "possible response" which seems to indicate that the House would have the chance to feed information directly into the policy-making process, short-circuiting, if you like, the link through the Ministers and the Council of Ministers. The other development is in terms of encouragement of, I think the phrase is, "the provision of mutual facilities for Members of the House and Members of the European Parliament". That is also stated and I suppose, broadly speaking, that means Members of Parliament and Members of the European Parliament should get closer together, which again would help increase the level of information and lock the two into a common programme.

96. Of course, what we have also is a reference to the Conference of Parliaments. This seems to envisage the meeting on a regular basis of the European Parliament with the national parliaments. Exactly what such meetings will do is difficult to define, is it not, particularly if you take Douglas Hurd's line—which he described before the Maastricht Agreement—that the European Parliament should hold accountable the Commission and the national parliaments should hold accountable the Council of Ministers. How do you see this Conference of Parliaments performing? What role do you see it performing?

(Dr Taylor) I also have great difficulty in understanding, on the basis of what is in this document, what possible contribution it could make. I have one further point to develop to do with Article 189b. I do not know if it is appropriate to make this point here or not.

97. I do not know what 189b is, perhaps you could tell us?

(Dr Taylor) 189b is the Article which gives the European Parliament essentially the right of co-decision. The point I would make on this is that it seems to be a less federal clause than the federalists would like to believe, because it does allow for the second veto by the European Parliament. It is also the context in which the Conciliation Committee is introduced. From the point of view of this House, if one does establish closer links between parties here and parties in Strasbourg, then this does mean that at least the opportunity would be created for attempting to orchestrate the development of a block in the European Parliament. In creating those kinds of links it increases the range of opportunities for national parliaments to manipulate (and perhaps the word is too strong) the develop-

ment of opinion with regard to 189b issues in the European Parliament, so that it makes available a kind of second stage of veto.

98. Do you think the European Parliament is effective at the moment in influencing Community legislation? Do you think that these proposals under 189b and other clauses will make them more effective in influencing legislation?

(Dr Taylor) The evidence I think so far relates to the co-operative procedure, and remembering that the cooperative procedure as in 189b applies to the relatively small area of legislation. The evidence appears to be that 189c, which is the old co-operative procedure, has helped the Parliament to exert influence upon the legislation, measured in terms of how far European Parliament amendments have been responded to positively in the legislation as it has appeared. There are figures on this, although I do not have them in my head, but one can take account of how many instances amendments have had an effect, and it is quite a reasonable score.

99. Do you not think that since the European Parliament is excluded from considering matters to do with the greater union through the pillars—the foreign affairs pillar and the home affairs pillar, and possibly the defence pillar later—that there is therefore a need for the national parliaments actually to meet together in order to provide that very essential thing for a democracy, to generate consent to being ruled by a majority? Because the lack of understanding between the national states is quite clear, even when you like to consider the definition of the word "federal", for example, the argument that took place on that took place because in different cultures it means different things. Therefore particularly with the pillar development—and of course, in my view (and I do not take Mr Vibert's view on the Council of Ministers) I do not think there is sufficient pressure for Ministers to account for their actions in the Council of Ministers—there is a strong necessity for national parliaments to meet and call those Ministers to account?

(Dr Taylor) I think there are two lines of argument: one is to do with the existence of a need and the possible way of solving that need. I would agree with the point you have made. It is possible that such a gathering of parliaments could take steps in that direction. It is a very large question, I think, and it is for the future. We do not know. The other argument is what was in the mind of the negotiators. One of the curious aspects of our discussions here is that none of us are quite clear about what was in the minds of the negotiators. What the difference was, for instance, between 189b and 189c is not entirely clear to me. One of the things that is possible, because it does in the Maastricht Treaty talk about the need to encourage further links between parties and there is in one of the Protocols a statement to that effect, is the need to encourage further links between national parties. Links to create European parties and the creation of such an assembly of national

[**Mr Wells** *Contd*]

parliaments could be seen as a part of that process of really creating constituencies, creating European parties, a proper European constituency base with those powers that are exercised within the framework competences extended to the Community.

(Dr Wallace) Whatever is in the minds of the negotiators, and I am sure there are many contradictory things, we have to live with the words as written down, which will be manipulated because people will have interests in manipulating them; some to manipulate them more extensively and some to constrain them. On the record of the European Parliament so far I think none of us are quite clear actually. There is a high correlation between parliamentary amendments to legislation and final legislation in the areas where the co-operation procedure has worked. Whether that amounts to real influence is slightly less clear. Whether it is an influence on important points or points of technical detail needs to be examined, and has not been properly examined. Whether it is a marginal influence or a more serious one we do not really yet know. Obviously members of the European Parliament are wont to argue that this shows an increasing influence. On the question of the areas that are outside that procedure, your point about the home affairs and the foreign affairs apart, I find it a little difficult to envisage a body which included parliamentarians from all of the national parliaments working in a coherent way procedurally. I cannot see what this kind of gathering is going to look like, other than as a conference. A conference may be useful from time to time for building bridges and developing dialogue, that is very valuable, but if what one is after is effective influence then surely one has to look somewhere else, and therefore one has to look in two different directions perhaps. If individual Ministers in the Council are not put under tough scrutiny by their own parliaments, then it seems to me down to those parliaments to do something about that. In this particular area we are just talking about the pillars, there is a particular opportunity there, it seems to me, for national parliaments in all Member States to be very activist. On the other point about control and looking for other ways of doing it, I do think the point about the parties is very important, and it relates to half a sentence that Mr Vibert uttered a few moments ago about the scope for pressure groups to influence the process as it stands. As it stands, because of the difficulties of effective parliamentary control at both the European and the national level in the Community, it is much easier it seems to me for well organised lobbies to insert themselves into the detail of Community legislation, both through their influence on Community institutions and through their influence on Ministers who go to the Council. Because the decision-making takes place in this curious way between the Commission and the Council as it does that is quite difficult to get at from the outside. It is quite difficult, it seems to me, for parliamentarians to produce the counterweight. In our national systems that is done partly by Parliament itself, but it is also done by the parties who make judgments about the relative importance of different sectoral interests. We are missing that entirely in the Community. It seems to me

because Ministers in the Council have got so many other needs to satisfy they cannot always give the political override that one needs to deal with the powerfully organised vested interests. To build up parties at a European level that would pull in some different versions of what the policy preferences should be and debate that out would be a very valuable addition to what is currently the case.

Mr Wells: If you had the misfortune, as I did, to attend the extremely bad tempered debate last night on the European budgetary matter you would also realise the very serious need for the development of understanding and tolerance between not just the individual parliaments of the 12, but also between the Commission, the Council of Ministers and the parliaments. It is a very destructive force and possibly the development of parties might help. That is certainly what the European Parliament think and they would like to destroy national parliaments, I think.

Mr Lawrence

100. It is possible for us to get quite a good idea of what is in the minds of the negotiators because we do speak to them and their masters when we go round as a Select Committee and we know what they say to us, we know what they say to other groups and, therefore, we have other information than the final documents at which they arrive. I think we can conclude from that that some of the negotiators are hell bent on forming a federal super-state, some negotiators—like the United Kingdom negotiators—are hell bent on holding the line, and some are in between. What I think we have to watch as a Committee is that there is a possibility that they do not actually have to be specific about their intentions in some of their agreements, because there may be an inevitable drift without making any specific declarations when they are negotiating these matters which might frighten the nationalists. If you do not say anything specific and the drift is inevitable, then people will not be alarmed. Yesterday I asked the Foreign Secretary, as I recall, if he did not feel that all the indicators were that there was a juggernaut so irresistible that we were heading for a federal super-state, or words to that effect. He said, no, he hoped we were not, and he pointed to the pillars, the intergovernmental aspects of the Maastricht Agreement, as indicating that it was not all one way. When I joined you a few minutes ago belatedly—I apologise for that—Dr Wallace was saying that it is really very difficult, if I understood her correctly, to justify coming to decisions about such important matters as immigration and justice behind locked doors, not exposed to public discussion, which, taking account of the subsequent discussions we have had about the ineffectiveness so far of national parliaments getting together, leads one to suppose that it is the European Parliament that ought to be discussing and coming to some final decisions about the intergovernmental pillars rather than the Commission. If that is so—and this is my question—is there not even a drift towards the European institutions away from national parliaments? Is there not, even on the element that the

[**Mr Lawrence** *Contd*]

Foreign Secretary chose to select as an indicator that we had not lost and were not going to lose more power, an inevitability that we will lose powers to Community institutions, *viz* the European Parliament? If that is so, then is not what Dr Taylor said in her paper to the effect that the Maastricht Agreement has not altered the underlying legal and constitutional circumstances of British sovereignty placed in question?

Chairman: That is rather a long question, I am afraid.

Mr Lawrence: A long introduction to a short question.

Chairman: We do not want to cover ground we have covered already. Would any of the witnesses like to comment a little more briefly on that?

(*Mr Vibert*) I am not sure that there would be a willingness of Member States to see some highly sensitive issues—for example, immigration—left to the European Parliament. I am not sure that that willingness to see that drift actually exists. I am also not sure that the possibility of national parliaments acting more effectively together might also not be possible in rather defined areas such as that which I suggested of the interpretation of subsidiarity. Of course, national parliaments have their different ways of proceeding. Nevertheless, I think Britain is not alone in being concerned about a drift towards over-centralisation and excessive intrusion. I think there are the beginnings of a mood change in Germany and other important countries. So if national parliaments reflected that mood they would find ways of working effectively. I do think it would have to be a rather small body, perhaps not more than 100 or 150 for a Community of between 20 and 25 Member States. It would have to be small to be effective but I think those sorts of things could be explored.

Mr Lawrence

101. If by working effectively you mean some kind of structure of decision making so that we would have to pool our decision-making process with other national states, that again is a loss of our sovereignty, is it not? If you are saying it should not be a structure, just a talking shop, a conference chamber, that is not going to achieve the end you have in mind.

(*Mr Vibert*) It would depend very much on how the delegates to that assembly actually worked and whether they went with instructions or not, whether they had flexibility. That would be one aspect. But if they took a decision that a certain area of legislation was not appropriate for Community legislation and, therefore, legislation at Community level should not be introduced there because it belonged to national parliaments, it would keep a certain area of legislation back within the national framework, and that is a perfectly legitimate and possible role to play.

Chairman

102. I think that is a very interesting idea you are introducing into the debate. Perhaps we could

have a few more thoughts on it. I think the Committee would like to ponder on it. You are really saying it is not merely a question of the parliaments and the European Parliament analysing legislation as it comes along but the national parliaments actually playing a role in deciding whether there should be such initiatives in the first place?

(*Mr Vibert*) Yes.

103. In fact, overriding the much vaunted and much treasured power of the Commission to initiate ideas which may lead to directives and regulations?

(*Mr Vibert*) Yes, that is the thought. One of the impulses towards centralisation in the Community very clearly is the monopoly right of the Commission to initiate; there is no doubt that works in the direction of centralisation. Although I think the definition of "subsidiarity" which has been included in the Maastricht Treaty is an important and worthwhile provision, I do not think that in itself is going to stop that behaviour. It may moderate it, and indeed the Foreign Secretary mentioned yesterday that it could influence the behaviour of the Commission, but the Commission will, in my view, still want to be the initiator and act as the initiator: that will work in the direction of increased centralisation. So if one wants to put greater teeth into that principle, that unnecessary legislation should not be carried out at Community level, then one looks for countervailing bodies. It seems to me very difficult to argue against the idea that national parliaments should themselves have a say in what needs to be done at Community level.

Chairman: We have a question we were planning for later on subsidiarity in all its meanings, obscure and less obscure. I do not know whether we might agree just to pursue the subsidiarity issue now that you have whetted our appetites about one more mechanism that might be brought into play to give it some definition.

Mr Lawrence

104. I did address the question to Dr Wallace. I do not know if she wants to answer.

(*Dr Wallace*) I have some problems with what Frank Vibert is proposing. We already have a very complicated decision-making system and tiering of bodies in the Community. We are all agreed that some of the results of that are less than good, but I am not sure whether the proposal to add another chamber of this kind, which is like a senate as it were, will necessarily help. I wonder whether one needs to pause for thought and reflect on the consequences in Switzerland of building in cantonal rights, which in a sense is what one may be thinking of in the Community, particularly an enlarged Community. We want an approach that will run for a Community which might have 18 or 25 members somewhere down the road if we are to have a kind of national parliamentary expression. Part of the reason why I am concerned is that I think we may be making things more complicated than will

[**Mr Lawrence** *Contd*]

be effective in a democratic or policy action sense. But I do not actually see this juggernaut towards centralisation driving down the road in front of us. If there is not, then obviously one is dealing with different issues. I think there are so many counter-vailing pressures in the Community, and this does take us to subsidiarity as well. There is not, it seems to me, unanimity of views within the Member States on this issue. There are some quite wide ranges of opinion across different Community countries about where to draw the balance between Community powers and powers of the Member States. There is a very strong strand in German political thinking, and there has been for a long time, about not pushing too much to the centre. They are more relaxed about foreign policy than we are, but that is not surprising given their history; but they are very unrelaxed about giving powers to the Community in some other areas——

Mr Wells

105. Monetary areas.

(Dr Wallace) ——and have thought about that very hard. We are talking about Member States which are very heterogeneous in character in many other respects. Enlargement will, it seems to me, be a great brake, if it goes ahead on centralisation. I think the issues we face are slightly different and therefore the remedies may need to be different.

Mr Jopling: I wonder if you could tell us how you see the progress of subsidiarity now at this stage, and how politically and legally significant those provisions are? In particular I would like to ask, do you think that we may see in the future some of the competences—I mean, for instance, on agriculture or the environment—being re-nation-alised and repatriated to national governments?

Chairman

106. It follows from what we have just been discussing as to whether the national parliaments could be one of the braking mechanisms in checking the flow of competence to the centre and indeed, as Mr Jopling has suggested, even accelerating the return of some to the nation states. Mr Jopling's wider question is to whether other forces, as well as national parliaments, could help in this process. That is what we are looking for, some reassurance that there are mechanisms and levers which work that will give body to the subsidiarity idea.

(Dr Taylor) This is where knowing something about the intentions of the negotiator I think is important, since I heard the Foreign Secretary's observation on this yesterday. I found them persuasive about ways of preventing the further extension of the Community's powers in areas that go beyond the purposes of the Treaty, according to the Maastricht agreement. I am less sure about what they mean for any weakening of those powers or return to the national levels. I think that is not the intention at the moment. So far I am at a loss to see how that could follow from what has been said in the Maastricht agreement.

(Dr Wallace) I have some difficulty in seeing how the Court of Justice will actually cope with subsidiarity cases. Of course they will only come to the Court after legislation has been made and is therefore subject to challenge. I think it will be quite difficult for the Court to say, "The Council of Ministers has so decided but actually we are going to override that as *ultra vires*", unless there is a very clear-cut case. Maybe that is not the important thing. Maybe the important thing is the insertion of the phrase in the Treaty albeit with some of the ambiguities that go with it. I think it does represent what is not just a British view but a much more widespread Community view, that we are all reaching the limits of what we can do on a collective basis. That is why I do not see the centralist juggernaut. I think there is real concern across the Community about what the Community can cope with: some of which is to do with the reasons we have talked about here this morning; some of which is simply to do with capacity. There is a sense of the Community being over-stretched. If you over-stretch it more things will not be well done and one can see examples of that already. The subsidiarity language is a reminder to everybody not to be hasty in continuing to assign new policy powers. I myself would have interpreted it a bit more literally at Maastricht than the negotiators did. I am not sure that I would have gone as far they did to attribute educational and cultural powers, even in a limited form, but regarded subsidiarity as something which should properly exclude those, but they took a different decision. I think we shall have some very interesting discussions about that. What I am a little uncomfortable about is the juxtaposition of the phrase on subsidiarity with this other phrase about the full *acquis communautaire*. If one wants to argue that maybe the time has come when you do not need as common a policy (and one can argue it in other cases as well as agriculture) I am not sure how those two phrases read out against each other. I would just add one other point which we have not mentioned and that is the reference to the Council of Regions. I see the subsidiarity discussion as having roots not only in the relationship between Member States and powers of the Community but also between other levels of governance and the Community. The fact that this conference of the regions has been inserted, albeit only in a very sketchy form, is a signal that people in many parts of the Community are grappling for ways of building in yet another level of linkage, at least in some countries, where there is an active provincial level of governance; and the subsidiarity point will take us into some interesting and very difficult debates in the Community, not just about member governments and Community powers but also lower levels of governance as well.

107. Surely, Dr Wallace, the doctrine of subsidiarity as enunciated to us suggests that it is up to the nation states at that level to decide best how much they want to apply the doctrine of subsidiarity? Any suggestion that at the centre of the Community there should be views which would dictate to nations at the national level how much

[Chairman *Contd*]

they in turn want to devolve powers to the lower levels of the region is itself an offence against the doctrine of subsidiarity?

(Dr Wallace) I think it does depend on which country you come from. If you are German or maybe Dutch you start at a much lower level of government and you cede often quite reluctantly either to the nation state or to the Community.

108. Can we have one more question on subsidiarity which runs through everything. Yesterday the Foreign Secretary helped us distinguish between two areas in which subsidiarity as an idea may help. One is what he called an area of commonsense within the Commission. They have got a lot of powers and they have been given a lot of powers over the years, they can either use these in a commonsense way or they can push everything to the limit. That is why he says subsidiarity may restrain them. You have also indicated that over-capacity may restrain them, although it seems to me that people in the Commission have endless capacity for new mischief and new barmy ideas. I do not think that is a restraint. He says that commonsense will be a restraint, and also the European Court of Justice will take into its mind the idea of subsidiarity in interpreting where competences lie and whether there are competences being abused and so on. We have also had Mr Vibert's idea that maybe national parliaments could have some say in the extension or the halting of the extension of competences. Is that a full picture, or have you got anything else to give to help on this front?

(Mr Vibert) I am not a lawyer but I think there are additional legal defences or legal developments which could be explored. Like Dr Wallace, I am very unhappy about this inclusion of the *acquis communautaire*, I think that is a very negative feature in the Treaty; but leaving that side, I think the developments one might want to see are, for example, in relation to the third indent of article 3b, the one the Foreign Secretary referred to yesterday that, "Any action by the Community shall not go beyond what is necessary to achieve the objectives of this Treaty". Like him, I think that is actually a rather important clause, and I think it could be developed more in the direction of what is in the US constitution about not exceeding express powers delegated to the centre. That would be a possible legal development. I think another type of provision which is in the Treaty which could be developed relates to the power of the Court of Justice to fine, because I think it does raise the question, on what basis does one levy fines? This opens a door, I think, to the assessment of fines on the basis of damage done to others. I think the principle of damage done to others is quite an important principle which could be developed as a principle for the Community: that if a practice within a Member State does not do damage to others, then maybe that is not an area where the Community should act. So for example, to take the environmental area, if Britain is polluting the

atmosphere through power stations which burn dirty coal that is damaging to others as it drifts across the North Sea, clearly that is a Community concern; but if we decide to replace the Winchester by-pass, it seems to me that is entirely our domestic concern. The question of damage to others seems to me rather an important concept in principle, so I think there are additional matters like legal doctrines—I am not a lawyer—which might be built into future revisions in the Treaty.

(Dr Wallace) That doctrine is already practised by the European Court of Justice in its other jurisprudence. If it were to develop in that way I think that would be a very welcome development.

Mr Shore

109. Is there not a danger here of losing our sense of proportion? What we are basically considering is a Treaty which enormously increases the power and competence of European institutions over great areas of economic policy, Economic and Monetary Union, aspirations of a single currency, the large areas of competence within the Treaty itself, research, development, consumer affairs, tourism—you know the list very well, an extension, although a small one, of the powers of the European Parliament, and now at least a bridgehead for the Community and for supranationality in the areas of foreign policy and the clear statement that defence is to follow. Against that background, do you think we are being a little bit obsessive about the importance of a mention of the possibility of subsidiarity in those areas of not such important policy which the Commission might, for purely sensible and common sense reasons, agree to relax like the point you made about the difference between the Winchester by-pass and the question of poisoning the atmosphere? Do you not think we are really dealing here with what is basically a sop?

(Mr Vibert) No, I think there is an important distinction between the Member States agreeing on what it makes sense to do collectively (and I happen to think it makes sense to try to work together collectively in areas such as immigration and foreign policy) and the processes for arriving there. I happen to think those processes are very important. I do not know that this Committee wants to get into the question of what, if anything, we have given away on monetary union. I think that raises some rather different issues, as I indicated in my note. I do not agree with your perspective.

Chairman

110. I think this subsidiarity issue is very central to our thoughts and I do not know if Dr Wallace or Dr Taylor would like to give any other reassurance on it. We have not talked about the Court of Justice in detail, as to whether that may act in a way that is less a force of centralisation, nor whether the Committee of Regions which Dr Wallace mentioned might be a counterweight to

[Chairman Contd]

centralisation. Does either of those areas give you any hope?

(Mr Vibert) I would like to say something about the Committee of Regions. I think yesterday the impression was given that this would be a rather ineffective body, like ECOSOC, and I am not so sure about that for two reasons. First of all, I think that there may very well be some rather sharply defined motivation operating in the Regional Council and that sharply defined motivation is to ask for assistance from the centre to the regions, in other words, they will be acting as a pressure group for cohesion funds, structural funds and so on. I think it will be a rather sharply defined pressure group acting in that direction. The second point I would make is to agree with what Dr Wallace has said, that underlying this creation is a theory about the constitutional evolution of the Community, and that is that there is a need for a third tier of government—the Community level, the national level, and the sub-national level, the regional level. The Council of Regions is seen by some as a step on the way towards that, formulating and fleshing out that third layer of government. So I think the future of that Committee like other areas of the Treaty requires a good deal of further thought. As Helen says, I do not think there is a juggernaut but I think there are tendencies and doctrines which one has not only to watch but which will work in certain directions unless we have alternative agenda and alternative proposals to put forward.

111. Just one other aspect of the forces influencing the character of the Community after Maastricht: you made a reference earlier to the European political parties and we had some exchanges earlier as to whether those parties would increasingly at European level form across boundaries and apply their varying views and ideologies that way, or whether they would continue to work within the framework of nation states' influence. Do you now, from your positions of expertise, sense that any changes are going on inside the French political parties, the Spanish political parties, the German political parties or the Italian, quite aside from our own here, about the part they should play in the centralisation versus decentralisation character battle of Europe?

(Dr Wallace) May I express that slightly differently, Chairman? It seems to me that the debate has not quite taken place around Maastricht at the political party level in the Community that one would have liked to see when the Community was facing some quite big questions. I for one would certainly hope a more wide-ranging debate would take place in and between parties before we come to the next intergovernmental conference, which may be 1996. So it is quite difficult to know, I think, what parties in any one part of the Community really think on some of the issues which this Committee is addressing. When the issues are ventilated in party debate, I do not think they will be looked at in quite this centralisation/decentralisation dimension. I think they will be

looked at from a slightly different perspective, which is whether in dealing with a particular policy problem—whatever that policy problem is; it might be immigration, it might be social policy, foreign policy or defence—it is at the European level or within the member State that is likely to produce a policy outcome that that particular party prefers, and on that I think we have much more to discuss than we have discussed yet. I think the outcome of that kind of debate would be to give some quite different answers from different political groupings as to where to draw the balance.

Chairman: I agree it is a difficult issue to focus on now. You may well be right, that may be the way they react. Could we then turn to one or two questions on yet another area which may be influencing the whole character of the Community after Maastricht, that is, enlargement.

Mr Wells

112. What changes do you think will be needed to Community institutions to cope with the widening of the Community to include EFTA countries and possibly later Poland, Hungary, Czechoslovakia and possibly other states in Eastern Europe and the old Soviet Union, Turkey and the Mediterranean "orphans"?

(Dr Wallace) The question invites a very lengthy answer. I will try to restrain myself. We are faced with very difficult choices on this. There are those who argue that if all we are talking about in the short to medium term is taking in two or three other countries, two of them being Sweden and Austria because those are the two EFTA countries which have applied, maybe you can then get by with only quite small consequential changes to the treaties—numbers of ministers, numbers of commissioners, numbers of parliamentarians and so on—which is really not a very big or exciting adventure; and that you come much later, when you are faced with a larger number of countries joining the Community, to a more radical overhaul. I am not persuaded by that argument for several reasons. One is that we are going to face maybe five or six EFTA countries applying for membership and that, therefore, we are talking about a quantum jump which requires more serious attention and not just marginal change.

113. Who do you add?

(Dr Wallace) Sweden and Austria have already applied, Finland and Switzerland quite possibly will apply this year, the pressure is then on Norway, and it is a marginal detail at that point whether Iceland and Liechtenstein also apply, except of course if they do, then what do you do with the Maltese candidature? The Community would then include some very small states and that gets one thinking about the very big question about whether it is reasonable for Germany and Malta to be treated in the same way in the Community's institutions (and it seems to me that is grotesque). Or simply to enlarge the size of the European Parliament *pro rata* in relation to its cur-

[**Mr Wells** *Contd*]

rent, not entirely scientific basis would, it seems to me, get terribly out of hand. Therefore, we may well have to think much more drastically about what kinds of changes. It seems to me that then affects not the Court of Justice, which is the one that is easy to adapt, but the other three main institutions which is quite a big question. If you then put alongside that the other question which is about Central and East European countries, I am a little sceptical as to whether one can envisage in the short to medium term, even on optimistic assumptions, Hungary being a member in the same way that one could imagine Austria being a member of the Community; the point from which they are starting is too different economically and perhaps politically. What we are going to have to investigate is ways of managing a quite different and much more intimate relationship with those countries, which I think has to go beyond the association agreement but cannot be enlargement as for Austria or Sweden yet. In order to do that we have to find some flexibility of institutions and maybe of jurisprudence to allow those countries to be, in some sense, partial participants. That takes one into very difficult territory. The Community's instincts, and I think this has been shown in the European Economic Area negotiations, faced with that request for flexibility and, as it were, elasticity, have been to be rigid rather than elastic.

Chairman

114. Do you have anything else to add?

(Mr Vibert) I agree with what Dr Wallace has said. I think it does present the British Government for the Presidency with a bit of a dilemma because it can take the Swedish and Austrian applications in isolation, if you like, and say this does not involve much change and it is easy to incorporate them; or it can view them as the first stage of a much larger and long-lasting process and, therefore, use this as a way of opening up some of these other areas that Dr Wallace has indicated. I would be very much in favour, and it is in Britain's interests, if it were viewed in that rather broader sense because of the reason Dr Wallace has indicated that their applications are to be followed in very short order by Finland, Norway, Switzerland and Hungary. So I see this as a start of a process and it would be more sensible to address some of those issues at the outset and then perhaps look at them much more thoroughly in the process leading up to 1996. I realise all governments are very tired after Maastricht and I think this was reflected yesterday, but I think to try and leave some of these issues until another Maastricht process in 1996 would really be very unfortunate, because it means some very important issues will be dealt with in exactly the same bad way as they were this time.

Mr Wells

115. Do you not see that one of the negotiating aims of the British Government is to in fact progress or speed up enlargement in order to defeat the federalist tendencies which they feel that they have contained in this Maastricht Treaty? Do you not, therefore, anticipate that in fact the British Government will press very hard for inclusion of not just two more, but the more the merrier, in order to dilute and submerge the possibility of a supranational state?

(Mr Vibert) I think that is a slight over-simplification. I think it is true that the British Government perhaps sees a larger Community as having to be a more flexible Community. I think that is fair, but to assume that that will actually be a counter against centralising forces is yet another assumption which I think remains to be seen. It depends very much on these applicants themselves. I do not think one can rely on that. I think there is a genuine national interest for economic and foreign policy and security reasons in having a larger Community. Again, there is the long tradition of British pragmatism of "let's take one little step at a time" or "as we've got Austria and Sweden on a plate let's deal with them in the simplest possible way", that would certainly be one way in which the Foreign Office might be inclined to treat the question. That has to be set against the rather longer term vision, and it is not clear at this point that the Government has made up its mind as to how to treat this.

(Dr Wallace) I think one has to be very careful about the notion of making the Community so elastic that it would then no longer be able to perform tasks which I think are properly assigned to it; and that the British Government has to think quite carefully about where it strikes the balance. The current Government attaches very great importance to having very tight rules to promote deregulation. You will only hold to that, it seems to me, with liberalisation really opening up the market, if the Community institutions are able to exercise some quite tough disciplines on Member States that may want to backslide, whether it is through the Council of Ministers, the Commission's supervisory and competition policy powers, the Court of Justice or whatever. A different British Government would no doubt have a different policy mix, but would want the Community to be rather effective in areas presumably that would touch on some of the social issues and cohesion and convergence issues, and would want the Community to be able to deliver effective policy and want other Member States to be subjected to the same discipline. We have to remember that federalism is a two-way street. We sometimes spend too much time worrying about the constraints on us and not remembering that we want constraints over the policies and behaviour of other governments in the Community as well. The challenge with enlargement is how to maintain enough discipline over each other so that we do not backslide without being so rigid that we cannot accommodate countries which have some very different views.

Chairman

116. Perhaps we could finally go on to two other points. Mr Vibert makes a whole series of

[Chairman *Contd*]

extremely positive and interesting recommendations which are a ready-made agenda for the British Presidency, and you may feel these should be taken up very seriously. One that was suggested was that there should be an office in Whitehall to concern itself with strategic and coordination issues relating to the European Union, and presumably you mean go through all the tasks you enumerate including tasks relating to enlargement. Could you just elaborate on that?

(Mr Vibert) I think that outside observers, as far as we can see, are always very impressed by the smooth working of the British machinery of government when it comes to day-to-day co-ordination, for example, the functions of the office of the UK representative with Brussels and how it liaises with Whitehall and gathers intelligence throughout the Community, on that kind of day-to-day co-ordination function. I have nothing which I would add to that. I think the issue is: is there sufficient thought being given within the machinery of government to some of these longer-term strategic issues which, as your questions indicate and as our answers have tried to indicate, are in fact very difficult issues. I think that is where the problem arises. I think that there is a need for a longer term unit concerned with this longer term perspective. As a longtime former bureaucrat myself, I am very well aware that planning units as such tend to be immediately sidelined because they do not have day-to-day responsibilities. So my suggestion is that the more important co-ordination issues also should be handled by this unit as well as perhaps the retrieval capacity, because many of these issues one is talking about—the longterm reform of the Community budget and so on—have a very long history and that history is extremely important. So I suggest the amalgamation of those functions within a unit of Whitehall. There have been suggestions that we actually need a Minister for Europe who pays full-time attention to Europe and I think there is some merit in that. It made me uneasy in the lead-up to Maastricht to see all those in the Foreign Office team going off in different parts of the world and not keeping their eye on the ball. I think that was unfortunate, given the importance of this particular event and I think that is the case for a Minister for Europe. However, I think within the British Cabinet system there is a hierarchy well established and the question is, where would the Minister for Europe fit within that hierarchy? So I think that is a very difficult practical issue. I have a feeling that between powerful well-established Ministers he would either become in due course a Junior minister or things would constantly be appealed to the Prime Minister. So I suggest the logical place perhaps, subject to people who know much more about the dynamics of cabinet government than I, might be directly within the office of the Prime Minister.

(Dr Wallace) I am intrigued but not quite persuaded by Frank Vibert's proposition. The Cabinet Office Co-ordination Unit is designed to do what it is you are asking for and is close to the centre of what constitutionally in our system is the centre of

government, collective cabinet decision-making. I tend to think that it is better to leave it with the Cabinet Office although one's views will vary depending on what one thinks the role of the Prime Minister is in relation to his or her colleagues. I think, however, Chairman, our problem has not been a machinery one as regards strategy on these issues. I think it has been a matter of political decision by ministers as to what they chose to determine were the important issues and that it is quite open to ministers of whatever kind of government to take a different view from those they have taken in the past, to take a different strategic appraisal, then to follow through the strategic need which I entirely agree has been very absent in the British policy. I think the machinery we have for following that through is quite a good one. It is for ministers to decide whether they want to approach it that way rather than the way they have in the past.

Chairman: One final question on Britain's position in the world.

Mr Shore

117. Commitment to a common foreign policy is expressed very strongly in the relevant clauses in the draft Treaty. What do you think are going to be the effects or implications of this commitment on foreign policy for the United Kingdom's position in other international institutions?

(Dr Taylor) With regard to the United Nations—another area in which I am particularly interested—clearly in the Security Council Britain and France have both tended in the past to insist upon the separation of items on the Security Council agenda from those items that are available for discussion by the members of the Community in New York. I have a sense that the way this is being formulated in the Maastricht Agreement actually reflects a weakening of that line and certainly there has been much discussion of it in the academic world, about how far the British and French can avoid, I suppose, two further steps. One is the step towards accepting a mandate from the Community and the other is, of course, beyond that having a Community seat. I sense in the Maastricht Agreement a step towards a mandate from the Community—it is not there yet—but certainly a commitment to much more discussion about Security Council matters than previously was the case. I think you are right that there is a relationship between the greater involvement of the Community in foreign policy and possibly beyond that defence policy, and the holding of that line in New York. The more there is a common foreign policy and a common defence policy, the greater the pressure towards yielding our permanent membership in favour of some kind of common representation.

118. It seems logical, if you are bound to be speaking with one voice over an ever larger area of policy, that your case for having a separate voice is bound to be undermined. Incidentally, I am sure you are correct in your interpretation of the

[Mr Shore *Contd]*

Agreement because I see Article B.3 of the Chapter on Common Foreign and Security Policy reads "In international organizations and at international conferences where not all the Member States participate, those which do take part shall uphold the common positions." That clearly is a very strong commitment but, of course, I suppose the answer to that—and I would like your comment on this—could be that, well, the common position has, of course, to be defined and certainly anything that followed from that, like a joint action which seems to have an even more commanding position of collective judgment. You would have to go a long way, in other words, along the procedure that is outlined in this part of the Treaty before you could say you were committed to a common position?

(Dr Taylor) Elsewhere in the Agreement there is, however, reference to the wording "without prejudice to our obligations under the Charter" and also in the United Nations since 1986 in fact you have had the development of this extremely valuable organisation between the so-called P5 group, which has worked very, very well, and I think the British and French have made some valuable contributions in that context. How the working of P5 can be reconciled with this apparent move towards greater consultation with the EEC group in the United Nations I think has yet to be seen, but I think there is tension there between those two systems.

Chairman: It would be odd, would it not, if the argument about the European Community having a voice at the United Nations were pushed too far because the European Community is not a country, not a nation, and is responsible for external affairs and economic matters of foreign policy but only those, however large that may be, and the other bits belong to the pillar. It would be even odder if a pillar turned up in the United Nations and said it wanted a seat because it was a pillar. So I think these are surely thoughts that could really be put on one side as absurd unless there are people planning to make a megastate out of Europe.

Mr Shore

119. On that very point, is it not obvious that the Community is not a country, is not a nation but is a state? Already the European Community is recognised in international law and there is a whole vast area and doctrine which we have not discussed at all about citizenship rights within the state which has not yet been tackled and explored. Surely I am right in this?

(Dr Wallace) In areas where the competence of the Community is clear, like the GATT, the Community is represented by the Commission and the logic is to do that at the stage where you have similar collectivisation of policy; one could make the same analogy for economic and monetary union in the IMF. That is all a long way away because the decision on economic and monetary union will not arrive till the end of the decade. In one sense there is no particular logic in having only some Community Members participating in the Group of 7. I do not think anybody is going to be in a hurry to push too quickly on these questions. We have to keep our eyes open to see from where the pressures will come from. I would simply add that there is an anomaly with a united Germany of that country being treated in so much less important a way, for example in the United Nations, than Britain or France. The old rationale for it is not quite there any more. This is not to raise scare stories about German irredentism at all; it is normal that a country which is recovering its confidence should want that to be reflected in its position. What the Germans have said pretty clearly is that they are happy to ascribe that to the Community, rather than to argue it for themselves. I think they mean that. The question is, at what point the rest of us will be under pressure to look at that question seriously.

(Mr Vibert) I would like to endorse what Dr Wallace has just said on the fact that our position in many of the international institutions is an historical anomaly; it reflects our position in the immediate post-war world rather than our current standing. A very good example of that is the Bretton Woods institutions. It might very well be in our interests to start with the World Bank to bring additional Community members into our seat, for example, so that kind of institutional evolution could be envisaged. However, having said that, I think much more important are the factual issues stemming from closer Community foreign policy co-ordination. I think an absolutely crucial issue over the coming years will be the US/EC relationship and particularly the role which Britain plays in that. Clearly there are grounds for seeing quite severe tension arising in that relationship which I think would cause great discomfort to this country. I think the US will also have its views on how the UK arrangements and international institutions are handling it, because it may in fact serve them to see us continuing, for example, as a permanent member of the Security Council.

(Dr Taylor) I disagree somewhat with that. It is true that the original allocation of power in the Security Council was that which existed in 1945, but I think there is a case for saying that other criteria have become very important. If one looks at the way the Security Council works, say, in relation to the Gulf crisis it is quite clear that Britain has something rather special to contribute. There is a case based on what the country can contribute to world peace and security on the basis of its experience and special skills in the area of multilateral diplomacy. That must be the case. There are certain reservations on our particular role in the Council and I am afraid it is true that the Japanese and the Germans, who are the chief claimants to taking a seat in the Council, simply do not have that experience and those skills.

Mr Wells

120. We had better keep them in their place.

(Dr Taylor) That does not follow in this case.

[**Mr Wells** *Contd*]

Chairman: I think on that exchange we will call this to a halt. We have many more hours of questions on many fascinating issues, this last one alone could take a whole session, but we must bring this session to an end. I would like to thank you very much indeed, Dr Wallace, Mr Vibert and Dr Taylor, for an extremely stimulating and interesting insight. Thank you very much indeed.

ISBN 0-10-279592-4

Printed in the United Kingdom for HMSO.
Dd 0508198, 3/92, C6, 3382/5B, 5673, 186357.

HOUSE OF COMMONS   SESSION 1991–92

FOREIGN AFFAIRS
COMMITTEE

EUROPE AFTER MAASTRICHT

MINUTES OF EVIDENCE

Wednesday 19 February 1992

Mr P Ludlow, Mr P Allott, Prof T Hartley, Mr J Lever QC and Prof J Usher

---

Ordered by The House of Commons *to be printed*
19 February 1992

LONDON: HMSO
£7.50 net

WEDNESDAY 19 FEBRUARY 1992

Members present:

Mr David Howell, in the Chair

Mr Dennis Canavan   Mr Ivan Lawrence
Mr David Harris   Mr Bowen Wells
Mr Michael Jopling

Examination of witness

MR PETER LUDLOW, Director, Centre of European Policy Studies, Brussels, was examined.

Chairman

121. Mr Ludlow, welcome back to this Committee. We had the opportunity of a discussion with you in this Committee earlier in the year, since when the Committee has had the opportunity not only of digesting your thoughts and looking at your paper but also of making our own inquiries in Paris, Brussels and Bonn, and indeed of holding further hearings here in London. So we regard this a bit as the second half of the match and would like to press you a little on some of the points you made to us when you came before us earlier. My proposal would be that our discussion would last about three-quarters of an hour. So could I begin by thanking you for coming a second time as Director of the Centre of European Policy Studies. We found what you said earlier very stimulating. Let us now pursue it. My first question to you this afternoon concerns the Maastricht Treaty which has yet to be ratified but is now in full draft form. I would ask you what really is your opinion about the basic nature of this Treaty and what it does to the Community institutions. Is it a significant step towards federalism, as some told us when we went to Paris? Is it a further step or stepping stone, as we often heard it called, along a straight extrapolation of the development of the Community and Community powers? Or does it mark in some way a change of direction? Could you give us some thoughts on that?

(Mr Ludlow) Yes. I wonder whether I could make (and really in a sense this does answer your question) three observations provoked by the Foreign Secretary's observations when he gave evidence to you?

122. Please.

(Mr Ludlow) I think when assessing the Maastricht Treaty, and indeed every other document that has emanated from the Community, it is worth bearing three general points in mind. The first is that the Community is, and always has been, an evolutionary process. It is a Community in full movement towards a goal, somewhat ill-defined but a goal which is still ahead of us. The early Treaties provided us with definitions of what was possible and, therefore, made the possible more probable, and I think Maastricht does this too. So to read Maastricht I think it is important not just to have one's legal hat on but also one's political senses in tune. One has to get a sense of what is the direction that it is directing us towards and not simply what is there in store. The second point is this: it is a curious phenomenon that we have now had two major treaty revisions, the Single European Act and this, but those who want to go furthest, as always, are dissatisfied. It does not surprise me at all that, as the Foreign Secretary pointed out, the Commission, some elements in the Parliament and undoubtedly the federalists outside expressed disenchantment with the Treaty, or disappointment with it—they did just the same about the Single European Act. M Delors expressed considerable reserve about the Single European Act in 1986 and Judge Pescatore, one of the leading authorities on the Community, actually said the Single European Act was a step backwards. So one would rather expect after a tough negotiation those who want to go fastest to be saying "This isn't really very much at all". The third point is this—and it has got to be said, I think. At the opposite end of the spectrum, the British Government (and British Governments of any colour I should hasten to add) has a pretty long record of misreading what the political intentions are amongst our partners. There are two basic mistakes which recur from the 1950s onward and I think it is important to put this in a perspective of forty years. One is that it is not serious, that it is wistful, to quote the Foreign Secretary. The second is that they are so divided amongst themselves that they will not actually get there. We have been caught again and again by the fact that they do take seriously the goals they set themselves. This has been a public agenda, not a private agenda—political union—from the beginning, 9 May 1950. It is against this background that I think we ought to assess Maastricht. It is not the end of the road. By its own definition, we shall meet again in 1996, if not earlier—I would sense rather earlier. But I do think (as I have said in writing in a paper I believe you have seen)[1] Maastricht is a significant document, an important agreement, which advances us a good deal further towards a goal which is, let us say, federal, though I would use federalism in a different way from that

[1] *Reflections on the Maastricht Council*, International Economic Insights, Jan/Feb 1992.

The cost of printing and publishing these Minutes of Evidence is estimated by HMSO at £4,119.

[**Chairman** *Contd*]

in which it is normally used in English. I think the essence of federalism is multi-layered government and decentralisation as much as centralisation; but the goal is (and I do not want to get caught on a word, I think the word is very misleading) that and I think Maastricht advances us towards it.

123. Yet when we discussed these things with ministers of nation states and some of the officials in the Commission and the Council of Ministers, they kept on about the dual character of the European Union which is now emerging: one part indeed federal, supranational, the other part inter-governmental and international. They suggested to us that the intergovernmental approach was strongly reflected in the Maastricht documents and Maastricht accords and indicated it was not merely a hiccough or temporary deviation in the march to federalism but a significant development in its own right. This is the point that you dismissed in your paper when you talked about the death-knell of intergovernmentalism. Those are strong words. We heard counter-arguments. Do you still stand by your view?

(Mr Ludlow) Yes, I do. Perhaps I could explain why. In order to explain why one needs to try to understand why the three pillars concept emerged. It emerged at the end of March last year in a pri-vate lunch between the Presidency and the Secretary-General of the Council, that is, the Luxembourg Presidency. Basically they had a problem. They had by this stage got a lot of pro-posals on the table dealing with a great number of subjects and it was quite clear, even from the Commission's paper it should be stressed, at February 1991 that everybody agreed that at least for the time being foreign policy, foreign affairs and security, and judicial affairs, would have to be treated in a different way from ordinary Community business. There was no dispute about this. The Commission paper itself admits this. The Presidency therefore, which was setting about at this stage a first draft of the new treaty, had basi-cally to choose between creating one treaty with derogations or creating a structure in which the differences were made more articulate, a three pil-lar structure. The Presidency in March opted for a single framework rather along the Dutch lines, but the Secretary-General and his colleagues pointed out that it would be both more elegant and politi-cally more sensible, given certain sensibilities of which they were aware, to go for a three pillar framework. Basically there was not much differ-ence whether you went for the single or three pillar structure because everybody admitted that we had to do foreign affairs and judicial affairs differently. So I think one has to see the three pillars concept as a tactical response to a problem which every-body recognised existed. Now, it was of course a politically controversial move because the single pillar concept, to which the Commission and feder-alists and the Dutch Government clung, had cer-tain symbolic overtones. It gave a message, a clearer message, of the federal goal, but the reality, even in the single pillar, would have been the real-ity that we have in three pillars because we were quite clearly, and you can test this by the Dutch draft that came out in July, August, September (it was drafted in those months) we were quite clearly going to do these things differently. The reality, therefore, it seems to me is this: that the dispute about the three pillars is much less important than those on the left and on the right, if one wants to use those terms, made it. What is much more important, to my mind, is as the Secretary General doubtless pointed out to you, or at least I imagine he did, when you saw him, and as the Treaty itself points out, that although we have three pillars, we have a single institutional framework. That is the basic unity. And that is why I would argue that intergovernmentalism, in the classic sense, is dead, or is on its way out. If you want to get a certain perspective on this, we do have intergovernmental-ism in the Treaties. The Single European Act, to be precise. Article 30 is a two pillar document. Article 30 is the one dealing with foreign policy in the Single European Act. Foreign policy is dealt with in quite a different way. It is dealt with through European political co-operation, through a classic intergovernmental method. What you have in Maastricht is something quite different. You have a different way of handling foreign pol-icy, particularly the provision that everybody par-ticipating—the Member States and the Presidency and the Commission—has the right of initiative, which is a very significant difference, and that the thing is not justiciable under the Court of Justice, but you have also, what is not in the Single European Act, a provision that foreign policy will be produced within a single institutional frame-work. That seems to me to be the heart of the mat-ter for two or three reasons; first of all, because it strengthens what I would suggest is the centralising tendency in these areas as much as in the Community, normal business. If you are going to handle foreign policy through the ordinary machinery of the Community, there will be a sim-ple physical centralisation. More and more deci-sions will perforce be taken in Brussels. It does not mean to say that they will be taken by the Commission, but they will be taken in Brussels. The political directors have been in the habit, as you are probably aware, of perambulating some-times it would seem as far away from Brussels as they could possibly get, but the political directors are now not put on the side (I think that goes too far) but are certainly auxiliaries to a central struc-ture in which the prime actors are, apart from the General Affairs Council, the Committee of Permanent Representatives and the General Secretariat. My own feeling about those who favoured the three pillar approach and felt it was very important is that they were actually straining after the wrong enemy. What they wanted to stop was the Commission getting more powers or being in effect entrusted with foreign policy. That actu-ally was not in the short term anyway a real dan-ger. What has happened is that decisions are now centralised in the normal machinery and I would guess, from what we know of the way in which

[Chairman *Contd]*

things have developed in the past, and again going back to the evolutionary approach, that this means that the three pillars will increasingly converge with the way decisions are taken and the linkages between decisions will become tighter and tighter and closer and closer.

Mr Wells

124. Is not the Secretariat to the foreign affairs pillar—certainly it was under the Single European Act—actually quite separate from the Commission and will this not continue?

(Mr Ludlow) The Commission is not the Secretariat. When I talk about the Secretariat, I am talking about what I think, as I said last time, is a very seriously under-rated institution. I think I quoted to you President Delors himself who said to me once that he fully agreed with my analysis, that after him the most powerful full-time official in the Community structure was the Secretary General of the Council, who is not a member of the Commission, Mr Ersboell, a Dane. What happened in Maastricht is essentially this: that the separate Secretariat for European Political Co-operation and the Co-ordination Committee for Judicial Affairs are now, in the case of the European Political Co-operation Secretariat is actually absorbed by the Council Secretariat and in the case of judicial affairs *de facto* also brought into the framework of the General Secretariat. This is not just procedurally interesting; it is politically very important. It is a further centralization of policy formulation, decision-making and has important implications also for implementation.

125. But it reinforces, if you like, the Council of Ministers, does it not?

(Mr Ludlow) Yes, absolutely.

126. It does not, therefore, as you were suggesting, actually enhance the Commission's powers.

(Mr Ludlow) I am afraid this is not a zero sum game. If you want to do the Commission down, this is not a particularly encouraging line. Of course it reinforces the Council. The main victor of the Single European Act, it is often forgotten, was the Council, but if the Council is made stronger and more efficient, the Commission benefits because the Commission has a far easier task in providing leadership in animating the Council, in, if you want to put it this way, even manipulating the Council if it has a Council which can genuinely decide. In European Political Co-operation you had the rule of unanimity, you had a structure which was, in its origin, outside the ordinary Community framework. You now have foreign policy brought into a body which is used to, not just when business is formally that of majority rule, but when it is just dealing with ordinary business, is used to cobbling coalitions together, arriving at decisions and deciding, "Well, we will let the eleven have it on this one because tomorrow we may need other allies". This is a very important step forward. Foreign policy is brought into a Council which is much more fluid, much more

mobile, much more effective than a Council dealing with European Political Co-operation in the old days could have been.

Mr Lawrence

127. What we are really concerned with is not so much how you define federalism, but whether or not power over our independent economic, so far as it exists, decision-making remains in our hands. Whether the national power in foreign affairs, in judicial matters, home affairs, immigration and also the powers of the national Parliament remain intact. Those who are not "federalists" are very concerned about that and that is broadly the attitude of the Government too. Now, when we asked every single interlocutor that we saw in Bonn and Brussels and Paris whether or not your thesis was the right one, whether we could rely upon what you were saying and particularly about the quote that the German . . . . .

(Mr Ludlow) The death knell of intergovernmentalism.

128. Yes. They smiled and said, "No, it is nonsense". Now, unless they are trying to con us, then it is nonsense. Why do they all say that? Maybe they are trying to con us. Maybe they are trying to say, "Well, just come along, chaps, and all will be all right", and then when we get there on the day, bang, the shutter will go down and we are no longer independent in any of these areas. It does actually require us to assume in all of them a degree of deceitfulness in their answers or their interpretations or their intentions that we do not like to assume.

(Mr Ludlow) No, I do not think it is necessary to assume a degree of deceitfulness. I think it is possible to assume a degree of self-deception which is born of the long-standing tension between the aspiration of the federal goal and the way the Community does it, which is not like classic federalism. What we have in the Community is certainly not a system comparable to that of the United States of America. To put it in two propositions, whereas the United States constitution rests on the principle of the separation of powers and a distinction between the federal level and state level being quite clear—the separation there too—the Community system actually works through the intermingling of powers. It is not a classic federal system. And so those who are, as in Bonn particularly where they also have a federal system, conscious of the differences between how we do things and how in some perfect federal world we might do things, will say to you—and they are right in a way "This is not a classic federalism". But that does not, it seems to me, actually meet the main point which I am trying to make which is this: that when governments enter into the Community they accept a degree of limitation on their sovereignty which, to my mind at any rate, is tantamount to transferral of sovereignty to a higher level. If I could put this in terms of the Treaty so it does not just look like my theory, they have changed Article 146 in the Treaty and the key word which they

[**Mr Lawrence** *Contd*]

have introduced into Article 146—this deals with the Council of Ministers—is where they say the Council should consist of a representative of each Member State at ministerial level authorised to take "binding" decisions for the government of the Member State. When you have taken your decision you are bound. The Governments have signed up and, whether it be by majority or not, if a government minister then comes back here and says something has been decided and Parliament does not like it, there really is no recourse on that point: he has committed his people in the process and that is the essence of the Council. This is what I was trying to say to you. It seems to me fallacious to see the Community constitution as it currently is and as it is developing as being, on the one side, three supranational institutions—the Parliament, the Court and the Commission—and, on the other side, an intergovernmental institution, the Council. The Council is in its own way just as supranational in the sense that *vis-a-vis* its members when those collective decisions are taken they bind the individual members. This is not just legal playing—I leave that to the lawyers afterwards. This is politically very significant because the whole has been consistently greater than the parts. They have produced, in other words, *vis-a-vis*, for example, German unification to take a recent example, collective views which do not reflect many of the things which individually governments were saying beforehand. Those collective views then become supranational in their authority, legal and political. If by federalism you mean, as I do, the introduction of multi-layered government in which there is a federal level which has in certain defined areas primacy both legally and politically over the subordinate instances, I would submit the system we have already, and the system still more after Maastricht, is in that sense federal.

129. I think I may have misled you. I did not actually make clear the basis upon which we asked the questions. I am one of those very concerned that we should not be sliding towards irrevocable supranationalism. Forget federalism for the Germans. It is plain we mean by something federal something different from what you mean. So we always talked about the surrender of more power, not whether or not we would surrender power. We have surrendered power but the surrender of more power under the five or six headings—justice, immigration, finance, foreign affairs, defence is something else. We put to all of them, are you not, like in Article 146 and a number of other articles, underpinning the slide so that we can never slide back and we are always sliding down the slope so that we are actually going to give up national power over these things? The answer was almost invariably—but not invariably—"No, you need not worry". That is why I say to you it was not just arguments over what we meant by federal, a misunderstanding of what we meant by intergovernmental, or not an adequate understanding of how much we had already slid. We were more positive than that. The Chairman was right, we found

your draft very stimulating and provocative, so we put it to everybody and everybody said, "No, no, no, the man is quite wrong. This is not the way we are going".

(Mr Ludlow) Well, I am interested and I have absolute confidence that you report faithfully. I would only argue that both the record of the Community and the Maastricht text itself suggest, if it is a slide—and I do not actually see it in such pejorative terms—that we are well down that slide and the slide will continue. Let us take another instance. We have introduced in the case of foreign policy the concept of joint action. How do we define a joint action? The European Council decides in certain areas we are going to do things together. The Council of Ministers then decides on the specifics of joint action. In Article C, paragraph 4, of the section dealing with common and foreign policy it says, "once the decision has been taken to commit ourselves to a joint action; "Joint actions shall commit the member states in the positions they adopt in the conduct of their activity." We are still defining the list. The Asolo list which was first discussed by the Community Foreign Ministers in Asolo in October 1990 is still the nearest approximation to what that list will be, I think, but once we have decided that in these areas we are going to take joint actions, if you would put it as a slide, we have slid further.

Mr Lawrence: We put Croatia to the Germans and they were most embarrassed by it.

Chairman: We want to press on. We have already taken up two-thirds of our allocated time. How does this analysis look when set up against the commitments on Economic and Monetary Union? Mr Wells wants to ask about that.

Mr Wells

130. Do you see the setting up of the Central Bank and a single currency as pushing the Community towards becoming a centralised United States of Europe?

(Mr Ludlow) Karl-Otto Pohl, the President of the Bundesbank, made no secret of the fact that, if you were going to have a monetary union—I think I quote exactly—federalism in this case would be of a very centralised character; in other words, you cannot divide monetary policy if you are going to have as the most important aim this monetary union, price stability. The short answer to your question is, yes, if we have a central bank there is one central authority and nobody else will get a look in, which does not mean to say we cannot through our participation in this institution as the United Kingdom, as France or whatever, have influence on its policy. But it is bound to be a central single decision-making body. I think one of the most remarkable features of the Treaty is this overriding commitment, which is even stronger than the Bundesbank's commitment to price stability, which leaves very little room for manoeuvre. So the short answer is yes.

131. But is it in character, other than the monetary union aspect of it, really very different from

[**Mr Wells** *Contd*]

the Bretton Woods system of monetary control that was abandoned in 1972 in favour of floating exchange rates which you now have? I agree you have the monetary union, but the objective of the two systems is the same, which is basically to stabilise the relationship between different moneys, different systems of money, internationally.

(Mr Ludlow) I would submit it is totally different and I would put it perhaps this way: we are now in a mini-Bretton Woods. Under the old Bretton Woods system our currency was linked with the dollar, which was the anchor currency. In the present interim phase our currency, as we are uncomfortably aware, is linked to the deutschmark. The fundamental difference between this transitional mini-Bretton Woods system which we have, which is the European Monetary System, and monetary union is that instead of currencies linked to one hegemonic currency, there will be one currency. And that is totally different. You cannot devalue or change your parity against one currency because you are one currency. The Scots may have pound notes which look different, but they cannot change their value unless they opt out of the Union.

132. It is clearly different from that point of view and I accept that, but the thing is, as you know, at the present time you are chained to the Deutschmark without any kind of representation as to how the Deutschmark is run and what you will get now is a system in which you will have a series of central bankers, as I understand it, sitting around a table from different countries and will have a say in how the monetary union is run.

(Mr Ludlow) I think this is a very important point, but it is not to be achieved by going back to Bretton Woods. We are not going back to a floating rate because we are deliberately excluding the devaluation or realignment option. The great appeal of Economic and Monetary Union, or monetary union, to most Member States is precisely that they will regain some of the sovereignty they have now lost to the deutschmark or to the Bundesbank, but it is not going back to the sovereignty that they allegedly had in the 1970s of free fall or free rise or whatever it was.

Mr Jopling

133. Can we come back to this House? I wonder if you could tell us what you see as the implications of Maastricht for the powers and working methods of this Parliament here and, besides that, how do you think Parliament will be able to make Ministers accountable for decisions which they take in the Council of Ministers and to what extent do you think, as a result of Maastricht, will Parliament find itself in a changed situation with regard to influencing those decisions taken in the Council of Ministers?

(Mr Ludlow) I think in answering this question it might be useful to make a distinction, which one should not exaggerate, but which is useful for analytical purposes, between legislative processes and political processes. I hope I am not being discourteous in this particular House, but it seems to me that in the areas which we have now already assigned to the Community, or which we propose to assign to the Community, in legislative powers this House has very little opportunity to influence the process, except if it got in at the very beginning by telling the Government, "Such and such a Directive is not going to go down at all well with us", I suspect it does that anyway. In terms of scrutiny of legislation, in the ordinary Community business the situation which already exists, which I think will become ever more the case, is that the initiative must lie with the European Parliament and that is where the action is in legislation. If I could go on just briefly about legislation. One of the uncomfortable features, to my mind, of the three pillars is precisely in fact the lack of democratic control particularly in the judicial area where it is not at all clear who is going to have parliamentary authority. There is a real chance, I think, that very important matters and very important decisions and legislative proposals will fall through the interstices. On the political side, inevitably if decision-making in foreign policy is concentrated in the Council of Ministers, and we are not just talking about the Commission but the Commission is the thirteenth member, I think we are going to go through a phase at any rate where we have to reckon on dual democratic control. It seems to me, and I do not think I should hide this, that inevitably the initiative will increasingly pass to the European Parliament too in terms of foreign policy. It seems to me also that the European Parliament should recognise this fact and choose to be much more effective than it has been. It already has powers that it could use to make life uncomfortable for those responsible for the development of the common foreign policy and so on. I think the initiative is moving in that direction, but at least for the time being the national parliaments could make life uncomfortable for ministers who will be collectively responsible for the development of foreign policy by letting their opinions be known beforehand or by letting their disapproval be known afterwards. One can see how sensitive governments are in the foreign policy area to national pressures in the case that has already been cited here of German behaviour over Croatia and Yugoslavia. The behaviour of the German Government in the Council of Ministers from July of last year onwards was a constant tribute to the strength of domestic opinion expressed not only through the Bundestag, but primarily through the Bundestag. I do not think that one should exclude the possibility that national parliaments, indeed the likelihood that national parliaments will for a very long time indeed have a major responsibility and a major opportunity to make sure that their ministers behave in ways which are more sensitive to national preferences and national priorities. I think in legislation you are going to see more and more that it is basically the European Parliament that plays the role, but in politics I hope the European Parliament will be more effective politically, but it would seem to me that national parlia-

[**Mr Jopling** *Contd*]

ments should exercise their might and main to ensure that their influence is felt too. I am not sure, having said that, that the provisions for conferences and so on are particularly going to help this forward. I believe, Mr Chairman, in one of the previous sessions you drew attention to the rather unsatisfactory experience of the Assize in November 1990 when, as far as I could see, 85 MEPs ran 175 national MPs largely I think because the national MPs could not get their act together. I suspect that is the way it would actually happen most times if you have these conferences. Your influence, is best exercised on your Government here and your Government then goes and bats for the country in the Council of Ministers.

Chairman

134. We were neutered by the decision for MPs to sit in party groupings rather than in national groupings. The moment that decision was taken, all effort by the nation states, our national parliaments, to influence this area was destroyed.

(Mr Ludlow) Yes, except that I think, if I may say so, you should not have been surprised about this because the development of the political families is one of the more important developments of the last decade or so. Community politics are now unintelligible if one does not take account, for example, of the solidarity of the Christian Democrat family. If one wants to predict how a European Council is going to go, it is a wise thing to look at the summit which always takes place beforehand of the Christian Democrat members of it because they constitute at the moment half the membership of the European Council. They feel a sense of solidarity. Pre-Maastricht they had a very important meeting where a lot of the decisions that were taken were already anticipated by their discussions.

135. But you would agree, would you not, that that, therefore, inevitably breaks the thread between the national legislatures and their democratic legitimacy and the Community institutions?

(Mr Ludlow) Yes.

136. There is no connection.

(Mr Ludlow) It makes it more difficult. As I would repeat, your principal chance of influencing the Community process must be through your leverage over your Member State which is a very important Member of the Community.

Mr Harris

137. Just as an aside, you might be interested to know that most of us read your paper appropriately enough on the train to Brussels and Paris and found it very interesting.

(Mr Ludlow) Good.

138. I want to ask about the Community institutions. You have mentioned perhaps some of the answers to my questions in your paper, but for the

record I will ask them. Which institutions do you think have been or will be strengthened as a result of Maastricht?

(Mr Ludlow) I think all of them, all four, plus, and this perhaps gives me a chance to mention it because I did not in my paper, one which is new and which I think is going to have a very important life in the future which is the Committee of the Regions. I have re-read the Treaty a lot since I did that paper for you. I think the regional dimension is very important in Maastricht and has now become more and more important. Going to the four, the main four, I think they have all been strengthened *vis-a-vis* the Member States. Going back to my original definition, that the Council is as much part of the supra-national structure as the other three, the Council has been strengthened because its decision-making structure is now simplified, its powers over the whole of Community business have been, as it were, clarified in one system, majority voting has been extended, its Secretariat is much stronger than it was previously and so on. The Commission has been strengthened because the Council cannot function without the Commission under the Community system. So if you strengthen the Council you strengthen the Commission. The Commission does not have an adversarial relationship with the Council; on the contrary it needs a strong Council to be strong, it cannot carry through decisions by itself, it needs to get them through a Council and a Council that is more efficient therefore makes the Commission stronger. Parliament has been strengthened, not as much as many parliamentarians would have hoped, but to my mind as much as it needs to be because it has still not, to my mind, digested all the powers it acquired through the Single European Act. The Court of Justice has been strengthened in a number of ways, not least, of course, in its ability to impose financial sanctions, but in other ways too. I think they are all stronger, but that in effect is a comment on the interlocking nature of the quadripartite system.

139. You would not say there is one big winner amongst those four, you would say the whole European network of institutions has been strengthened?

(Mr Ludlow) Yes. Going back to the original conversation, which is why I am a little surprised you got the messages you did, I did my post-Maastricht round, following in some cases or indeed preceding you, and I put together a picture such as the one I portrayed there largely on the comments of those who were involved. One of the striking things was that each of them had a different view of who had gained. To some it was the Commission that had been the great gainer, to others the Council. The conclusion I drew from it, and I draw also from reading the Treaty, is that actually everybody gained.

140. You mentioned the Committee of the Regions. This is something which interested us greatly during our visit to Brussels. Could you per-

[**Mr Harris** *Contd*]

haps say a word about why you think it is going to be so important, because it is going to be consultative, is it not? Do you see it as really strengthening the links between regions and the Commission in particular, in other words, the regions perhaps trying to bypass Whitehall and national governments? Is that what you think its importance is?

(Mr Ludlow) I think Maastricht to a very large extent in this area actually legitimised or codified the situation which has been developing. This is not something which they are creating, it is something they are acknowledging. One of the facts of life in Brussels over the last five to ten years has been the development and proliferation of regional representation, dealing directly with the Community. The German Lander led the way. All of them have offices in Brussels; all deal directly—sometimes to the considerable embarrassment of the Bonn Government—with the European Commission, and this example has been followed by regional authorities from all over the Community, including regional authorities from this country. So Maastricht to a large extent was acknowledging a fact of life: regions are here, they have begun to organise themselves. There are various trans-national European regional organisations, the Association of European Regions, etc. Maastricht was, therefore, to some extent, simply acknowledging what the state of affairs was; but as always, as with the Single European Act which did the same thing in other areas, by acknowledging it, it gives a further push forward, it institutionalises what at present is a fairly chaotic system. I would myself anticipate that you will see an increasing regionalisation of decision-making and of consultation in certain obvious areas, the administration of the structural funds being one. I would actually take the agreement that the British Government has made this week with the Commission over the funds for Scotland as being a sign of what we are going to see again and again, that the regional dimension is asserted by Brussels as its condition for giving its money. This has, of course, mind-boggling and rather fascinating constitutional possibilities because does this mean—I raise this as a question—that the German Lander who have been very much making the running are going to become the role models for regions all over the Community? It may seem rather fanciful but I do not think it is entirely out of the question. What was striking in the Maastricht process itself was that sometimes the regional representatives of the Lander were actually present with the German delegation in the negotiation of the intergovernmental conference. At one point it is actually alleged (with some dismay one of the stronger personal representatives put it to me) that a Lander representative even tried to grasp the microphone but was ruled out of order. But there is a very strong regional presence and several countries, particularly Germany and particularly Belgium, would see this as certainly not going to wane in those countries but rather to spread.

141. You mentioned the European political families and the importance of them. How do you think this is going to develop? Do you, for example, see my colleague Mr Ivan Lawrence in years to come standing as a Christian Democrat for this place? Do you actually see it developing into full-blown European political parties?

(Mr Ludlow) I can scarce forebear to say I think he would have to come to terms with the social protocol of the Maastricht Treaty before that could happen. The answer is yes. I think we will see political confederations, political families, we even already have them. I cannot help contrasting, if I may say so, the behaviour of the European Democratic Group in the European Parliament—the Conservatives—with, if I may say so, their national comrades. Because they have to work in a Parliament where, if they do not belong to a particular group they are marginalised. The system is such that, if you are one of the smaller players, you are constantly marginalised. Hence, to take another development which is not without interest, Giscard d'Estaing decision to join the EPP, because he did not like being a member of a small group. I think you will not see a total elimination of small parties—by no means; you will certainly have some which stay doggedly on—but there will be an increasing convergence towards two main political families, the Socialists and the Christian Democrats, though interestingly enough if the British introduced proportional representation, they might slightly delay that process by greatly strengthening another political family, the Liberals, because the biggest Liberal Democratic party in Europe with proportional representation would be the British one.

Chairman

142. Although we read that the Italians are considering coming to our system because they find proportional representation so unsatisfactory.

(Mr Ludlow) I agree.

Chairman: How would all this picture of ever more binding central decisions square up with a Community of 17 or 23 countries?

Mr Canavan

143. You state in your paper that deepening is a precondition of widening but that widening will nevertheless entail further modification of the EC institutional structure. Could you elaborate on that and, in particular, tell us what changes you think will be necessary to the Community institutions to cope with widening the Community to include the EFTA countries plus probably Poland, Hungary, Czechoslovakia, plus possibly other states in Eastern Europe and the former Soviet Union and maybe even Turkey and the Mediterranean "orphans"?

(Mr Ludlow) I think on this one, perhaps to take the question abut deepening and widening, to my mind—you know where my sympathies are—the Community was absolutely right to give priority to deepening over widening, because had we widened two years ago instead of going through the Maastricht process, I think there was a real

[**Mr Canavan** *Contd*]

chance that more fragile institutions would have been overrun or diluted, or whatever metaphor you want to use, by much greater numbers. I think we are now equipped with a more robust institutional machinery which can, if one wants to use the word, cope with enlargement. If I could just develop this argument a little further, I do not think that widening, certainly in the first phase, will in any way weaken the Community. On the contrary, to take one rather specific example, it seems to me that the inclusion of the four or five EFTA states before 1996, which now seems quite possible if not probable, will actually make the early rendezvous with economic and monetary union likelier than it would have been without, because they are almost without exception strong currency countries who will join the majority, making it possible to proceed faster towards monetary union. If we move on, as I trust we will—and you will remember from my last time here I advocate a much more systematic approach to enlargement than is currently on the table—to a Community of 24 or 30, clearly we are going to have to modify our institutions. We cannot have, I would guess, a system of one Commissioner per country and we certainly could not have a system of one Commissioner per country and two for the bigger countries. We would have to make much more use of majority voting, qualified majority voting. We would have, and I think I commented on this last time, certainly to consider the weighting of voting by a country. The situation where Luxembourg has a fifth of the voting power of Germany is already odd. It becomes even odder if you then put Malta or other very small countries in a similar situation. So there are any number of institutional changes which will have to be made. The real question is: do you have to change the system absolutely? Jacques Delors' argument when he was really anxious about deepening taking priority over widening was in order to cope with all these newcomers we would really have to make a qualitative leap to a highly-centralised system and indeed a very different system like a classic federation. I said when I was before your Committee last time, and I do not think I need repeat it, that it does seem to me that we could develop the present system in which the Council of Ministers still has the decisive voice even in a Community of 24 to 30, but it is not going to be easy.

144. We did hear evidence from some quarters in Germany and elsewhere that the Treaty on European Union would in fact, whether we liked it or not, make it more difficult for Eastern European countries to join and it will take them longer to catch up, as it were, and, therefore, postpone their entry date well into the next century. What do you think of that?

(Mr Ludlow) Again I am somewhat mystified by the motivation. The motives of your German interlocutors becoming increasingly fascinating because Germany has in fact been collectively one of the main protagonists of a very radical enlargement policy towards the east and, as you will remember, the German Foreign Minister only a few weeks ago was saying that we must take Czechoslovakia, Hungary and Poland in fairly rapidly, so if they were saying this as you say they were, perhaps some of them are beginning to think that Maastricht was not so good after all, but there we are. The point, I think, is this: in every enlargement we have made it possible for those who are not ready or who have special problems to have periods of transition, to have derogations. The Spaniards and the Portuguese are full Members of the Community politically, but they are not yet full Members economically. It does not seem to me that the admittedly very backward state of some of the candidate countries in the east is in itself a bar to membership, as long as we get our derogations, our transitional regimes right. It will be difficult, but I think we could do it, so I do not think we have to see the Maastricht Treaty as basically making it impossible for these countries to come in; on the contrary, I think it means that we have got a structure in which we can actually make life easier for them. If I may say just one other point on this, going back to the weakening which might come through enlargement. One of the things which is very striking indeed, and this applies to the EFTA countries who used to be our allies against the six in the old days, if you go round prospective candidate countries, and I do not think that this is mere tactics, all of them profess very strongly indeed that they do not want to come into a Community which they weaken by joining. In other words, they accept the present situation and the intentions declared in Maastricht as a basic point of departure for their own membership.

Chairman: Mr Ludlow, time is up, I fear. We are very grateful to you for coming back a second time. You have painted a picture of a great machine rolling forward which makes us almost feel a little powerless to do anything about these ineluctable processes. Now, whether that is right or whether that is not right, the way you presented it is extremely stimulating and challenging and has set all our minds a-whirl and we will now have to see how your thoughts can be fitted in with our conclusions. In the meantime thank you very much indeed for coming.

Memorandum submitted by Mr Philip Allott, Trinity College, Cambridge (EC 239)

THE EUROPEAN COMMUNITY AT THE PAIN-BARRIER

THE SIGNIFICANCE OF THE MAASTRICHT TREATY

I

In a leading article some twenty years ago, the *Times* newspaper divided supporters of European integration into two camps—European idealists and European imperialists. The idealists are misty-eyed about the transcending of the nation-state and the final burial of German, French and British nationalism in a new kind of political system. The imperialists pine for the 19th century. If Prussia-Germany, France and Britain were Great Powers then, why should not Germany-France-Britain be a Very Great Power now? In the Maastricht Treaty which was signed on 7 February, we can watch as a struggle that has gone on for more than twelve centuries takes on its latest and most subtle form. It is a world-historical event with worldwide implications.

Maastricht is a voluminous set of legal texts, but the superficial analysis which is treated as received wisdom is that it is a crude amalgam of three different approaches.

The British government wanted to enhance the intergovernmental aspect of the EC at the expense of its supranational character. They wanted to exclude from the EC system things that they would rather deal with internally, and to include in a rather loose parallel system, not fully integrated into the EC system, governmental activities that can profit from common action, including foreign policy and security questions, and to provide for limited intergovernmental co-operation in a number of other fields. The French wanted to incorporate Germany's potential economic hegemony into the legal sovereignty of the EC so that, step-by-step through the rest of the decade, the national economies would be substantially integrated in a single Economic and Monetary Union. The Germans wanted to put their economic power into the EC system, with its vast market of 320 million people, but only into an EC system which is made as reliable and efficient as a well-ordered nation-state and which would not be a perpetual drain on German resources.

Every line of almost all the Maastricht texts can be read as some sort of a resolution of these conflicting attitudes, simply because such may well have been the actual attitudes of the politicians and bureaucrats who negotiated the texts. They put such ideas into the instructions that they gave to themselves before the negotiation. And, when the negotiation is over, they mark their score-cards accordingly for the benefit of public opinion, a public opinion glad to have so straightforward an explanation of such obscure matters. As each of the governments listens to the echo of their attitude in public opinion, the self-reinforcing loop of so-called "national interest" is formed, to be carried forward into the next stage of the EC's development.

The European idealists must be confused by Maastricht. It seems to imply a much greater cohesion of the member States in the future, but it seems to involve a significant weakening of the communitarian character of the EC, in which the Council (where national governments have the power) will become the *de iure* and not merely the *de facto* supreme power, and above which has been added a completely new entity, called the European Union, of which the nationals of the member States will now become citizens, as a sort of second nationality. There is also a new body called the European Community, which seems designed more or less to replace the old European Economic Community, but which seems to leave in existence the European Coal and Steel Community and the European Atomic Energy Community. Economic and Monetary Union is apparently not itself a community or a union. It is a special aspect of the other communities and of the European Union.

The years of talk about creating, in the minds of the citizens, a sense of loyalty and attachment to the EC is not worth much now, given that the new total structure will be as obscure as the Holy Roman Empire. One may be called upon to die for the EC in war, but one will not be able to say quite what it is that one is dying for.

The European imperialists might find Maastricht rather exciting. Under the banner of "Forward to the 19th century", they can proclaim a mighty European pillar of that new world order which is due to emerge, any moment now, from the ashes of the Cold War. Equally exciting, there will begin during the 1990's a process called Enlargement or Widening—chilling abstract words of a kind favoured by diplomats down the centuries to describe something which will profoundly affect the lives of millions of people. In a slow-motion replay of the Congress of Vienna, every other state which can fairly claim to use the brand-name "European" will be brought into the European system, as an EC member or else held by mutual agreement in the EC's overwhelming force-field.

But the idealists will not give up. Under their banner of "Never Again", they will continue to argue that the vision of the EC was a vision of a world beyond the European system of the 19th century and of a world far beyond the horrors of the European system of the first half of the 20th century.

To predict who will win and how the EC (or EU, or whatever it will be called) will behave as a world power, it is necessary to go beyond the attitudes of politicians and bureaucrats and public opinion. The Maastricht agreement is the product of the interacting of the particular obsessional neuroses of the Germans, the French, and the British. Together they have reached a pain-barrier. If they cannot force their way through that barrier together, the future of the EC is in danger. The idealists will be permanently frustrated, because the three life-threatening nationalisms will not be overcome. The imperialists will be permanently frustrated, because the EC will be condemned to be a second-rate and ineffectual Great Power.

II

The Maastricht Agreement can be presented, at the most superficial level, as the outcome of a conflict between the policies of three governments. At a deeper level, it can be seen as the outcome of a conflict between two philosophies of European integration. But it can also be seen as yet another chapter in the long story of the lively interaction of three strange and complex national characters, national characters which are rooted in obsessional neurosis.

The obsessional neurosis of the British is called Freedom, of the French is called Security, of the Germans is called Order.

The British have fostered a fantasy of Freedom for some twelve centuries. They conjured up something called "the ancient rights and liberties of the English people" as a way of taming a series of essentially foreign kings. They forced one king to acknowledge the interesting idea in Magna Carta and got rid of two kings in the 17th century in the name of the same idea. In the 18th century, foreign observers, to the surprise and pleasure of the British, found that the idea of the remarkable political freedom of the British could serve a useful purpose in their own pro revolutionary endeavours. In the American and French Revolutions the idea took on a magical wonder-working quality and, in the 19th century, the British themselves used it again to justify the transfer of power to a new ruling class.

The idea had always been full of fantasy, because through all this time the only true freedom of the British people was the freedom of one privileged class after another, from the medieval barons to the 19th century bourgeoisie.

The protection of British freedom through the Balance of Power became the beginning and the end of British foreign policy. And the imposition of freedom through unfreedom on other peoples all over the world took on a sort of blithe sense of duty, as part of the long-term preservation and enhancement of the freedom of the British people.

As Britain faces the challenge of the EC, the latest continental ruse, it is not surprising if they bring to it their illusion-filled game of Freedom.

The French are in the unfortunate position that the Rhine is not the English Channel. They are in the fortunate position that they have a long-matured national consciousness founded on a justified, if also a fantasised, sense of achievement. With reason, they might see themselves as entitled to a place alongside, say, China and India among those nations which have sustained the excellence of their high culture over a very long period—at least 12 centuries in the case of France. The French ruling class has been able to retain, right up to the present day, a sense that all the rest of Europe is in some sense provincial and, if this is true of Europe, how much more might it be true of the rest of the world!

The fact that wars are not fought with the mind of the intellectual nor the hand of the artist put the French at a disadvantage in the cruder forms of conflict between the nations, at least until an unFrench Napoleon Bonaparte inspired the nation temporarily to British or Prussian levels of aggressive militarism. On three occasions from 1871, they have had to accept the fact that they are inherently and hopelessly vulnerable to the physical power of Germany.

When you believe that you have something very precious to protect and that you have no obvious means of protecting it, you are liable to suffer a neurosis of Security. In the EC, the French see themselves once again in their eternally precarious situation, giving others power in order to retain power over themselves.

In the 19th century the Germans conjured a German nation out of the medieval Teutonic mists, and the idea was very useful in making a new German state. The evident and cherished diversity of geographical Germany and of the German peoples meant that the new state-structure had then, in its turn, to play an unusually important part in sustaining the new-old nation. This reciprocal reinforcement of nation and state in Germany generated a neurotic interest in Order, which may have played a part in their rich high culture but played a less significant part in their untidy political culture down the centuries.

Following an outbreak of ultimate disorder, in the Third Reich a neurosis of Order developed into something more than a neurosis. Following the Third Reich, a new state-system was created which has now become the state-system of all present-day Germany, a constitution which may rank as the most intelligent and successful piece of purposive social organisation in the history of the world, rivalled only, perhaps, by the social organisation of Venice in its glory days.

In these circumstances, it would not be surprising if the Germans display neurotic symptoms when they are called upon to submerge themselves finally in some quasi-state-system which they may dominate economically but which might undo them politically.

The intricate obscurity of the Maastricht Agreement is the product of such neuroses, which are at the heart of the three forms of nationalism. The troubling question is—will Maastricht contribute to the overcoming of the nationalisms or is it the waste of a last opportunity, in this century, to overcome them?

Even a more or less detached observer might feel a sense of nervousness in contemplating what will be the post-Maastricht EC. The intricate structure of Austria-Hungary a century ago was also the handiwork of highly intelligent bureaucrats. In the post-Maastricht triad of European Union, the European Community, and Economic and Monetary Union, it would, of course, be grossly over-fanciful to detect any echo of Austria-Hungary, Austria, and Hungary which were respectively and charmingly designated as *K. und K., K.-K., and K.* (Imperial and Royal, Imperial-Royal, and Royal). What we can say is that history shows that inappropriate constitutional structures tend not to last.

And there is another strange echo of Austria. According to a famous saying, of which Austria was not ashamed, Austria had been content to let others fight its battles (the Gulf War?) while it became great through marriage. *Tu, felix Austria, nube.* Post-Maastricht EC will continue its aggrandizement through the dynastic agreements of so-called Enlargement. But external ambition will not cure internal weakness. There is reason to believe that the EC will not overcome its inherent, possibly terminal, weakness unless it has the courage to do what Maastricht consciously failed to do, unless it reconstructs its internal constitution.

III

There is one point at which the different nationalist neuroses of Germany, France and Britain might have been expected to interact fruitfully in their approach to the future of the EC, namely, in relation to the internal constitutional structure of the EC. The system is not a realm of order for the Germans, nor a realm of security for the French, nor a realm of freedom for the British.

The cause of the constitutional inadequacy of the EC is not difficult to identify. It lies in the fact that the EC is neither diplomacy nor democracy but both at the same time. Those who created the structure in the 1950's, with an intelligence and a clairvoyance comparable only to those displayed by the makers of the US Constitution, endowed the EC with three of the essential attributes of a constitutional order—organs of the constitution and, hence, a separation of powers; the Rule of Law in the hands of a powerful supreme court; and a parliamentary body.

But, contrary to what were probably the expectations of the founders, the life of the EC came more and more to be dominated by the Council, the body where most of the important decisions are negotiated, even if they are eventually adopted (by the Council) in the form of laws which apply in all the member states as ordinary law, overriding all national law.

In all modern democracies, law-making has taken on more and more of the character of negotiation, especially between the executive or the legislature and special interests. But, in the EC, the special interests concerned are not merely those of interest-groups and lobbies, important as they now are in the EC system. The most important special interests continue to be *national interests*. In other words, at the heart. of the system, there is an activity that feels a great deal more like the conduct of a strange new sort of foreign relations than like the conduct of a strange new sort of liberal democracy.

It has been traditional in Europe that the conduct of foreign relations has been integrated weakly, if at all, in national Democratic processes. It is too important, urgent, and difficult for such crude treatment.

So it is that the pain-barrier now facing the Community can be stated quite precisely. Given that very large areas of national law and government are now integrated into the EC system and given that, during the 1990's, very much more will be so integrated, including eventually the commanding heights of the national economies, how can diplomacy at last let go and hand over to democracy?

If this step cannot be taken, the EC will not be able to act as a Very Great Power, the EC will never transcend the three competing national isms, and, it must be said frankly, the danger of pathological nationalistic developments will remain.

In other words, the idealist and the imperialist philosophies of the EC could have been reconciled at Maastricht, if only a few extra pages had been added to the hundreds of pages of legal texts. Those pages would have contained a new Constitutional Act for the EC, comprising four things in particular.

(1) A formal statement of the nature and purpose of the EC which does not use the stale old categories of federation or confederation but builds on the splendidly rich idea of Community. The European Community, it would be said at last, is not the continuation of diplomacy by other means but the continuation of democracy by other means. We have opened up our political systems to each other and we are now seeking the public interest and the common interest of the Community, and not merely an aggregation of the national interests of the member states.

(2) A provision on the vertical distribution of power in the EC, including a locating of residual sovereignty. Maastricht includes a fatuous text on so-called *subsidiarity*, which says that things will only be done at the EC level if it is necessary to do them at that. level. What is needed is a provision which makes clear that the EC system is not merely a horizontal relationship among member states and among EC organs. It is a system of integrated and distributed power from Brussels through the national governments, the regions, the counties, and the cities, down to the village.

(3) A set of codified fundamental rights. It is an insult to the future citizens of the European Union to tell them that codified fundamental rights are absolutely essential to control the power of government in every aspect of government other than government by and through the EC. It is one of the rare oversights of the founders of the EC that they made no provision for fundamental rights, and the European Court of Justice has been left to conjure a feeble shadow of such rights out of thin air.

(4) The transformation of the European Parliament into a legislature. The EP, as it is at present allowed to function, is an institutionalisation of all the futility of the national parliaments. The central and critical role of national parliaments, achieved through centuries of struggle, as the focus and symbol of the will of the people has been cynically withheld from the EC system. It is an insult to the citizens of the European Union to say that legislation and taxation must be formalised in the member states in parliaments, and to go round the world preaching parliamentary democracy, when the EC system itself is anything but a parliamentary democracy.

Of course, national parliaments are full of fantasy, hypocrisy and illusion about their own status and powers and, of course, there will always be a power-struggle in the EC, as in all constitutional systems, among the organs of government—and the Council might continue to dominate a real European Parliament, as national executive branches in many countries tend to dominate national parliaments.

The EC system will never be a realm of freedom, order, and security until there is a real EC political system, engaging the citizens at least as much as they have been engaged in national political systems.

The cause of this failure of constitutional development is again not difficult to identify. If you had asked Henry VIII or James I in England or Louis XIII or Louis XIV in France for something on the lines of the four points noted above, you would have been greeted by a vigorous lack of enthusiasm. So long as the constitutional development of the EC is in the hands of national executive branches, politicians and bureaucrats and diplomats, with noises-off from national parliaments who fear losing their last vestiges of importance, the resistance to fundamental change will be almost insuperable.

In the past, we, the people of Germany and France and Britain (not to mention the United States), have found our various ways of overcoming that resistance.

7 February 1992

Memorandum submitted by Jeremy Lever QC, All Souls' College, Oxford (EC 245)

1. European Community law operates at the following levels:

(a) Between the Governments of the Member States *inter se*, between them and the Community Institutions and between the Community Institutions *inter se*.

(b) Between the Community Institutions and private persons (individuals, companies etc.).

(b) Between private persons and the Governments of the Member States.

(c) Between private persons *inter se*.

2. The Treaty of Maastricht will have important effects at each of those levels. The following describes a few of those effects, by way of example.

3. However, a preliminary comment of general relevance concerns the principle of subsidiarity as expressed in article 3b, 3° of the EC Treaty, as amended. The Foreign Secretary suggested to the Committee both that subsidiarity was a good deal more complicated than a dispute as to what was a Community matter and what was an entirely national matter and that, as a concept, it was "actually common sense".[1] For the lawyer, the question is whether subsidiarity raises "justiciable" issues, that is issues that can be determined by Courts, using normal judicial techniques.

4. My own view, which may turn out to be wrong, is that the European Court of Justice will ultimately find that it must choose between:

— applying the principle only where the Community Institutions have been guilty of manifest error or misuse of powers or have otherwise misdirected themselves (that is not substituting the Court's judgment for that of the Institutions but performing the traditional role of "judicial review" of the judgment of a non-judicial body); or

— risking the politicization of the Court and taking up a substantive position of the Court's own in the vexed areas of "State rights".

A. AT THE INTER-GOVERNMENTAL/INSTITUTIONAL LEVEL

5. The political/constitutional implications of the Treaty will be broadly familiar to the Committee (almost certainly more familiar to it than to a mere legal practitioner). To the European Community lawyer, it seems evident that monetary union is already implicit in the concept of a common market, as interpreted by the European Court of Justice. The question before Maastricht appeared to be whether monetary union implied economic union as a *legal* necessity; if not, it could scarcely be doubted that a single market and monetary union without economic union would lead to increasing German economic hegemony *de facto*. See again generally the perceptive comments of Professor ver Loren van Themaat, cited in the footnote to paragraph 3 above.

6. The Committee, at Issue 3, refers to the power of the European Court of Justice to fine recalcitrant Member States (Article 171 of the EC Treaty as amended). That provision and Article 104(c), paragraph 11, are remarkable, and perhaps unique, in the history of inter-State relations. Both provisions permit the imposition on a Member State of financial penalties:

(ii) Article 104(c), paragraph 11, 4th indent:

— "Fines of an appropriate size" may be imposed on a Member State by the Council for failure by the Member State to comply with measures imposed by the Council for the reduction of a national budget deficit, being a reduction which is judged necessary by the Council.

(ii) Article 171:

— The Court of Justice of the European Communities may impose on a Member State "a lump sum or penalty payment" for failure by the Member State to comply with a judgment of the Court (a penalty payment is a fine of a periodic nature which continues to be incurred as long as the person on whom it is imposed fails to comply with the relevant order).

7. It is presumably felt that the loss of face resulting from being fined would be worse than the loss of face resulting from being identified as a defaulter. A Member State fined by the Council will be able to

---

[1] For a brief, but I find very helpful, discussion of three different aspects of the principle of subsidiarity, see the Appendix to these Notes which contain an excerpt from an article (Common Market Law Review, vol.28, 291–318, 1991) by Professor P ver Loren van Themaat, a former Director General of the European Communities Commission and a former Advocate General of the European Court of Justice.

apply to the European Court of Justice to annul the Council's decision. But there would seem to be no appeal procedure so far as fines imposed by the Court are concerned.

B. AT THE INSTITUTIONAL/PRIVATE PERSON LEVEL

8. Article 108a, paragraph 3, empowers the European Central Bank, under conditions established by the Council, to impose fines and periodic penalty payments on undertakings for failure to comply with obligations under the ECB's regulations and decisions. As always in Community law, persons to whom a decision is addressed (including a decision imposing a fine) and persons who are directly and individually concerned by regulations or decisions addressed to others have the right to apply to the European Court of Justice (generally now the Court of First Instance, which is the lower Court) for annulment of the decision. However, this widens further the area where private persons are liable to be subjected to fines for "wrongful" conduct, without the safeguards that we in the United Kingdom generally associate with application of the criminal law. A fine on a company for alleged infringements of the Rules on Competition of the EC Treaty recently amounted to over ECU 70 million: the growth of "quasi-criminal" Community law is, therefore, of considerable practical importance.

C. AT THE PRIVATE PERSON/MEMBER STATE GOVERNMENT LEVEL

9. The European Community Treaty now creates a right for nationals of a Member State not merely to go to another Member State in the course of an economic activity (for example free movement of labour) but a "right to move and reside freely within the territory of the Member States" and to vote and stand as a candidate. at municipal elections and in elections to the European Parliament in the Member State in which he resides: Articles 8a and 8b.

10. Title VI (Provisions on Co-operation In the Fields of Justice and Home Affairs) of the Treaty of Maastricht provides for co-operation in relation to a number of matters of very great significance for the individual (see Article K1, listing asylum, rules governing the crossing by persons of the external borders of the Member States, immigration policy, drug addiction, international fraud, judicial co-operation in civil and criminal matters, customs co-operation and police co-operation in various areas). Article K3, paragraph 2(b) permits the Council, acting by a qualified majority, to take measures implementing joint action in the enumerated areas. We have yet to see whether those provisions will result in the creation of new Community law rights and liabilities as between the Member States and private persons in these important areas.

D. AT THE LEVEL OF PRIVATE PERSON INTER SE

11. The 2nd Protocol (Concerning Article 119 of the EC Treaty) has very important implications in private law. By a judgment of 17 May 1990 in a case called *Barber* v. *Guardian Royal Exchange* the Court of Justice ruled that sex-related differences in normal retirement age under contracted-out defined benefit occupational pension schemes were prohibited by Article 119 of the EEC Treaty. The view generally held before then had been that that was not so. The Court further ruled that its judgment should not be given retrospective effect in proceedings brought after the date of the judgment ("the temporal limitation"). There was considerable doubt about the meaning of the temporal limitation and whether it applied not only to contracted-out but also, by analogy, to contracted-in schemes. If the temporal limitation were given a narrow interpretation, the additional cost to British industry was variously estimated at between £5 billion and £40 billion, depending on the precise interpretation adopted and the assumptions made.

12. The 2nd Protocol should remove these doubts and confirms the position taken by amongst others the CBI and the National Association of Pension Funds in this country that, whether the scheme in question was contracted-out or contracted-in, no additional liability is incurred in respect of pension attributable to service before the date of the judgment in *Barber*, 17 May 1990.

13. This highlights a more general problem. Where the European Court of Justice "interprets" one of the Treaties and does so in a way that produces consequences that are unacceptable to the Member States, then even if the Member States are unanimous in that view, there is nothing that they can do to remedy the position otherwise than by further Treaty.

14. The 14th Protocol (On Social Policy) to which the United Kingdom is not a party, is likely to generate a mass of Community law rights and obligations enforceable as between employees and employers: British firms' subsidiaries located in other Member States will of course be affected by the Social Charter.

A general observation

15. Community law takes priority over national law in the legal systems of the Member States including the United Kingdom. The Treaty of Maastricht thus constitutes a very important *corpus* of *legislation*. Ordinarily, at least in this country, such legislation would be published in draft and those with

political, economic or personal interests, with their specialist advisers, would have a chance to comment on the policy and the drafting of each provision, with at least potentially an effect on the final outcome. The constitutional arrangements within the Community do not permit of such debate; and the ultimate "take-it-or-leave-it" decisions of the national legislatures may be felt not to be an adequate substitute.

One question is whether, before 1996, the national legislatures and the European Parliament could conduct a detailed scrutiny of this great mass of new law, so as to make constructive suggestions for its modification and further development.

17 February 1992

APPENDIX

PROFESSOR PIETER VER LOREN VAN THEMAAT

COMMON MARKET LAW REVIEW 28: 219–318, 1991. PAGES 310-311: OF THE PRINCIPLE OF SUBSIDIARITY

Firstly the principle means, among other things, that the *economic union should support the national economic policies. It should take the place of these national policies only as far as necessary for attaining the agreed objectives of the economic union.* If one accepts the conclusion of the preceding section that an economic union should be justified in the first place by the common desire to compensate at the Community level the loss of powers to correct the outcome of market-mechanisms at the national level, this aspect of a principle of subsidiarity becomes particularly relevant. The principle also means, then, that *national economic policies, as far as they are not affected by the legal or the economic effects of the completed common market—and to a lesser extent by the effects of a monetary union—should not be transferred to the community level.* As far as they may, but not necessarily need, affect in their turn the proper functioning of the common market (for example, state aids and other distortions of competition by measures taken by Member States) or the attainment of the agreed objectives of the economic union, only possibilities of corrective measures at the Community-level should be provided for.

Secondly the principle means that the *Community measures taken within the framework of an economic (and social) union should leave as many powers in the hands of national authorities as possible, without affecting the attainment of the agreed objectives of the economic union.* Among other things this means that *the implementation, or at least the daily application of the policies of the economic union should be left to the Member States, as far as the transnational character of the nature of their objectives do not require implementation and application at the Community level.* It should be remembered, in this context, that it follows already from the case law of the Court of Justice, that for example the maintenance of the primary and secondary rules of the Community having direct effect (most of the rules on the establishment of a common market, as well as regulations, decisions and even some elements of directives) is already the task of national courts. The daily administrative application and to a limited extent also the implementation by additional regulations of the Common Agricultural Policy (for example, with regard to criminal sanctions) has also to be left to Member States. As the practical implementation of Article 100A shows, it would also be possible to formulate a principle that directives should be preferred to regulations as much as is possible without affecting the desirable degree of uniform implementation of the objectives to be achieved.

Thirdly, in order to safeguard the greatest possible degree of economic sovereignty for Member States as well as an economic order characterized, like the present Treaty, by the primacy of the guiding and politically neutral role of the market (see Article 2 and the abundant body of case law of the Court of Justice on the role of the concept of the common market) one could formulate, on the analogy of Articles 5 and 57 of the ECSC Treaty, a *"principle of the least possible measure of intervention".* This could imply for example that macro-economic interventions should be preferred as much as possible to micro-economic interventions.

EUROPE AFTER MAASTRICHT

Memorandum submitted by Professor J A Usher University of Exeter (EC 240)

The main changes effected by the Maastricht Treaty on European Union were clearly indicated in the FCO Memorandum (EC 204). The present observations do not therefore attempt to present a comprehensive account of those changes, but rather to present, in note form, an indication of a number of points which appear to be of particular legal interest or importance.

1. The "Union": In December 1991, the European Court held in *Opinion 1/91* (with regard to the European Economic Area) than under the existing Treaties the Community already had the objective of achieving a European Union and of attaining Economic and Monetary Union.

Specific mention might be made of art. F(2) which appears to elevate the Court's case-law on fundamental rights to Treaty status.

2. *The Institutions*

2.1 The Council and European Council: The new Treaty appears to draw a subtle distinction between the European Council in the context of the Union (art. D) and intergovernmental co-operation (arts. J4 and J8) and the Council "in the composition of the Heads of State or Government" in the Community context (arts. 109J and 109K on EMU). Previously the Heads of State or Government do not appear to have acted as the Council of Ministers, although the current European Monetary System is based on a 1978 Resolution of the European Council (at the time an undefined act of an undefined body).

With regard to the "ordinary" Council, the new art. 146 requires it to comprise Ministers "authorized to commit the government of that Member State", which could have consequences for the scrutiny procedure. The problem has also been faced of calculating a qualified majority where the Council comprises representatives of less than 12 Member States (in the context of the excessive deficit procedure, under EMU provisions where certain Member States have derogations, and under the Social Policy Protocol). The solution in all cases amounts to a qualified majority of two thirds of the weighted votes of those Member States entitled to participate, whereas the basic qualified majority of 54 out of 76 is a 71 per cent majority.

2.2 European Parliament: The Parliament is treated as joint author with the Council of legislation adopted under the art.189B procedure (see arts. 173 and 189), whether it is referred to as co-decision or negative assent. In other respects the case law of the Court with regard to the status of the Parliament in the context of judicial review is confirmed.

It may be wondered whether the requirement that the members of the Commission be approved by the Parliament and that they hold office for the same term may lead to a change in relationships between those institutions.

2.3 European Central Bank: It may be observed that this will be a bank with a certain degree of legislative authority, able to issue binding regulations and decisions (art. 108A).

2.4 European Court of Justice: Dare it be suggested that one of the most important amendments is the abolition of any automatic requirement that the Court should sit in plenary session in certain cases (art. 165). This could help remove the backlog of cases before it.

While the United Kingdom would appear to have been a strong partisan of amending Article 171 of the EEC Treaty to allow for sanctions to be imposed against Member States which do not give effect to judgments given against them under Article 169, it may be surmised that it envisaged such sanctions largely being employed against other Member States. More seriously, it may be observed that the ECSC Treaty has envisaged sanctions from the outset, and that these sanctions do not appear to have been used. It might be suggested that what is more important is the existence of the judgment of the European Court holding that there has been a breach of Community law, on the basis of which those affected may be able to seek remedies at the national level, particularly now that the Court has held in *Francovitch* that there may as a matter of Community law be a duty on a Member State to pay damages in certain circumstances to those injured by its breach of Community law.

On the other hand, while a fine or penalty may give a public indication of the seriousness with which a continuing breach of community law is regarded, and may also give a public indication of the primacy of Community law, it may be doubted whether they would have internal legal effects unless pitched at such a level as to require further revenue to be raised.

It is of course already the case that Community payments may be withheld where a Member State has acted in breach of Community law with regard to the expenditure of Community money, and it may be submitted that in this context such a sanction is likely both to be effective and proportionate.

3. Subsidiarity: The new art. 3B introduces a requirement of subsidiarity in areas which do not fall within the Community's exclusive jurisdiction, and a general requirement that any Community action should not go beyond what is necessary to achieve the objectives of the Treaty. This assumes that a clear distinction may be drawn between exclusive and non-exclusive jurisdiction; however, it may be suggested that even matters on which the Community has no express jurisdiction may become a matter of exclusive jurisdiction once the Community has acted in that area. Furthermore, there have long been Treaty provisions which have only allowed Community action if it was necessary (for example, art. 235, art. 130R), and in the context of capital movements in *Casati* the Court took the view that necessity was a political question for the Council to decide rather than an issue for the courts.

4. Protocol on Social Policy: It might merely be observed that the Member States which signed the Social Charter in 1989 took the view that its aims could be achieved and must be achieved under existing Treaty provisions. All those Treaty provisions remain in force, and a number of them allow majority voting. If an argument were to be put that the Social Policy Agreement provisions agreed by the 11 are more specific and should therefore be used in this area, it may be submitted that arguments based on Community solidarity might well lead the Court to uphold the use of provisions which would bind all the Member States.

Examination of witnesses

MR PHILIP ALLOTT, Trinity College, Cambridge; PROFESSOR TREVOR HARTLEY, London School of Economics; MR JEREMY LEVER QC, All Souls' College, Oxford; and PROFESSOR JOHN USHER, Exeter University, were examined.

Chairman

145. Gentlemen, thank you very much indeed for sparing time from your extremely busy lives to join us this afternoon. We are very grateful to you. I know you have been listening during our previous session with Mr Ludlow so you will have a flavour of what our concerns are already, which is a very good thing because you have hit the ground running, as it were. We value enormously your wisdom and knowledge on the legal implications and aspects of Britain's involvement in the European Community, insofar as they are discernible, of the Maastricht Treaty. We would really like to start with a very fundamental question which is what is the legal personality of this Union? Is it an international entity which will replace the UK as a member of the UN and the Commonwealth? Is it a new legal existence or are we just imagining things? Let me start, if I may, with Mr Lever. Could I ask you to tell us about the legal personality of this forthcoming Union?

(Mr Lever) It clearly is a unique animal and if you look around for precedents, I do not think that you will find any satisfactory precedents. It has a number of the legal characteristics of a federation, but it also has a number of the legal characteristics of an international and supranational organisation. It has, and Philip Allott will correct me if I am wrong on that, but I think it would be recognised as having legal personality in international law, yet it is not exactly a state.

(Mr Allott) Mr Chairman, it is a terribly difficult question that you have asked. If you had asked about the European Economic Community, there would have been no difficulty. It is unquestionably an international legal person and one which behaves in countless ways as an international legal person. The European Union, and I must say I have only seen the Treaty relatively recently, I am at a loss to say what it is. I find it very difficult to place it in the mind. It will have citizens, and that, one might think, is the first distinguishing feature of a state, an international legal person. It will have international functions and some sort of institutions so that makes it something like an international organisation which is not a state, but which is another sort of international legal person. So my guess would be that rather like the EEC itself, it will evolve into an international legal person *sui generis*, of its own kind, with its own capacities and other states in the world will simply have to accept it, and there will now be, therefore, a second thing in addition to the EEC in that there will be a *sui generis* European Union.

(Mr Lever) Could I just add something to that? Mr Allott has said that he has only recently seen the Treaty. I think that is true of all except the most well-informed people who happen to have access to drafts and so on. If on occasion today we plead ignorance, we will not be pleading privilege but real ignorance. Speaking at any rate for myself, I would say that there are many people who might be able to answer three times as many of your questions as I—that would mean they would answer 6 per cent rather than 2 per cent, leaving 94 per cent rather than 98 per cent unanswered. Anybody who claims to answer more than 92 per cent is almost certainly a quack.

146. Perhaps rather than answering, we can speculate together on the basis of your considerable experience of international legal matters. I agree with you, we do not any of us know enough to assume firm answers. If I may pass to questions with that thought, we heard Mr Ludlow telling us earlier what many others told us—it is all going to turn out to be one ball of wax because decisions taken by the Council of Ministers, whatever hat they are wearing, are binding. What is the legal force that binds them? By what penalty are we, the citizens—and I will come to citizenship in a moment—charged if we fail to be bound? Who sends whom to collect the money for us to pay the penalty? Who drags us to which prison if we fail to pay the penalty? How does this binding process gain force and reality?

(Professor Usher) Before turning to that, could I go back to your initial question, then hopefully that will make it slightly easier to try to deal with the second supplementary to it. If I might say so,

[Chairman Contd]

to my own way of thinking, in trying to classify the union just as in trying to classify the three communities which still, of course, remain, it is extremely dangerous to try to fit them into other models. They have their own existence, they have developed their own ways and you can try as hard as you like to categorise them into federal, confederal, intergovernmental, or whatever else you like, analyses. In the last resort, they are themselves and we have to try to deal with them as they are, because to try to fit them into other categories really means you are inventing a new heading for other categories. In the first place, having said that, the Union to my way of thinking is a most curious monster, nonetheless because it proclaims itself to be founded on the European Communities which continue and which undeniably do have legal personality, which do have enforceable legal rules which we have been used to now for nearly twenty years. So in that sense it is a continuation of the same thing. What is rather startling though is that one of the most important attributes of the Union, the idea of Union citizenship, has as a matter of law been inserted into what is now to be called the European Community Treaty; it is not in the Union bit of the Treaty but has been inserted into what we are now told we are to call the European Community Treaty which everybody no doubt still refers to as the EEC Treaty. That is rather odd. You have Union citizenship dealt with specifically in one of the binding Community Treaties giving rise, I have little doubt, to enforceable legal rights and obligations.

(Professor Hartley) I think part of the problem, going back to your first question, is the relationship between the Union and the Community or Communities. In the international sphere, one question is this: if a country, say Japan, signs a treaty, with whom do they sign? I assume it is with the Community and not with the Union: therefore, the international personality, I assume, would be the European Community rather than the Union. I say that because the EC Treaty Articles concerned with international agreements come in the old EEC Treaty, now the EC Treaty, or whatever you call it. So I assume it will be with what was previously the EEC and is now the European Community. So I would have thought it is that body which would have an international personality with a very weak personality for the ECSC and Euratom unless they are somehow swallowed up by the EC. What the function of the Union is on an international level, as distinct from the Community, is something which I do not know and I do not know whether Philip Allott knows. I think that is the big problem.

(Mr Lever) Maastricht must be read as a political document as well as a legal document. If you say about some questions "That is a political question rather than a legal question", it does not detract in any way from its significance. Then you ask, what is the force of the decisions? The force of the decisions is clearly Community law. It is Community law that is the glue that holds the Community together and there will be a host of problems that will emerge from Maastricht and the lawyers will ultimately sort them out and thus advance the political objective.

Mr Lawrence

147. International law is the law of states.
(Mr Lever) No, Community law.

148. Take the situation in the wider international law: is not international law the law of states—public international law?
(Mr Lever) It is the law that generally governs the relationships of states towards each other, but Community law, although governing the relationship between states, operates rather differently from public international law of a traditional nature.

149. But that is the law, the commercial law. It is mostly commercial law that is the Community law.
(Professor Hartley) Not only commercial law.
(Mr Lever) Also constitutional law—hence the fact that I was privileged to appear for the European Parliament when it was sued by the Council and one was concerned with the application of Community law.

150. What you are saying is for the European Union or the European Community to have an entity it does not have to take the form of a state.
(Mr Lever) Evidently, I think, that has to be our answer to you. But we are all saying to you, I think, the same thing, that this is a different animal from anything that we or other lawyers have encountered in the past and it is difficult for us to pigeonhole it.

151. Suppose Britain were to enter into some kind of a contractual relationship with another state and was sued, could it say "It is not us. We are obliged to have behaved in this way because we are obliged by our Treaty, our Union Treaty, to go along with the rulings of the Union"? Would that be a defence?
(Mr Lever) It depends on the Treaty. If you take something like the Bermuda 2 Civil Aviation Treaty, a number of the obligations there entered into by the United Kingdom towards the United States are to use best efforts, and there I think it is generally accepted that, if the United Kingdom found itself unable to combine the twin duties of that and Community law, that would be an answer to the charge that it had not used its best efforts, in the same way that it is an answer for the United States Government to say it was constitutionally prevented from doing this or that. But, generally speaking, Treaty law is regarded within Community law as itself a superior law and therefore, generally speaking, the public international law obligations that had been accepted would be regarded as a good basis for action within the Community itself.

[**Mr Lawrence** *Contd*]

(Professor Hartley) It is a bit more complicated than that, I think. First of all, the United Kingdom's ability, capacity or right to enter into international treaties is limited by Community law. If we wanted to sign an agreement with Iceland on fishing rights, we could not do it because that is a matter for Community law. So, first of all, our rights are certainly restricted by Community law and, if we tried to do something which was against Community law, to sign a treaty which they said we should not do, we could get the Commission bringing an action against us in the European Court, saying "You have no right to do that." Secondly, it is true that international law is regarded in some sense as higher than Community law by the European Court, but only, as far as treaties are concerned, if they are binding on the Community and not otherwise, so that if the UK went off and did something on the side which was contrary to EC law, we might be bound in international law, but the Community would disclaim all responsibility and we could find we could not deliver on that treaty and we might thereby incur liability towards the third country; but the Community could say, "Well, we are not bound by it and it is not our problem". It is quite a complex situation. I do not think you can think that international law automatically overrides Community law; it may in some cases. If the Community itself signs a treaty with a foreign country, then that treaty probably would prevail over Regulations passed by the Community, but that is because the Community itself is bound by it.

(Mr Allott) I just want to say that Mr Lawrence's hypothetical situation has arisen on various occasions and it arose very prominently at the Law of the Sea Conference because we said there that we cannot carry out certain obligations in the Law of the Sea Convention because these are matters within Community competence. The other contracting parties with a single voice said, "That is intolerable. You cannot undertake international obligations and tell us that because of some internal goings on you cannot carry out those obligations". What they insisted on and what we did in the end was to conclude a protocol listing matters within Community competence. It is the first time that it had ever been done and the Community normally says that it is impossible to list Community competences.

(Professor Hartley) For the very good reason that Community competence is growing all the time and, therefore, they do not want to list it.

(Mr Allott) We told them it was inconceivable to do, but in the end we did it.

(Professor Usher) The other side of the coin of course as to international personality and the capacity of the Community with regard to the rest of the world is of course the willingness of the rest of the world to enter into binding treaties with it and that has been going on within the sphere of its competence and indeed some would say within the very extended sphere of its competence for very many years. Indeed under the Coal & Steel Treaty, where in fact there is no express Community

power to enter into trade treaties, the United States in the early 1980s simply was not willing to sign steel quota arrangements with the separate Member States and the Community had to use the very general Article 95 of the Coal & Steel Treaty to give itself power as a Community to sign an agreement with the United States. They simply were not interested in negotiating with the separate Member States.

152. To some extent we are restricted already and we have had the example of the law of the sea and there are many other examples of our restrictions. What the people will want to know is just how far more are we going to be restricted either by Maastricht, the first stage, or by full monetary union in 1996 if we sign up or by the almost inevitable, if you listened to Mr Ludlow, supranational powers which will then be operated from Brussels with or without the democratic restraint of the European Parliament. It looks to me as though whatever remaining rights we have in areas over which the European Community has some competence at the moment will be pretty substantially further diminished if we sign up to anything which approaches the Maastricht intention. Is that right or will we still be able to have protocols with the Union to exempt us?

(Professor Hartley) The European Court has said that as the internal powers grow, the external powers automatically follow suit, at least once they have been used; so if you give the Community an increased competence internally, then that pulls with it increased competence externally and once it has been used either internally or externally it cuts out the Member States. I am not quite sure how that doctrine would apply to things like defence, security, justice, and those areas, where they may not pull with them. I am not sure how it would apply to them, but certainly any area where you give them internal power, including social affairs, monetary or anything else, that would give them the external competence as well and in time could take it away from the Member States. It is a constantly growing area.

153. It is not just a question of us being tied to European Community law, but we actually have to defer to the decisions of the European Community in any contract or relationship that is entered into.

(Professor Hartley) And we lose internationally the power to act internationally in certain areas as well.

Chairman: Could we turn to the question of these powers and how they affect us as individuals. We have already mentioned citizenship. Mr Canavan has a further question on that and then we would like to come on to the constitutional rights of all of us under this rather enormous arrangement.

Mr Canavan

154. What does the provision for citizenship of the Union actually mean and how will it affect UK citizens?

[Mr Canavan *Contd]*

(Mr Allott) Again, if I may say so, Mr Chairman, it is a terribly difficult question because there is no real guidance in the text as to what it means and they have simply put this sentence in, but it appears to be the case that the net result will be that we will all become dual nationals of some kind.

(Professor Hartley) Maybe we are already. We have got our little red passports now which already say on them, do they not, "European Community"?

(Mr Allott) Yes, but I think clearly the intention is that we will become dual nationals, that is to say, we will become British citizens and citizens of the European Union. That is what our passport does say. That of course is rather similar to the British imperial position where we were, and to some extent still are, dual nationals in relation to the Commonwealth. At the moment we are British citizens, and Commonwealth citizens. We are already dual nationals, so the British will become triple nationals, so to speak.

(Mr Lever) I think, and I will be corrected if I am wrong, the practical implications at least include the fact that now we all have the right to go and live in another member state, not necessarily to work, but to reside there. That, I think, is really a new right because in the old days there was free movement of labour, but it was in one's capacity as a worker, free movement of services, but not, I think, as a matter of law, the right to reside. Secondly, you will now have a right to vote in the municipal elections and to stand as a candidate in the municipal elections in another Member State, to vote in elections to the European Parliament and to stand as a candidate in another Member State. Those are new rights. I think lastly, although here again somebody better informed than me will correct me if I am wrong, if you find yourself in trouble in Kathmandu or somewhere like that where there is not a British consul, but there is a German consul, you will be entitled to turn up at the German consulate and say, "I am a citizen of the Union. For heaven's sake, help me", and he will not say to you, "You are not one of my flock", but he would be obliged to do for you what he would do for any other citizen of the Union, including a German citizen of the Union, I think.

(Professor Hartley) I agree with that. On the citizenship point, John Usher I am sure also has views on this, but it actually says that a citizen has the right to reside, et cetera, "subject to the limitations and conditions laid down in this Treaty", and "this Treaty", I think, means the EC Treaty and that does give rights to workers and various people subject to certain conditions of public policy, public security and public health. It also refers to measures adopted to give it effect and we have those already. I am not entirely sure whether this adds anything.

(Professor Usher) Could I just say on that particular point that I agree entirely with Trevor Hartley. Although it is a nice statement in Article 8(a) it actually does not really add much to the existing state of the law. In principle, certainly since the end of 1990, you can freely move and reside in any other Member State unless you are, I believe it is called, a genuine and serious threat to a fundamental interest of society. On the other hand, though, there is one very important point about the citizenship of the Union. Dare I suggest it is actually a subordinate or subsidiary citizenship because it depends on your having the nationality of a Member State and it is still, I am sure, for the Member States to determine who are their nationals and it is only if a Member State says you are one of their nationals that you would then acquire in addition the citizenship of the Union.

(Mr Lever) A declaration confirms that is to be determined according to the laws of the Member State.

Mr Wells

155. Does that give the Union the capacity to control migration across its borders?
(Professor Hartley) Of whom? EC citizens or third country citizens?

156. Both—first of all, to define a citizen who crosses your border.
(Professor Hartley) To define who is an EC citizen?

157. Who can become a German citizen.
(Professor Hartley) No, Germany decides who become German citizens. The United Kingdom decides who are British citizens. Any British or German citizen automatically becomes a Union citizen, except for certain classes of British citizen who will not become Union citizens because Britain says they do not count for that purpose. So there are certain categories of British citizen who are not EC citizens in the old terminology, Union citizens in the new terminology, because the United Kingdom made a declaration that they are not. So really it is the Member States that define who are their citizens and, as John Usher said, as a result collectively define who are the Union citizens. Of course, it does mean, if Germany decides to give its citizenship to a new group of people who did not have it before, automatically they become Union citizens and, therefore, have the right to come here. So if Greece thought "We'll give Greek citizenship to all Cypriots", then they automatically would have the right to come here. If we wanted to give British citizenship to all Hong Kongians, unless some other member state could pressure us in not doing that and cutting them out, *prima facie* they would then be Union citizens. So each country can in one sense define who is a citizen of the whole Union but, once you have that citizenship, you can move freely within the Community, subject to the exceptions we have been talking about—public policy, public security.

(Mr Lever) That problem has existed even before Maastricht in that, for example, Professor Hartley has referred to Hong Kong citizens where we limited the number to whom we would give right of citizenship in this country. The

[**Mr Wells** *Contd*]

Portuguese, I think, granted Portuguese citizenship to all the citizens of Macau. Therefore, there was this odd situation that everybody in Macau could come and work in this country by virtue of his Portuguese citizenship—maybe after the end of the transitional period, but subject to that—whereas many citizens of Hong Kong would be unable to do so; and sooner or later it would seem that, just as immigration policy and control of the external borders is going to have to be the subject of co-operation, so too will extension of citizenship because of the implications for all the other Member States.

(Professor Hartley) I have heard of Hong Kong citizens who have not been able to get the right to come here under United Kingdom law who have gone to Macau and obtained Portuguese citizenship (which apparently is quite easy if you bribe the right people), become Macau-Portuguese citizens and then, clutching their Portuguese passports, are planning to come in here.

Chairman: I think this Committee is beyond being surprised at the way people get passports, on which we have heard many fascinating lines of thought. Could we move on to more about the character of this animal and, in particular, whether it has a constitution—the Rome Treaty, the European Union Treaty—or needs a constitution, as Mr Allot's paper is suggesting.

Mr Wells

158. Mr Allott's paper argues that four things are missing from the Maastricht Treaty—I am surprised it is only four. But the four are stated as being: a formal statement of the nature and purpose of the European Community; a provision setting out the vertical relationships between the different institutions of the Community; a set of codified fundamental human rights of citizens of the Union; and the transformation of the European Parliament into a legislature. What we would like to know is whether you are arguing for the Treaty to become a basic constitution for a European state.

(Mr Allott) Mr Chairman, I obviously have no wish to advocate the creation of a European state. I hope that the general tone of my paper would suggest that with the development of the state, particularly in the twentieth century, one of our great misfortunes is the great power of the executive branch in the state system. But at the same time what one would want is for the Community to develop into something we would want to be citizens of, and at the present time it seems to me that it is something which is neither a satisfactory diplomatic activity nor a satisfactory democracy and even in narrow terms, in British interests, is deeply against our ultimate interests. Our interests would best be served, it seems to me, by a Community in which we were obviously extremely influential but which also satisfied our very long and arduously established tradition of liberal democracy. I would be very glad if this great monster of the European Community in some sense evaporated overnight. There is a great deal to be

said for it, but we are caught ever more into this great and untidy, chaotic morass that is now being created. All I am arguing is, if it is going to exist, then it has to begin to satisfy the requirements of liberal democracy. If you call that becoming a state, well, then, one would have to say that. But a state is the last thing I want. I want some completely new kind of political system which serves British interests but which is also in accordance with British traditions.

Mr Lawrence: Quite right—we all agree with that.

Chairman

159. Does anybody else have other ideas on that?

(Professor Usher) If I could add a couple of comments, first of all, dare I say in this place, if having a formal list of fundamental rights is part of the characteristics of something we want to belong to, then we have a problem with this country as we currently are. Leaving that on one side, I am not sure I see such a dichotomy between what I think Philip Allott called diplomacy and democracy. In a sense, yes, we are used to democratic systems of government in such political organisations as we belong to. On the other hand, the diplomatic side of the European Community consists of the representatives of democratically elected governments, and I think they quite seriously believe—and, indeed the large number of civil servants I meet in the Civil Service College from time to time quite seriously believe—that that is a proper exercise of democracy, it is not the case that the Community is run in an anti-democratic manner. Just as, dare I say it, within some states one has to reconcile regional and national interests, I see a continuous balancing, but not a sudden resolution, of the problems between central democracy, dare I say, in the form of the European Parliament and strong representation of the national democracies through the ministers. In fact, Maastricht takes it one small stage further in favour of the central democracy, but not a huge step. Nonetheless, the Single European Act also made a very small step which many cynics thought would not work because it required the European Parliament to get an absolute majority—half plus one—if it was going to have any influence. I believe many commentators thought that would never happen. It has happened. They have had very considerable influence. Although Helen Wallace thinks much of their influence is on technical matters—I am not wholly convinced of that—I think their political influence has extended considerably. This represents another stage. A balance has to be maintained; we are not suddenly going to get rid of nation states, you somehow have to have their adequate participation in the decision-making process. Yet, as more and more becomes common, there is a place for some form of central democracy which I see the European Parliament as performing.

Mr Lawrence

160. The question is, how far is the nation state as a legal entity tied to the European state which it is now joining? You have already answered this question for me, but it is not just a question in the way you just put it of a democratic representation. We are talking about what the legal status is. We have examined that problem.

(Professor Usher) If you are looking at it in terms of the legal status, of course I did perhaps rather provocatively some ten years or so ago publish a little book called The Irreversible Transfer?, admittedly with a question mark after it, to describe the relationship between national law and Community law. In a sense I would see it as some form of shared activity though in which the Member States obviously through the Council still have the major policy-making role, but, nonetheless, whilst the political reality is membership of the Community, there are in truth certain powers the Member State cannot exercise and which can only be exercised through the joint mechanisms of the European Community and historically the areas which are matters of joint exercise have increased and Maastricht increases them further.

(Mr Lever) But, as parliamentarians, you surely are right to be concerned that Parliament does not participate in the legislative process, and when I say "Parliament" I do not mind whether you are thinking of the national Parliament or the Community Parliament, Parliament does not participate in the legislative process in the way in which we have become accustomed to think that it should.

Chairman

161. That is of course a thought in our minds as to whether this central democracy, as Professor Usher calls it, really adds up to a systematic form of accountability, and can it actually work logistically with twelve, let alone seventeen members and goodness knows how many languages and people coming from hundreds, if not thousands, of miles away, certainly hundreds of miles away, representing huge constituencies or, in the German case, none, and can this kind of central democracy work? That is in our minds. Then there is also in our minds the different question which is the question of irreversibility which Professor Usher has mentioned. Have we, as a national Parliament and a source of legitimate authority, really surrendered powers irreversibly or have we kept the right to secede if we wish, if we change our minds? Is there some higher law which takes from us that power?

(Professor Hartley) I dare say that depends on whether you are looking at it from the point of view of Community law or English law, UK law. UK law clearly says that we can leave if we want to. Parliament passes another Act repealing the European Communities Act and as far as UK law is concerned we are out. That is what the law says. I am not saying what the politics is or what the economic price of leaving is, but if you want the strictly legal answer, we could do it any day with a simple Act of Parliament passed by a simple majority with no referendum and we are out. That does not mean that that is the position according to Community law, as interpreted by the European Court. The Treaties themselves do not make any provision for leaving. I think the only country which has left is Greenland and there they negotiated their withdrawal. They said they wanted to withdraw and would the Community agree and they negotiated the terms, which rather implies that you cannot walk out and you have to ask to leave. There are those two different points of view. You can take whichever one you want.

Mr Lawrence

162. Does the European Court recognise the principle of the supremacy of the British Parliament?

(Professor Hartley) No, it does not.

163. Well, then whatever the British Parliament may say, are we not bound to any Treaty agreement we have made with the European Community?

(Professor Hartley) Yes, and if we pass an Act repealing the European Communities Act in whole or in part or whatever, the European Court would say that that is invalid to the extent that it conflicts with Community law. The House of Lords, in its judicial capacity, might take a different view, and I believe it would, but there are those two separate ways of looking at it.

Mr Lawrence: I agree with you from the practical point of view that it would not agree.

Chairman

164. Mr Allott, you wanted to disagree?

(Mr Allott) Chairman, I am sure you do not want a full debate on this very famous and difficult question, but I just wanted to register a slight disagreement with what Professor Hartley has said. There are those of us who take the view—and here there is a danger of the well-known principle of four lawyers, five opinions—there are those of us who take the view that the supremacy of the British Parliament has been terminated by membership of the European Community. The supremacy of the British Parliament, an invention of the 19th Century, included two principles: one, that there was no limit on the power of Parliament; and, secondly, that no court could question the validity of an Act of Parliament. Both of those have been terminated by Community law. There is now a limit on the power of Parliament and it cannot validly enact Acts of Parliament contrary to Community law. Secondly, there is a judicial review in the Community Court where it can set aside British Acts of Parliament if they are in violation of Community law and they can be held to be invalid by the European Court. So an Act of Parliament which purported to go against the Treaty as a whole, which does not include a withdrawal provision, could very well be held to be invalid. In that sense we have lost our right to

[**Chairman** *Contd*]

secede by Act of Parliament. Obviously we could do it because Acts of Parliament are pieces of paper and so clearly physically we could do it and produce the relevant pieces of paper and the House of Lords as a court might produce the relevant piece of paper, but from a legal point of view, I would say, contrary to Professor Hartley, it is not possible legally in English law, the law of the United Kingdom, to do that.

(Mr Lever) If we were to do it, it would be a political, rather than a legal, act. We would have, as a political matter, seceded from the Community, but we would be in breach, as Professor Hartley has said, of our public international law obligations because the Treaty is not limited in time and makes no provision for secession, but, nevertheless people have before now taken political acts of that nature if the situation has become for them intolerable and there is not now, as there was by the time of the American Civil War, a federal army and, therefore, there would be no possibility of——

(Professor Hartley) Not yet!

(Mr Lever)——no possibility of the Member State that wished to secede as a political act being held by force, but this is not, I believe, the real problem that confronts this Committee. The problem that confronts this Committee is that you are presented effectively with a take-it-or-leave- it Treaty; and even within the Community it is not possible to fill up quite as much paper as that without making some fairly substantial changes and those changes undoubtedly are moving towards a greater measure of decisions being taken as a matter of law not explicitly by Her Majesty's Government. It may not be, as a matter of fact, a loss of power as great as the legal loss of power, but, nevertheless, a substantial change will have been wrought and wrought without the normal democratic processes that we associate with parliamentary government having been gone through.

Mr Harris

165. Could I ask Professor Usher a question which is perhaps put to all parliamentarians with increasing frequency by keen young people who want to get into politics and they say to someone like yourself, who has had experience of both places, "Where should I go? If I want to play a meaningful political role in 20 years from now, where shall I go? Shall I try to get into the. European Parliament or shall I try and come to Westminster?" What sort of advice would you give?

(Professor Usher) That is a very good question because I do actually get asked that question in real life sometimes. Until very recently I suppose I would have said to come here because that traditionally is where the powers are, but if I am honest, my own impression, and I have to say this, even though I worked for the Communities in a different institution, I used to think of the European Parliament as a talking shop and nothing else and I have to say that its work since the Single European Act has made me think that it does indeed have some real political powers.

People like Giscard d'Estaing, I think, would not be involved with it unless they thought there was something worthwhile to be got out of it, I do not know, and I think, looking long- term, at any rate it will be at least as important. Whether it will be more important, I do not know, but within the sphere of competence of the Communities, yes, it will be a place where I think you can make a political career, but that is my personal speculation and my training as a lawyer does not qualify me to give you any more informed comment on that than anybody else.

Chairman

166. Everywhere we go, including hearing evidence here in London, we are told when talking about the accretion or accumulation of power in Community institutions and the rising authority of the European Parliament, "Don't worry, the principle of subsidiarity will safeguard you": this will be taken into account both in the European Court of Justice and with common sense by the Commissioners in their use of their already huge powers. Indeed, one Commissioner even told the Committee they were thinking of drawing up a list of items that could be returned to the nation states, powers that had been given to the Commission by previous Acts of previous national legislators—they now thought they should return them to the nation states. What about this principle of subsidiarity? Mr Allott has a reference to the "somewhat fatuous" clauses in the Maastricht documents. My heart is a bit with him, I must confess. From this chair, they seem very, very vague, these ideas about who decides how long the piece of string is. On the other hand, if we could get such an attitude built into the whole spirit of the Community that the aim was not to centralise all the time but to decentralise and put back to the member states, that surely would be a very healthy thing. Would you like to defend your "fatuous" adjective?

(Mr Allott) I would prefer one of my colleagues who takes the positive view to speak.

(Mr Lever) Can I tell you what I see to be a possible contribution that one can make as a lawyer to your question. The acid test is to ask what happens if the Community decides to take such an action and one or more Member States take the view that the taking of such action infringes the principle of subsidiarity. Who is to decide, because it is not a very precise question that one is asking; some measure of discretion, some measure of judgment, I believe will often be involved. As I see it, the problem that will confront the European Court of Justice then will be whether they are to approach the question as themselves judges of subsidiarity and inevitably, if they do, become to a greater degree politicised, or whether they are to undertake the traditional role of courts when called on to review the actions of political bodies, the judicial review function which asks rather limited questions about whether there has been a manifest error, such unreasonableness that no reasonable body addressing its mind to the

[**Chairman** *Contd*]

appropriate questions could reasonably have concluded what it did—the sort of questions that you, Chairman, when you were a Minister, were always being warned by your officials might be asked about your actions in this country on a judicial review. That is a very much more limited exercise and you may feel that, *unless* there is a political will on the part of the Commissioners to restrain themselves and really to think only about the big things that affect the Community and have to be done at Community level, it may be that writing this in as a legal matter is not going to be all that significant.

(*Professor Usher*) Could I just say one or two things. First of all, my impression on looking through the information I was sent, particularly of the evidence given by the Foreign Secretary before you, was that he seemed particularly pleased not just with the subsidiarity clause but also with the general necessity clause introduced into the Treaty. On the subsidiarity point and the way the Treaty is drafted, it is only subsidiarity as between the Community and Member States, not subsidiarity in any more general sense of whether local bodies might be more appropriate. Leaving that question on one side, of course, there is already at least one Treaty provision with a subsidiarity clause in it, Article 130R, introduced by the Single European Act with regard to environmental legislation. I am not aware that that has ceased the flow of environmental legislation from the Community or has given rise to any challenge from anybody that the Community should not have done it. A second issue arises from the fact that the subsidiarity clause only applies to matters which do not fall under the exclusive jurisdiction of the Community which I indicated in my brief paper, to my way of thinking, indicates a fallacious view: that you can easily identify what is exclusive Community competence and what is not, whereas the reality is that even in areas where there are no specific powers, once a Community has acted, that is it, it is Community competence. If I can give one simple example involving the United Kingdom, there is an EEC Directive on car headlamps enacted under general powers; nothing in the Treaty says the Community shall have power to harmonise car headlamps, nonetheless there is legislation on it. A few years ago we tried to introduce the concept of dim-dipped headlights; you cannot drive on sidelights when the ignition is switched on. The Commission took us to the European Court over it on the basis that we had unilaterally introduced a type of headlight that was not envisaged in the Directive and the Commission won. The Court said now there was Community legislation on the matter Member States could no longer legislate. To think there is a zone you can clearly call exclusive Community competence to my way of thinking is a trifle naive.

Mr Lawrence

167. Are you saying the doctrine of subsidiarity is nonsense because it cannot apply once the European Community has taken a decision?

(*Professor Usher*) Once there is Community legislation on a particular area, yes, I would say it is.

(*Professor Hartley*) That does not count for the legislation under challenge. He and I are saying the same thing. That does not count for the legislation you are challenging before the Court. If there is a previous regulation which everybody accepts and after that they pass a new regulation on the same thing, you cannot then bring in subsidiarity on the second one because the first one has occupied the field and made that Community jurisdiction and, therefore, subsidiarity does not apply. But if it is the first time they have legislated in that field, then you might be able to argue that it is not exclusively Community competence, partly it is and partly it is not. Then you could bring in subsidiarity. But I agree with the previous people, Mr Lever in particular. I doubt very much whether it would get you very far in the Court, except in a very extreme case. But if you look at judgments of the Court, whenever it is a question of the jurisdiction of the Community versus that of the Member State, the Community wins. So they strike down Community legislation on other grounds—human rights or a Treaty—but if it is simply a Member State versus the Community, the Community wins. Subsidiarity really is simply that question; it is, which is it—the Member State or the Community? So I think it would have to be a really glaring and extreme and excessive example before the Court would take action, which was really the case, as Mr Lever said, in the Wednesbury case—was it so unreasonable that no reasonable person would do it?

168. Is the Court likely to say "We find ourselves unable to resolve what is essentially a political question and therefore we refuse to give a ruling on it. This must go back to the Council of Ministers" or whatever the power is that makes the decision, or in your view will the Court always accept the challenge of having to rule on subsidiarity?

(*Professor Hartley*) I think what the Court would do would be to say, "To decide this question we have to decide whether it can be more easily or better dealt with at a higher or lower level and we would give the Council a certain margin of discretion and only if they are clearly wrong would we strike it down", because obviously if they have passed a measure, by definition they think it is better dealt with at the Community level, and the Court I think would say, "We will give them a certain margin of error or discretion", and only if they feel they are clearly wrong will they strike it down. If it is something which a reasonable person can accept, even if we do not accept it, then they would let it stand; so they would not refuse to rule but they would simply say "The Council has a certain area within which it can err. It is not a gross error. It is not clearly wrong. Therefore we will not interfere."

(*Mr Allott*) Mr Chairman, could I just make two brief comments which I hope are constructive? One is that I think in the German constitution there is a provision on subsidiarity, or rather I would prefer to call it vertical distribution of

[**Mr Lawrence** *Contd*]

power, where there is a fairly careful statement of what the conditions are for determining whether a thing should be dealt with at this level or that. I would have preferred to have seen something like that. If we had anything in the Treaty, we could have almost the German text on it. The second point is this: I was very interested also to read what the Foreign Secretary said about this and I was surprised he was so relaxed on the point that it would ultimately be dealt with by the Court. That is not a very British point of view normally, but I detected that really one should see this in a much wider context, namely why he is so pleased about it is obviously that he thinks it changes the nature of the discourse in the Community, that it will give a basis for a completely different kind of discussion when legislation takes place. On that he must be right, that there will be a new kind of discussion, and he is very pleased to have that anchored now in the Treaty. But, secondly, I would go so far as to say that this was a great British achievement in a still wider sense, namely that it really re-orientates the nature of the Community. I think it really suggests, in the text of the Treaty itself now, that the Community is not this great powerful monster, that I keep referring to it as, which sucks everything into itself, but that the whole structure of it is federal in a vertical sense, that is to say, that it is a distribution of power including a distribution downwards, and I really do think that the British should be congratulated on seeing that by putting in a provision which in its drafting is completely fatuous, you can nevertheless change, help to change, the constitutional nature of the Community I really think that is why they are pleased with the provision.

(Mr Lever) The Foreign Secretary, I think, took a different view as well about the clause from what, if I understood Professor Usher correctly, was his view. I think Professor Usher, if I understood him rightly, was saying that the subsidiarity provision would not apply where the Community had exclusive competence and that was not the view of the Foreign Secretary on pages 21 to 22 of your transcript (Qs 29 and 30): he took the view that by having separated 3(b) and having got it into a separate paragraph at the end of 3(b), (he said he put up his hand at that moment and not everyone had realised what had gone in), that it had made a fundamental difference. I would not want to express any view as to the significance of the second paragraph, but I thought I should just mention that to you.

(Professor Usher) Just a quickie on that one. Yes, what in effect they have achieved is to get a general "necessary" clause, if I can call it that, into all Community activity. However, the Community provisions which have been used to extend the scope of what the Community is doing, above all Article 235 already has a necessary clause in it and it has been used more than 800 times, including things like giving, it appears, open-ended guarantees for loans in Poland and Hungary on the basis that they have some historical and cultural link with the Community, but I am not sure that on any strict reading that really falls within the Community objectives.

Chairman: I think on the question of subsidiarity we are very nearly in the realms of psychology where one is hoping to change the basic attitude of the 20th and 19th Century that everything is done better on a bigger and more central scale. I think, on that note, our time is up. Your valuable time has been useful to us. We are extremely grateful and you would not forgive me if I claimed that we are all clearer in our understanding of Community law and constitution than we were before, but we certainly have many new questions running in our minds by your thoughts and particularly by your very valuable papers and we really do treasure the time and wisdom you have shared with us on these matters. There are obviously many things which have not been pursued to the depth we would wish, and should you wish to pursue matters and put in further notes to us, they will be extremely welcome. Thank you very much.

HMSO publications are available from:

HMSO Publications Centre
(Mail, fax and telephone orders only)
PO Box 276, London, SW8 5DT
Telephone orders 071-873 9090
General enquiries 071-873 0011
(queuing system in operation for both numbers)
Fax orders 071-873 8200

HMSO Bookshops
49 High Holborn, London, WC1V 6HB   071-873 0011 (counter service only)
258 Broad Street, Birmingham, B1 2HE   021-643 3740
Southey House, 33 Wine Street, Bristol, BS1 2BQ   (0272) 264306
9-21 Princess Street, Manchester, M60 8AS   061-834 7201
80 Chichester Street, Belfast, BT1 4JY   (0232) 238451
71 Lothian Road, Edinburgh, EH3 9AZ   031-228 4181

HMSO's Accredited Agents
(see Yellow Pages)

and through good booksellers

ISBN 0-10-282692-7

HOUSE OF COMMONS SESSION 1991–92

FOREIGN AFFAIRS COMMITTEE

EUROPE AFTER MAASTRICHT

MINUTES OF EVIDENCE

Wednesday 26 February 1992

Sir Ralf Dahrendorf

Ordered by The House of Commons *to be printed*
26 February 1992

LONDON: HMSO
£4.95 net

223–iv

WEDNESDAY 26 FEBRUARY 1992

Members present:

Mr David Howell, in the Chair

Mr Nigel Forman   Mr Ted Rowlands
Mr David Harris   Mr Peter Shore
Mr Michael Jopling   Mr Michael Welsh
Mr Jim Lester

Examination of witnesses

SIR RALF DAHRENDORF, Warden of St Antony's College, Oxford, was examined.

Chairman

169. Sir Ralf, good afternoon. I would like to extend a warm welcome to you on behalf of this Committee and thank you for coming before us this afternoon to share your views on the pattern of change and development in Europe, particularly after the Maastricht meeting and the Treaties which have not yet been ratified but have now, I think, been published. We are particularly pleased you are able to come because you have a very broad vision of these matters having been a European Commissioner, a Director of LSE and now Warden of St Antony's College Oxford. We are looking forward very much to hearing your views as part of our inquiry. Thank you very much.
(Sir Ralf Dahrendorf) Thank you.

170. Could I begin with a question which you may feel provides a peg for you to develop a theme if you wish or we will come back to your ideas later, I am very happy to leave to you how you wish to answer. The first question, and I believe the central question for us in this inquiry, is, are these Maastricht agreements, the Maastricht documents, as significant as the history of the European Communities or indeed the pattern, the structure, the new architecture of Europe? Are we going to see changes as significant as those that turned out to emerge from the Single European Act and originally from the original Rome Treaty or is this something less than a major turning point, a major historical point in the development of Europe? A general question, please let us have your opening thoughts.
(Sir Ralf Dahrendorf) Thank you very much, Chairman. Thank you for asking me to come at all. My views are those of an informed citizen, no more, and so I am sure, in fact I know, you have seen many others whose views have to be taken more seriously. They are also the views of an informed citizen who while a convinced European has for long been somewhat sceptical of the European Community. So there is a history of my own approach to the European Community which, after all, as we know it, has always been a distinctly second best institution in the sense that it was created after the Council of Europe had failed to deliver its initial promise, after the European

Defence Community had foundered in the French Parliament and after two attempts to create a political union had failed. People then got together and set up what under the circumstances was the best they could have but no more. I make this remark advisedly because I see Maastricht above all as two things—and I am speaking with the candour for which some people know me—it is in the first instance yet another attempt to stretch the Treaty of Rome and the arrangements which have grown from the Treaties of Rome and Paris into new directions. These attempts have been made for a very long time. From time to time one has used Article 235 in order to introduce elements on which Member States could agree but which were not exactly in the Treaty, in the common work of the Community. More recently—and I notice this is particularly true of the Maastricht Treaty— attempts have been made say in Article (I think it is) 109F to add on new objectives of co-operation but all this 'added on to a Treaty which is essentially about a creation of a customs union. So some of the new developments, as I see it, sit a little awkwardly on this Treaty and have a slightly forced quality, a process on which one could say a lot. I will not bore you with my own recent experiences in that respect. Maastricht is another attempt to move out of the strait jacket of the original Treaties, I am not sure it is easy to do so. The second point is that I have come to feel, if you pardon my putting it in this metaphor, that in many ways Maastricht was a Summit which looked in the rear mirror rather than out of the forward windscreen. It was the completion of a particular process rather than addressing itself to what I would regard as truly major issues ahead of all Member States of the European Community and indeed the whole of Europe in a wider sense. So it may be an important event but it is an important event which closes a chapter rather than opening a new book.

171. Sir Ralf, those who say, as you have just done well, at root what the Community was about and indeed what this country which we are in now thought it was joining was a customs union or Common Market, are often then replied to with references to phrases like "ever closer union" in the original Rome Treaty or to some of the ideals of

[Chairman *Contd]*

Jean Monnet or other Europe builders who liked to assert from the start this was a great construction for building a federated European nation. What do you say to that?

(Sir Ralf Dahrendorf) It has been true from a very early point that different members had different motives when they were talking. There was a school of thought right from the beginning (and here one can actually go back to the Coal and Steel Community which was the only real construction by Jean Monnet) there were those who took the view that there was an inescapable process which led for example—and I am only half ironical in putting it in these terms—from the idea of a customs union to a common policy in those areas where there was no market like agriculture, a Common Agricultural Policy with common prices to a unit of amount in which these common prices were expressed to monetary union to political union. This is a school of thought which can still be found in Brussels. It is a rather Cartesian notion of how political processes proceed. There is another school of thought which tends to think that perhaps there is a great deal of verbiage and highfalutin' language about what is actually happening and one should look at what is happening. One should deal with what is happening and as a consequence deal with them in their own right rather than assume an automatic process which has been set in motion and cannot be stopped. I confess I belong to the latter school.

Mr Rowlands

172. I was struck by your reference to the Treaty as a customs union, not only because politicians have added and embellished and extended it in the most recent ruling of the European Court of Justice on the EFTA agreement but the European Court, as I understand it, ruled it did not agree with that arrangement because the arrangement conflicted with a fundamental objective of European unity, something greater than a customs union because, in fact, the EFTA arrangement was reinforcing the customs union principle which was the European Court of Justice, as I read it, setting the base on which they overruled the agreement that it was in conflict with some greater objective, namely European unity in its broader sense not in a narrower customs free trade concept?

(Sir Ralf Dahrendorf) There are two answers to this. Even a free trade association, if it is taken seriously, needs a dispute settlement machinery. It is interesting to see how North America is struggling with this. There is such machinery in the North American Free Trade Agreement which has supra-national qualities, that is it actually overrides the US, American and Canadian, courts and incidentally, not unnaturally, this is one of the main problems which arise in connection with the extending of that agreement to Mexico. It was to be expected that a serious customs union would involve legal machinery which is more than the sort of machinery which would be set up in international treaties. In part—I say in part—the European Economic Area, Economic Space agree-

ment, ran into difficulties with that aspect of the European Economic Community and its customs union. There is another aspect to this which is that it is perfectly true, that the machinery of the European Community contains elements which are not strictly necessary for customs union and which undoubtedly have their origin in the history to which you, Chairman, alluded, that is to say Jean Monnet and the original ideal of which there is even more in the Coal and Steel Community Treaty than in the Treaty of Rome if you read that closely. It is also true that the European Court has certainly throughout the 20-odd years I have followed it tended to interpret the institutional arrangements of the Community extensively rather than restrictively on all occasions. It has been cautious but it has been an extensive interpretation and I would see a combination of both in this particular reaction. I agree, it raises a very interesting question about the quality of the whole institutional set up.

Mr Shore

173. The strategy of the Rome Treaty as you described it from a union into many larger areas is perhaps no more vividly demonstrated than in the creation of a European Union which has apparently taken place, or will take place, when Maastricht is ratified and within that European Union. To the immense surprise of tens of millions of Europeans all over the Continent and these islands, we are to become citizens of this European Union. No-one has really spelt out for us very clearly what it is to be a citizen in this new structure, this joint European Union, have you the faintest idea what is involved in this citizenship?

(Sir Ralf Dahrendorf) First of all, the notion of a European Union first gained official status many years ago at the Summit of Paris in 1972 when President Pompidou actually introduced it and it was part of the Summit Communique then. It was an attempt, if anything, to avoid terminology which would have a specific meaning in constitutional institutions of any member State and to indicate that what was being created here does not readily fit into any of these constitutional arrangements. I for one never read too much into that particular concept except something with which I strongly agreed which was that we in Europe cannot easily be described in traditional constitutional terminology. I gather, and as it happens I have had quite a long conversation with the Spanish Prime Minister about this, I gather Spain was particularly eager to introduce the notice of citizenship without having a terribly clear concept of what it involved. It certainly does not involve the sort of thing which I, and I have written quite widely about it, and you would assert as one of the many key concepts for describing a panoply of rights and entitlements which go with membership of a society. I understand Prime Minister Gonzales was thinking of the sort of thing that is already happening, that is EC Channels for passport control at airports and elsewhere and a number of things of that kind rather than the full concept of citizenship. There is

[**Mr Shore** *Contd*]

a deeper issue than this which is perhaps more academic than political.

Mr Forman

174. Is it possible on European Union that it was the habit of the European Community for so many years to have the first draft of any Treaty or legislative proposal written in French and that has changed a bit now but it certainly used to be the case? The phrase "union politique" which is the French presumably for European Union, means no more and no less than political unity and the weight of the word "unity" could be a great deal less threatening to the British or the sceptical mind than the word "union" in its organic and familiar sense. In much the same way "controle" has a softer meaning than the English word "control". I remember at the time of the Schumann Plan Cripps and Atlee and people like Bevin were terrified of the French word "controle" when actually the meaning was softer than the English equivalent. Would you like to comment on this problem of vocabulary?

(Sir Ralf Dahrendorf) I have had a chance to read the evidence you have heard so I do not need to repeat anything which has been said. The issues of language are truly complicated when it comes to federalism or sovereignty. Union in my view is a simpler case. I just mentioned the Summit of Paris in 1972, I was present on that occasion and I can vouch that the word union was chosen by everybody because it did not mean an awful lot, not in order to describe any particularly clear sector of unitary institutions but to say: "We want to act together and if we want to give this a name union is as good as any". Now things may have changed since then and union may have become a stricter constitutional term, that particular process has escaped me.

Chairman: Let us pursue this animal, this union, and see what it contains?

Mr Lester

175. Sir Ralf, the distinction between inter-governmental activities, decided on by the Council, and the supranational activities of the Community *per se*, initiated by the Commission, do you think that distinction is one which can be made to last—we heard quite a lot of evidence about that distinction when we were in Brussels—or in your opinion will the Commission eventually come to take the lead in all the activities of the European Union?

(Sir Ralf Dahrendorf) I am not sure about the latter, I think it could go the other way. Since 1969 when the notion of co-operation in the field of foreign policy was first agreed on by the then Community of six there has been this second strand of very close inter-governmental co-operation which in my view has been rather effective. I remember when my alas long deceased friend Andrew Shonfield gave his Reith lecture at the time of the British entry he made quite a point of what he called the habit of co-operation and the way it developed. He had great hopes for the habit

of co-operation. I regard the inter-governmental side of European Union as above all the one method of developing this habit of co-operation. If I listen to what turns up here, there and elsewhere, it has gone a long way. A lot of people find it easy to pick up the phone and ring their opposite numbers in other countries of the Community and the Commission is not particularly involved in that process. On the other hand I have seen in the evidence some detailed descriptions of the thirteen at the inter-governmental table and the role of the Commission there. I am aware of it, we all are, that the 12 often find it useful to have somebody who actually acts more as a secretariat rather than as a full member. This is a process which has been going on for quite a while and will continue and in my view is quite likely to lead co-operation into fields which are at least as important, probably more important, than those which the first Treaties are about.

Chairman

176. So you do not have a picture in your mind which has been suggested by some witnesses of the Commission and the Commission machinery gradually gobbling everything up and these pillars which have been supposedly erected by the Maastricht accords being subsumed into a great Commission pyramid?

(Sir Ralf Dahrendorf) I think that is very unlikely, and one must not get excited when the Commission produces papers about a subject which is outside the Treaty or not yet agreed on. When I was in the Commission I had to kill a whole lot of these papers on all sorts of subjects and it was easy to do because they had no future anyway but as it happens in this country anyway the press is rather interested in any such Commission document and in many cases they have no real relevance to what is going on, what is going to happen.

Mr Wells

177. Could I put it to you, Sir Ralf, that it has been said that this habit of co-operation, these union pillars, if you like, seen in German eyes when we went to see them in Bonn, they are stepping stones on a road to a supra-national organisation. Further evidence laid before this Committee suggested that, in fact, the takeover of the Foreign Affairs and Political union by a secretariat of the Council of Ministers is an indication that that is an inevitable process that is going to take place. They seem to avoid the logic that there is a difference between the Council of Ministers' secretariat and the Commission but nonetheless they see this as an establishment of the supra-national state. Do you see it that way?

(Sir Ralf Dahrendorf) Here we really get into an extremely important issue of language and the use of language in political discourse. This is a country in which politicians tend to be quite precise when they describe this process of co-operation. Some of the other Members of the European Community

[Mr Wells Contd]

have a different kind of political culture where people are much less precise and much more prepared to say things which they know are not going to happen in their lifetime and thereby indicate that they are prepared to go a few steps in a certain direction but not to indicate they are prepared to go all the way. This difference in political culture is at times worrying and it is not easy to deal with for those who sit around the table, especially the Council of Ministers or the European Council. Having said that, it is I think quite clear that all over the Community you get three views. You get a view which says whatever we do now is only a stepping stone to a truly federal, in the American sense, United States of Europe and perhaps a European superpower alongside two others or one other and lots of bits or whatever one's analysis is. You get this view here, of course, and there are quite a few friends of mine who are fervent pro-Europeans and mean by European the creation of another superpower and to some extent Britain regaining a quasi-imperial status by way of participation in the Community. It is just conceivable this view is rather more widespread in a number of Continental countries for a number of different reasons which one could spell out. At the other end you get those who essentially see the Community as a customs union with a few bits and pieces in between. Then, thirdly there is this curious idea of union which is groping for something which does not really exist yet and which will undoubtedly take longer to create than some people think. Now you are more likely to hear the first view in Bonn but it exists everywhere—which is not to say that it is going to prevail.

Chairman: I think Mr Jopling has a question which really carries on from this.

Mr Jopling

178. With your unique experience starting in the Federal Republic and then going through the Commission to this country, could you explain to us what you understand by the enthusiasm in Germany for a federation of European states? I wonder if you could tell us to what extent you think that aspiration might conflict with the sovereignty of the British Parliament here which is a matter which obsesses many people here within this building.

(Sir Ralf Dahrendorf) I should not really say much about the mood and motives in other countries, especially since you have been travelling. In the early period of the European Economic Community it was quite clear that European co-operation was one method for Germany to return to the community of nations and since it was coupled with a great deal of profound soul searching about the German past—which led many people to feel that the nation state had perhaps been the wrong vehicle to express political aspirations—the combination of this national interest and the view of the nation state led a lot of people to embrace some other political community, however fictitious and remote it may be. I think that was clearly, right through the 1950s, a fairly widespread

motive. I do not want to take too much of your time but when the Treaty of Rome was ratified by the German Parliament Ludwig Erhard made an extraordinary speech. In nine-tenths of the speech he called the Treaty of Rome an obstacle to international free trade which had created a regional set of arrangements which were totally contrary to his universalism, but he said in the last 10 per cent: "Young Germans need something to believe in and the only thing they can believe in these days is Europe, therefore I am going to vote for the ratification of the Treaty". I mention this by way of illustration. I think now the position is a very interesting one and you are much better at assessing it than I am. You would need a pretty serious analysis on the rather complex national interests in a semi-inchoate form beginning to be expressed in policies of the continental European countries. I am sure you have found the German position is much more ambiguous and much more complicated.

Chairman: Yes, I think we have.

Mr Rowlands

179. I wonder whether in fact our assessment of German attitudes to the Community is based upon its history of a state being half a state or three-quarters of a state and we have not been able to think through in any international firm policy terms or Community terms the impact, not over a year or so but over a longer period, which German unification is going to make. Would you from your assessment believe you would see in a five or ten year period a real sea change in German attitudes in different directions from the last 20 or 30 years?

(Sir Ralf Dahrendorf) My guess is much worse than your information but if by real sea change you mean a turning away from Europe I would say no, though if you mean a rather less emotional and idealistic attitude to what Europe is about I think that is very likely. We have seen significant changes in France—do not forget—which you will also have noticed especially at the time when there is a growing tendency to explain some of the shifts in domestic political preferences by France's enthusiastic Europeanism of the 1980s. I do expect changes and I think monetary union will tell the whole story. What will happen in that area will tell you what is actually going on in people's wider sense of where they belong and where they should go.

Chairman

180. I think we got a very ambiguous message as you suggested in this Committee's visit to Bonn even about monetary union. We talked to some people from the Lander (there is a question we will have later on the Committee of Regions) who said they look for a Europe in which the smaller sub-national communities have a major role and the major national community, which is Germany, this vast and united Germany, would have a lesser role, powers would be devolved to the Lander and

[**Chairman** *Contd*]

raised to the Community and the nation is not very important. Yet we heard against that people saying the deutschmark was the symbol of post-war German successes and its evaporation or merging into something European would be a very considerable assault on the idea of the United State of Germany. Which of these sentiments is tomorrow's view because that is what we would like to hear?

(Sir Ralf Dahrendorf) So would I!

Mr Forman

181. Can I just explore this from a different angle. One of the characteristics, Sir Ralf, would you agree, about the German set up is that the position of the Lander is to a large extent more entrenched than any other sub-national political union in any part of Western Europe. I say that, for example, because of their entrenchment in the Bundesbank and Grundgazetz in fundamental law, about as inescapable as you can make them. Does that not set Germany apart from any of her partner nations in the Community? Does it not mean we ought to pay a great deal of attention, if we are trying to get to the bottom of these matters, to what the leading voices of the Lander think and want for Europe?

(Sir Ralf Dahrendorf) I am sure that is the case. I have not read a truly impressive analysis of the precise role of the Lander in the Federal Republic because you see the strangest aspect of the Lander is how little power they have in their regions. The main power of the Lander is actually federal and is through the Federal Council. A long time ago I was a Lander MP and I can well remember parliamentary debates on such subjects as: "This House should decide to ask the Lander Government to intervene with the Federal Government so that in Brussels the following decision is taken", which is almost like a student parliament rather than a real parliament, that is you are asking three times removed someone else to act because there is not the power, but the federal power of the Lander is quite considerable. What you see is an assertion of federal power and that is emphasised by the fact that the political complexion of the second chamber is once again different from that of the Federal Government. I see it more in these terms than in terms of the power which, for instance, the Catalans have in Spain which is much greater. In a sense you are not likely to see a Spanish Government in the next 10 or 15 years not based on a coalition between a national party and the national representatives of either the Catalans or the Basques or both, that is power based on a local constituency or regional constituency which would become quite awkward.

182. The point I was seeking to make, just to clarify, is that the power may be to a degree top down and homogenised at the time in the Bundesrat for the Lander, but it is nonetheless real because of the importance of the coalition-building and the number of issues where it is necessary for the Federal Government to get a majority in both houses.

(Sir Ralf Dahrendorf) Yes. The federal level is extremely important too, therefore if the Lander ask for greater representation either in this Council of Regions or in some other way by having embassies almost, they can have it.

Mr Lester

183. Is there not a subtle pressure in that the political unions are based very much in the Lander and, therefore, members of the Bundestag and Bundesrat tend to look back over their shoulders within the political support of the Lander because that is where they are elected and where their opportunity to get elected comes from so they tend to look backwards rather than forwards in some ways?

(Sir Ralf Dahrendorf) It is a fair point, though like politics everywhere it is much more complicated.

Chairman: There is another concept which comes out of the German mind. This may be going into your past but you must forgive us, we would like to explore.

Mr Rowlands

184. For the first time included in the Treaty is the principle of subsidiarity, Sir Ralf. I wonder if you could tell us how you assess the significance of this subject. Do you think, as we have heard from some witnesses, this will act as a deterrent power over the Commission, it will think to itself: "We had better not try to proceed and initiate proposals in this or that direction because of subsidiarity, this could be challenged, this could be subject to subsidiarity" or whether the European Court of Justice might start to rule that actions by the Commission or Council conflict with this principle and, therefore, with the Treaty clause? Can you give us your assessment of how you see the principle post-Maastricht?

(Sir Ralf Dahrendorf) On the principle itself you have seen Helen Wallace who has written or co-authored a very informative paper on subsidiarity. It is of course originally very much a Catholic concept and it is more about the state coming into the picture once the family fails than it is about the sort of thing for which it is used now. It was originally really saying essentially the family should look after the infirm and needy and if it cannot then public agencies should. It is now being used to say there should be a presumption in favour of the smallest political or administrative unit when it comes to a decision. I think the answer is quite straight forward, it will depend totally on the Court of Justice

185. Totally on the Court of Justice?

(Sir Ralf Dahrendorf)—whether this is a concept which has meaning or not. In principle the Court of Justice could use it quite extensively, I wonder whether it will.

[**Mr Rowlands** *Contd*]

186. Given what you said earlier that there had been a tendency by the Court of Justice to be "European" extensive rather than restrictive, I do not find very much comfort for the support of subsidiarity in that.

(Sir Ralf Dahrendorf) I am not suggesting comfort, I am trying to answer your question and tell you how I see it. I think that is the way it will be defined. It will be very hard for the Council of Ministers to say the Court may think environmental issues are best dealt with at European Community level but we believe that, whatever it is. It will be hard for any other institution to overrule the Court in its decision on subsidiarity. That is where it will be decided.

187. What about the function of the national governments saying: "We believe you, the Commission, and therefore the Council of Ministers believe, this is an issue which should be subject to subsidiarity"?

(Sir Ralf Dahrendorf) I suppose national governments have been doing that all along and have said no we are not prepared to take a decision on particular research programmes in the framework of the European Community because they are best looked after by non governmental or arm's length institutions in our own country. That is one of the motives which enters into a country's behaviour in the Council of Ministers. You cannot say subsidiarity is impossible and should never happen, it will not be as simple as that.

188. If you say we are going to be very dependent upon the Court actually in these things, do you think this Article is sufficiently clear in the way it has been drafted to give a good steer to the European Court of Justice that it should find in favour of subsidiarity as in the balance of argument as opposed to finding communautaire?

(Sir Ralf Dahrendorf) If it was totally clear we would not be so dependent on the Court. I suppose the political question is do we want it to be totally clear or is it, in fact, quite possible to live with it and with the possibility for every government to interpret it as it sees fit?

Mr Shore

189. Does not the whole issue of subsidiarity become important only in the event of a federal union? Who decides otherwise, if it was a more limited Treaty, what such a principle would mean? Once you start thinking in terms of layers of Government in which the supreme higher layers, are the European layers, then the whole argument becomes alive, and who defines subsidiarity defines the nature of the union.

(Sir Ralf Dahrendorf) I agree.

Chairman

190. Do you see that as leading to an unravelling of some of the existing powers which have been assigned to the supranational element which already exists?

(Sir Ralf Dahrendorf) If you look at it very closely there is not really an awful lot that is truly supranational. I am struck time and again by the limited importance of the supra-national elements of the European Community as we know it today. Most of the interesting developments have happened alongside these, outside these and in other ways. So for the moment, and since I do not believe in the functional progression from a Common Agricultural Policy to Federal Political Union, I do not see that particular thing happening.

Mr Harris

191. How do you think the Commission views this? Do you think they have a rather different view than you do, Sir Ralf? Do you think the Commission sees itself as becoming or indeed perhaps even now as a real Government of Europe or as an agent to national Governments' collective decisions?

(Sir Ralf Dahrendorf) First of all, I do not believe there is full agreement within the Commission, that would be very unlikely. Secondly there is always a temptation if you sit—I do not think they sit on the thirteenth floor of the Berlaymont any more, they had to move out,—if you are in charge of an administration which produces documents on virtually everything, to believe that you are governing virtually everything. So there may be a temptation in the Commission to believe that their actual influence on what happens in Europe is greater than it is. I think the budget tells the true story, including the very peculiar distribution of its elements. That is the vast importance of the Common Agricultural Policy and the relatively minor importance of a whole lot of other areas which are much talked about. While I think some in the Commission may have a slightly different view, there are others I am sure who have a realistic position. One would also like to see Mr Delors in a French national position and then compare and make up one's mind what he really believes.

192. I take it you do not see all this developing into such a point that we have European ministers for trade or anything else, or foreign affairs?

(Sir Ralf Dahrendorf) Trade, as you know, is a peculiar example which you have chosen there because of the relevant Articles 113 and so on which for a customs union quite naturally suggest there should be a degree of common action but it falls far short of a Minister of Trade because the Commissioner in charge has a committee representing Member States with which he or she has to consult and consult in ways which are rather different from persuading a national Parliament and finding a majority there. Trade is not the best example to choose for the presence or absence of something which could be compared to a Minister. I think in trade and agriculture and otherwise only very limited areas you do have quasi ministerial rights through the Treaty of Rome in Brussels.

Mr Jopling

193. Fishing?

(Sir Ralf Dahrendorf) Sure, agriculture and fishing, the whole complex of the Common Agricultural Policy and the customs union.

Mr Harris

194. Surely the powers of the Monopolies and Mergers must be also developing in that way, are they not overriding?

(Sir Ralf Dahrendorf) It is an interesting question. It is the question of the famous conditions of a full customs union and does it apply to certain things? Yes is the simple answer to your point but if you look at it closely it is by no means undisputed.

Chairman: Where does monetary union fit into your thesis? Is that consistent with this customs union or is that not a huge leap forward?

Mr Welsh

195. Is the European Economic and Monetary Union feasible across the whole of the Community or is it your opinion that we may just have a fast track group of countries with strong economies progressing faster than others towards a single currency?

(Sir Ralf Dahrendorf) I believe one can say categorically there will not be a monetary union of the 12 present members of the European Community this decade and I would be surprised if there was one in the next decade. The next question is what is (a) feasible and (b) likely? Feasibility is a question of definition. Maastricht offers a definition, a fairly detailed definition, and as you know well, and you do not need me to repeat it, following that definition it will not be easy to find six of the present 12 Member States on the dates suggested in the second Maastricht paper to form a monetary union by 1997 or 1999. It will not be easy. It is not totally impossible but it is not terribly likely. However, the six, if one found them, would not necessarily all wish to go along with it and that is where the likelihood has to be added to feasibility. If I do that, and if I think of a Community of 12, I am bound to wonder just how real the project is. I was a witness at the first attempt to create economic and monetary union and at its failure. The attempt was made between 1969 and 1971 and the failure happened in 1971. I, therefore, have a very strong sense that—pardon the word—it is almost arrogant to believe you can plan ahead economic and monetary processes of this importance and order of magnitude over a period of six years, that it is enough for a few people to sit in any one place and to say: "If we cannot agree by 1997 it will happen anyway by 1999" and make it come true because monetary union is a very big objective and there are a whole lot of processes which are not controlled or controllable by the government sitting around the table in Maastricht which may appear between now and then.

196. On that basis it is possible there could be a fast track of six or less?

(Sir Ralf Dahrendorf) Yes.

197. Could you visualise the other countries that come in from EFTA being in that fast track and other countries which are in the 12 at the moment not being in it?

(Sir Ralf Dahrendorf) Quite frankly, whether Austria is a member or not it will be part of any monetary union which includes the German mark so membership is almost not relevant to being a part of the fast track. I suspect if Sweden and possibly Finland were to be members before long they would be very interested in this process, so I think the answer to your question is yes it is possible, you will get a much less tidy picture than some may wish to see.

Chairman

198. You are saying there should be a greater deutschmark zone including people who might or might not be members of the Community and there will be the rest of us?

(Sir Ralf Dahrendorf) I think the key question here, as in so many other things, is the relation between Paris and Bonn, Berlin, or perhaps in this case Frankfurt.

Mr Welsh

199. This, of course, is going to make it a lot harder for any eastern country to come in, it is hard enough as it is. This will push it back another 10 or 20 years, would you agree with that?

(Sir Ralf Dahrendorf) As you probably know I feel very strongly about that, that was the point of my initial remark about rear mirrors and windscreens. We should do everything in Europe to water the tender plant of democracy in the new democracies. I can think of no more important issue in these key areas, so whatever I say will be coloured by it. Curiously some of these countries believe they would not have any particular difficulties with those issues which we believe are the most difficult. They would like to be within the Common Agricultural Policy and it may be some of the rest of us, not I am glad to say Britain, would be more sceptical about their coming in than they would be about coming in. They may have slight illusions about the implications of being a part of the fast track monetary union because I happen to share your views on this. It is interesting how East Europeans are rather unsophisticated in their thinking about money. It is part of this process of printing a new currency and then being surprised it does not work. That is true for their attitude towards monetary union. If you have them here you will probably have seen they will not object to monetary union.

Mr Rowlands

200. When we were in Paris the theme there was the keenness of the French for monetary union which is somehow that they will have a shared

[**Mr Rowlands** *Contd*]

decision making process on the position of the deutschmark, of the currency, whereas at the moment all they can do is follow the decisions of the Germans. Do you think that is a French illusion that somehow by monetary union they will get a share in the decision making process, in fundamental decisions on currency and economic policy that flows from it?

(*Sir Ralf Dahrendorf*) When we were discussing monetary union in the early 1970s the great dispute was between the German so-called "economist" and the French "monetarist" view. First of all, the Germans said: "You have to get your economic policy right and then we can talk about economic union" and the French said: "First we have to align our currencies and the economic policy will follow by itself". In this respect France has undergone a fundamental change since 1983, it is one of the greatest changes in the economic policy field over the last 10 years. Today France has the identical position of that of Germany with respect to the economic and monetary policy and in relation to the two it is only on this basis that the questions that become real. It is because it is perfectly possible for France to join a currency area, say with Germany, that the question of influence is more than an academic question. Having said that, yes, I think this is a very strong French motive.

Mr Forman

201. I felt we let Sir Ralf off a little bit lightly, can I try this question on him. I realise Sir Ralf is a sociologist or political scientist rather than a lawyer but since the language of Article 3b as it is in the Maastricht Treaty is essentially normative rather than descriptive I wonder if he could comment more on the language. Does he believe the phraseology which is there, and I remind the Committee of the words: "In areas which do not fall within its exclusive competence, the Community shall take action in accordance with the principle of subsidiarity only if and insofar as the objectives of the proposed action cannot be sufficiently achieved by the Member States and can, therefore, by reason of the scale or effects of the proposed action be better achieved by the Community"—think the interesting word there is "sufficiently". It is not saying what is the situation in the United States where all rights which are not specifically allocated to the federal level are reserved under the constitution to the member states, it is saying it is more normative and iffy, it is giving ECJ a bigger role. How does Sir Ralf believe that form of *ultra vires* doctrine at European level is going to be interpreted?

(*Sir Ralf Dahrendorf*) I have both texts, the last one before Maastricht and the Maastricht text. The first says, "can be better achieved by the Community", "sufficiently" came in at the very last minute. It remains, and that was my whole argument. If I may say this in parenthesis, you say you have let me off too lightly but I do not know what my role is here, it is certainly not to give you

more than one person's view, the person who has thought about these things and is part of the para-political debate and no more, so do not pay too much attention to what I say. It strikes me that this is the sort of phraseology which would have to be defined by case law.

202. Yes.

(*Sir Ralf Dahrendorf*) It would be perfectly easy for me to argue that the Common Agricultural Policy cannot sufficiently be achieved by the European Community but requires regional break-up into regional policies because it is closely related to inheritance laws and geographical conditions and what have you. Where am I having the escape in relation to 3b, probably nowhere because I think the Court will probably uphold the Common Agricultural Policy. So I am afraid it remains to be seen where the first important contentious case is. It may well be in the field of environment, in the widest sense.

203. They have a tradition of upholding the *acquis communautaire*, that is a natural instinct. One feels in areas of new proposed Community law where it is uncharted territory it is possible, using this terminology that we have both lighted on, that the judgment can fall in favour of the nation state and the supranational level, or, either or and in some cases, in favour of, the sub national level as well.

(*Sir Ralf Dahrendorf*) Yes.

Mr Harris

204. Would fishing be a good example of that because the Court has, after all, on this question of flagging vessels really driven a coach and horses through the whole issue of national concept under the fisheries policy? Taking up the point of Mr Forman obviously there is a strong regional interest, particularly in the implementation of fishing policy. Do you see that as an area where the Court could have a major impact?

(*Sir Ralf Dahrendorf*) Yes, I do not feel sufficiently expert to say anything on that.

Chairman: Before opening up the vista a little, could we turn to the European Parliament and the structure of things post-Maastricht?

Mr Harris

205. I am wondering how you see the European Parliament post-Maastricht? Does it have any real chance to hold the Commission or the Council of Ministers properly to account or do you think it is an institution which might have that objective but really that is wishful thinking?

(*Sir Ralf Dahrendorf*) It is very hard for institutions to get away from their history and even their origins. One must never forget that in the original Treaty the Assembly was an afterthought, that is there was a complete institutional system consisting of Commission, Council of Ministers and Court of Justice and it was the insistence I think of the Dutch, the strong insistence of the Dutch,

[**Mr Harris** *Contd*]

which led to the introduction of the Assembly and throughout the history of the Community it has been one or two members who have insisted Parliament has to be given more rights. I think Maastricht adds relatively little to that. I think along with that there is one simple but very complicated trick which could give Parliament a role which would be for Parliament to appoint the Commission and in that way actually sit at the table of the Council of Ministers through the Commission but that is not likely to happen. There was no indication in the run up to Maastricht that any Member State was particularly eager to do that and I do not remember Parliament even asking for it. So I think these are quite minor adjustments in the role of the European Parliament.

206. So Germany I suppose is the country which says it has the greatest desire for powers to be given to the European Parliament? From what you say you do not think that will happen for a very long time, if at all? Is that what you are actually saying?

(Sir Ralf Dahrendorf) I find the whole system in this respect very unsatisfactory but you asked me a factual question and the answer to that is yes.

207. Can we look at some of the other ideas, some ideas contained in the Treaty. You made reference, the Chairman made reference, to the Committee of Regions, how do you see that developing? Again, when we were in Brussels certainly some significance was being attached to the proposal for a Committee of the Regions. Do you think that will be a body eventually of some significance or is it just meant to be yet another institution tacked on to rather a lot which are there already?

(Sir Ralf Dahrendorf) It has obviously got some significance and it will have some significance if only because it is a new body. Those who are initially appointed or elected to it will wish to have some influence to it. It is a large body, I forget the number, 113 regions, maybe even more which have been identified. So it is not easy to see—it is almost a second chamber—how it will work. If your question is, is it likely to have a significant influence on legislation in the Community framework, I doubt it.

208. And the Conference of Parliaments, is that a good idea in your opinion or a bad idea? Will it have any effect at all?

(Sir Ralf Dahrendorf) Since I was always in favour of an indirectly elected European Parliament as long as there are no proper Parliamentary functions for it, because of the link between Europe and national Parliaments which were established, as long as there is an indirectly elected Parliament I tend to favour everything that strengthens this link.

Chairman

209. You do not think that link does exist or the thread is broken from mega constituencies or lists all over Europe?

(Sir Ralf Dahrendorf) I rather think so.

Chairman: That is interesting. Could we turn to a broader scene. There are those who think that everything we have talked about so far which went on at Maastricht was a bit of a sideshow and there is a big European drama unfolding which wise Europeans should have their eyes on.

Mr Lester

210. You argued in your article in the Financial Times that we have to include the new democracies of Eastern Europe if we do not want to pay a high price "in external protection, internal divisions and moral shame." Do you think the Association Agreements with Poland, Hungary and Czechoslovakia are sufficient to bring those countries within the markets of the Community and reinforce their fragile democracies? Do you see their main purpose of enlargement as being economic or political?

(Sir Ralf Dahrendorf) I see the main purpose as being political. I am pleased the Association Agreement exists and when I wrote my little book "Reflections on the Revolution in Europe" two years ago I did in fact advocate precisely this way forward. I have since changed my mind and I now feel full membership in the institutions is a political imperative and the reason for this is the following. The new democracies like all new democracies are extremely vulnerable. Most of the defence against forces which may undo what has been gained has to be marshalled within these countries but there is a marginal, and perhaps more than marginal, importance of a degree of external constraint which is exercised by being part of a club, almost by being a member of organisations which have this constraining power. It is a curious and for some certainly regrettable fact that some international organisations have a greater restraining power than others. One could imagine in theory that the Council of Europe with the European Convention—and it's emphasis on human rights and rule of law—would have the greater restraining power, unfortunately that is not the case. It is useful, I am delighted they have become Members quickly. I think it will make a lot of difference for those trying to find their way through institutions and texts in some cases which help especially the rule of law. But, despite the experience of the Greeks at the time of the Colonels—that was the suspension of Greece at the time—there was no feeling that the Council of Europe is where it is at. One must not do certain things or else everyone will get upset. There is such a sense about the European Community for the moment, it is among the strong international institutions like NATO and I believe membership of NATO is exactly the sort of constraint that would be an element of reference for those who are defining the new democracies. They can say: "this would go down very

[**Mr Lester** *Contd*]
badly with our friends in the European Community". They can go further and say: "This will lead to trouble in the European Community". That is what Felipe Gonzales said when he campaigned for early Spanish membership, first in the EC and then for early Spanish membership in NATO. We heard the same view from Vaclav Havel for the East Central Europeans. They are prepared to pay the economic price, those who defend the new democratic institutions are prepared to pay the new economic price in unemployment and in other respects in order to have a degree of political certainty. I think we have a very great responsibility.

211. Do you think the way to deal with the economic tide is a very long interim period?
(Sir Ralf Dahrendorf) Yes. Instead of having seven years before and seven years after I would like to fold the entire transitional period inwards and find arrangements which make it possible immediately for them to sit at the table of the Council of Ministers as full members despite the fact there is a 14 year transition period in important economic respects.

Mr Wells

212. You see membership of the Community as being an underpinning—I do not think we can use "guarantee"—of the democratic influences or forces at work and that is what their membership would assist?
(Sir Ralf Dahrendorf) Exactly.

213. If that is so do we not have to enlarge even further than we are thinking of at the present time?
(Sir Ralf Dahrendorf) The answer may well be yes. I think, however, it will be a very important signal to start with the three. I hope they remain three and do not become four. It will be a very important signal to others, to begin with Poland, Czechoslovakia and Hungary.

Mr Forman

214. Can I ask for your observation: early enlargement or folding in all three in Central Europe into the Community would surely create expectations both ways, it would certainly create expectations in those countries of what they would hope to gain by being in the Community, including the rule of law, political values and market support. It would create experience, if you like, in the public opinion of existing member states, many of whom would find interests strongly in conflict with those of the new members. Is Sir Ralf so confident the Community could digest this very big change in the sort of timescale he suggests, economically and politically?
(Sir Ralf Dahrendorf) Curiously the main threat, if that is the word, and it should not be, is economic. The main effect of membership is on the economy of present members, because sometimes in my more cynical moments I describe the European Economic Community as an organisa-

tion to defend declining industries, and of course these declining industries are precisely the ones with which the Eastern and Central Europeans would compete: agriculture, textiles, steel, you name it, we are talking about the industries which are doing badly at home. They would be able to compete presumably from a fairly low wage starting level, like Portugal, for a while, and they will be a little uncomfortable because we are talking about countries of quite significant economic potential. Portugal was just palatable but Poland is a country like Spain, that is much more difficult.

Chairman

215. This surely is the bottom line: if there are hundreds of tons of wheat from the Danubian Plain and beef from Poland and cheap shoes from Poland and low cost furniture from Czechoslovakia about to sweep into Europe there will be vast resistance and we will not be able to deliver, or hope to, through Community membership for those countries even if they want it.
(Sir Ralf Dahrendorf) You must allow me to defend what is right even if you have to defend what is possible.
Chairman: That is a sentiment that appeals to this Committee.

Mr Welsh

216. I agree with your view, if we believe in open markets and free markets we should accept them in, there is no point in putting barriers up. Should we not go a little way where individual countries could allow them in, should we not let them in without visas, is that not recognising they are citizens of Europe anyway? Why should they apply for a silly little piece of paper to visit our country? Would that not help them, so they are really accepted as Europeans, if you will accept the terminology?
(Sir Ralf Dahrendorf) Yes. It is amazing how much even symbolic acts—this is more than a symbolic act—help. It is no accident the concept of East European time has disappeared in the area of Central Europe. They want to be a part of the area which for the moment starts in Brest and ends in Brest, starts at the Polish/Ukraine border and ends at the Channel. Yes is the unambiguous answer.

Mr Rowlands

217. Two points arise out of that. We shared very strongly some of the sentiments you have expressed in our last Report about the importance of the bolster of democracy and the value of belonging to the European Community. Presumably that places a clear condition that states succeeding will in fact remain democratic? We have not really been properly tested in the Community yet, no Greek Colonels have taken over within the Community. We would surely make it a clear condition that resolution of disputes of the Croatian kind or Slovak/Czech kind are going to be resolved by political dialogue and

[**Mr Rowlands** *Contd*]

interchange rather than weapons and war as a condition of belonging?

(Sir Ralf Dahrendorf) I must be careful not to be led too far from my knowledge to my passions. I certainly agree, one of the unfortunate weaknesses of the European Community is that it has done relatively little to spell out the value of conditions, as it were, of membership. There has been a sort of assumption you have to be a democracy but that is another one of those words in many respects which have had different interpretations in different places. I would very much like to see that. Ultimately I would like to see a merger of the Community and the Council of Europe, then one could see what one does with some of the values embodied in the Council of Europe and the Convention.

Mr Lester

218. That takes you to a vast number of countries, 23 are now involved in the Council of Europe. How wide do you see the Community becoming? Where does it end? What is "European"? We really appear to take on many poorer countries. Chancellor Kohl was very clear you should not take on another Spain, Portugal and Greece. In taking on the three countries you mentioned there would be quite an economic responsibility, particularly in view of what we have seen in German unification. I wonder how strong the relative economies of the Community can be in terms of the relative expansion?

(Sir Ralf Dahrendorf) Well, I would indeed be inclined to exclude from your present perspective for the European Community, say, Byelorussia and I think there are a number of other questions we have to be clear and honest upon, Turkey is one of them. I can see a Community which extends —the Council of Europe is growing all the time so it is hard to know how many Members it has on any given day—I can see a Community which extends to about the size of the Council of Europe as we know it at this present moment. I do not think we can afford—you are not doing it actually but I have seen it in these papers—to use institutional arguments against European necessity. I think it is very very weak to say; "We do not know how the Commission would work, would there be enough space in Strasbourg for all these MPs?", that is a very frail answer.

Chairman

219. My own sentiments are with yours Sir Ralf on this, those who think otherwise would say you are turning the Community, this mechanism, this Group of 12 with its interpretations and languages into a vast rally of 20, into a jamboree. This has ceased to be a Community. Is that what you and is that what London wants?

(Sir Ralf Dahrendorf) A Europe which does not face the question of the new democracies will become so inherently implausible it will not become a deeper Community at all but it will

tempt some of its existing Members to begin their own national policies, to set in motion their own national policies beyond the boundaries of the Community. We have no option, what we have an option to do is give harder thought to the way in which one can run a Community of some cohesion despite this larger membership.

Mr Rowlands

220. Does not an enlargement of this kind, does that not make in some way the structures envisaged in Maastricht rather irrelevant and as you say it was the end of a chapter and in fact we have to start, not again, but Maastricht does not lead us to the solutions that enlargement will cause in institutional terms.

(Sir Ralf Dahrendorf) That is very largely my view and I was pleased to hear expressions of a similar view from the Government and occasionally from Mr Delors too. He is now hinting that there are new problems and we really have to face up to them so I think perhaps there is a growing recognition of this fact.

Mr Wells

221. Does your answer to the question before last not also suggest that the natural trading boundaries, the natural cultural ties, historical connections of Europe extend, of course, far to the eastwards and, of course, are related to Germany's particular position, Germany and for that matter Poland, Austria, Hungary and Czechoslovakia whose connections and trading relationships traditionally were eastwards and therefore the centre of the European Community we are now looking at has, with the end of the Cold War, moved eastwards and we must recognise that. The centre is Germany and the problem is Germany.

(Sir Ralf Dahrendorf) This is partly the case and partly things have changed. When the East Central Europeans say Central Europe they mean West, they do not mean Central Europe in the old prewar, let alone pre First World War sense since they have become very Western in their orientation and that is really what they want. In fact, the last thing they want is to be part of some German bloc, so those who suspect an extension of the Community in that direction would strengthen Germany's position may well be wrong because you do not have to go too far and talk to too many people in Warsaw, Prague and Budapest to know their notion of where they should go. For the present political, intellectual and media class, Europe is a very Western notion so it is not a reconstitution of the traditional boundaries let alone trade flows, it is the creation of a Europe which in cultural terms is Western and in economic terms I hope is open.

Chairman

222. Could this Europe about which we are talking embrace a democratic Ukraine, a democratic Russian Federation, as our Prime Minister and the Foreign Secretary have both suggested it could?

[**Chairman** *Contd*]

(Sir Ralf Dahrendorf) One day could be a very long way away. I have my doubts about them but one enters an area of judgments for it is not altogether easy to give a rational argument.

Mr Rowlands

223. Where does this put Britain, very much out on a limb really, on the periphery, if it is seen to shift? I read a book on someone sailing down the Danube which described the civilisation, the culture and the history of the whole of Central Europe. We have not shared it. We have not belonged to it. Do you think Britain is very much going to be a fringe part of this new Europe of 20 plus?

(Sir Ralf Dahrendorf) I wonder whether if one reads what I have said over the last hour or hour and a half, one could not easily conclude that it is a perfectly viable policy for Britain and it's broad European policy. Geography does not determine where one is in this game, it is more what kind of values do you represent, how confident are you of your policies and how do you introduce them into the discourse with others whether Britain is at the centre of things or at the margin is entirely a matter for decisions, not a matter for some geo-political world spirit or anything of that kind.

Mr Forman

224. Sir Ralf, what you have said assumes the European Community for all its history, and indeed its future, has not been engaged in something akin to building of new European nations. I suspect there are many people in the Community who think that is exactly what it is engaged in. One knows from history any form of nation building, whether in the last century, this century or the next century, is bound up inevitably with geography and bound up with your point about institutional arrangements. You as a political scientist surely appreciate if this larger Community you ideally would like to see became ungovernable in some sense because it had gone beyond one's critical mass, what is one to do, one is undermining the achievements of the last 40–50 years?

(Sir Ralf Dahrendorf) To give a slightly oblique answer, there are moments when I fear what we will see in the next five or six years is not ever closer union but a whole lot of centrifugal tendencies. As far as Europe is concerned, including the Europe of the present 12, this may well be a period in which a reasonable balanced firm institutional view of what Europe can and cannot do emanating from Britain will be quite central in order to keep together what otherwise might take us into new inter-war or the pre-First World War period.

Chairman: I think that last answer strikes a strong chord with the Committee. Thank you very much for sharing your thoughts with us this afternoon. You have left us a little wiser, not necessarily less confused, but with new vistas opening up. Thank you.

Printed in the United Kingdom for HMSO.
Dd.0508219, 3/92, C6, 3382/5B, 5673, 189379.

HMSO publications are available from:

HMSO Publications Centre
(Mail, fax and telephone orders only)
PO Box 276, London, SW8 5DT
Telephone orders 071-873 9090
General enquiries 071-873 0011
(queuing system in operation for both numbers)
Fax orders 071-873 8200

HMSO Bookshops
49 High Holborn, London, WC1V 6HB   071-873 0011 (counter service only)
258 Broad Street, Birmingham, B1 2HE   021-643 3740
Southey House, 33 Wine Street, Bristol, BS1 2BQ   (0272) 264306
9-21 Princess Street, Manchester, M60 8AS   061-834 7201
80 Chichester Street, Belfast, BT1 4JY   (0232) 238451
71 Lothian Road, Edinburgh, EH3 9AZ   031-228 4181

HMSO's Accredited Agents
(see Yellow Pages)

and through good booksellers

ISBN 0-10-284892-0

FOREIGN AFFAIRS COMMITTEE

EUROPE AFTER MAASTRICHT

MINUTES OF EVIDENCE

Wednesday 4 March 1992

Mr Michael Jay, Mr John Goulden CMG, Mr Martin Eaton and Mr Michael Arthur

---

Ordered by The House of Commons *to be printed*
4 March 1992

LONDON: HMSO

£5.80 net

WEDNESDAY 4 MARCH 1992

Members present:

Mr David Howell, in the Chair

Mr David Harris	Mr Ted Rowlands
Mr Michael Jopling	Mr Peter Shore
Mr Jim Lester	Mr Bowen Wells

Examination of witnesses

MR MICHAEL JAY, Assistant Under Secretary of State, European Community, MR JOHN GOULDEN CMG, Assistant Under Secretary of State, Arms Control, MR MARTIN EATON, Deputy Legal Adviser and MR MICHAEL ARTHUR, Head of European Community (Internal) Department, Foreign & Commonwealth Office, were examined.

Chairman

225. Gentlemen, could I begin by welcoming you to the Committee. I think I am right in saying that three of you, Mr Jay, Mr Goulden and Mr Arthur, have kindly been our guests before. Mr Eaton, am I right, you have not been before us before?

(Mr Eaton) Not yet.

226. Welcome, and I hope your colleagues have not given you too gloomy an assessment of what to come is like. We are very grateful to you and we want really to pursue some rather more detailed questions this morning on the Treaty of European Union agreed at Maastricht and follow up the evidence given to this Committee by the Foreign Secretary on 4 February and subsequent evidence and indeed informal meetings the Committee has had in Paris, Brussels and Bonn. Could I just say for ground rules, please would witnesses have no hesitation about coming in on questions, even if the question is not initially directed to them. Could we begin with what was agreed at Maastricht and what will need to be ratified by the parliaments of the Community, namely the Treaty on European Union. Perhaps I should direct this to Mr Eaton, who is the Deputy Legal Adviser, but others please come in. What changes will be required to the law of the United Kingdom to ratify that Treaty and what other consequential amendments to United Kingdom law will be needed to carry through the decisions taken at Maastricht and agreed by this Government?

(Mr Eaton) Mr Chairman, the essential change would be, as in the case of the Single European Act, that the parts of the Maastricht agreement which amend the European Community treaties should be given the force of law in the United Kingdom. Those parts which do not amend the European Community treaties would not be given the force of law and I am referring particularly to those parts concerned with the common foreign and security policy and those with justice and home affairs. That would be the essential change.

227. Those, for instance, parts of the social document agreed and signed by other members but not by Britain, would they involve any law changes here or is our position that we are insulated from all changes flowing from those provisions?

(Mr Eaton) Those would not require any change here, no.

Mr Wells

228. Will this require a Bill?

(Mr Eaton) Yes.

229. It will require a Bill?

(Mr Eaton) Yes.

Mr Rowlands

230. Simply incorporating the amended Treaty?

(Mr Eaton) Yes, that is right. It will specify that those parts of the Treaty of Maastricht which amend the European Community treaties should be Community treaties for the purposes of the European Communities Act 1972. It will be very similar to what was done in the European Communities (Amendment) Act in 1986 which gave effect to the Single European Act.

231. That will be the model we should follow, will it?

(Mr Eaton) Yes.

Mr Jopling

232. Will it be the same sort of length as that Bill? I cannot remember how many clauses that was.

(Mr Eaton) It was about five, I think, Mr Jopling, and yes, I would imagine it would be a similar length.

Mr Rowlands: And virtually unamendable in the sense that we would be only ratifying the Treaty?

Mr Jopling: Take it or leave it.

The cost of printing and publishing these Minutes of Evidence is estimated by HMSO at £2,919.

Mr Rowlands

233. Is that right?

(Mr Eaton) Yes.

234. When you say that, what about all the monetary union agreements which were made at Maastricht? Would they also be incorporated within the same one Bill?

(Mr Eaton) A good many of the things which I think you are referring to are protocols to the Treaty and anything that is a protocol is part of the Treaty, so as a protocol to the Treaty of Rome, as amended, that would also be given effect in this way.

235. So the protocol, for example, limiting the level of public expenditure in the various stages, that would be incorporated within our legislation by this Bill?

(Mr Eaton) I am slightly uneasy about answering questions on the EMU part because that is more a Treasury responsibility, but certainly I think any protocol concerned with EMU would become part of our law, yes.

236. And in one Bill?

(Mr Eaton) Yes, indeed.

Chairman

237. Do you, Mr Eaton, or do any other witnesses, know about ratification in other Member States and whether their methods and timing are going to be roughly the same as ours or whether there are any major snags looming up?

(Mr Jay) Perhaps I could answer that, Mr Chairman. The procedures vary between Member States or among other Member States and the timing of ratification will depend on different procedures in different Member States. Some seem to think there should be no difficulty about ratification quite quickly and others may have difficulty in ratifying within the timetable envisaged, in other words, to enable the new Treaty to come into effect on the 1 January 1993. Two Member States, Denmark and Ireland, are obliged by their constitutions to have referenda as part of the process of ratification. At least one other Member State, France, may decide to have a referendum. That, as I understand it, is not yet decided.

Mr Lester

238. How about countries which may apply to become members subsequently? Will they have a whole new Act to follow which will incorporate the Single European Act and the Treaty of Maastricht as part of whatever they have to sign up to and ratify before they can become members?

(Mr Jay) Yes, the applicant Member States would have to accept the Treaty of Maastricht as it enters into effect early next year.

Mr Shore

239. Could I for one moment revert to the business of the protocols and their force in terms of the legislation? As it presently stands, the British opt-out position is incorporated in a protocol, is it not? Would I be right, therefore, in thinking that that opt-out would be enacted in terms of the legislation that we intend to put before the House?

(Mr Jay) The whole Treaty, the part of the Treaty of Maastricht which includes the amendments to the European Community and the protocols which are attached to the Treaty of Rome, which includes the protocols on economic and monetary union and including the protocol which reflects the opt-out clause, will be included in the amendments to the European Communities Act which will be enacted during the rest of this year.

Mr Wells

240. Is it proposed to put some high-sounding preamble in front of this yellow document as was done in the Single European Act with disastrous consequences for us?

(Mr Jay) The yellow document does include a preamble already right at the very beginning. The section which has at the bottom "UP/UEM/en/IV" is the preamble to the Maastricht Treaty, where it says "Resolved to mark a new stage ..."

241. Nothing more?

(Mr Jay) Nothing more. The document you have in front of you is the document which was signed by Member States in Maastricht on the 7 February and that is the document, unchanged, which will need to be ratified by all Member States during the course of this year.

Mr Rowlands

242. I am sorry to come back on this, but we are learning as we go along. You have just said that the whole of that yellow document will be, as it were, incorporated within or ratified by a Bill. Is that right?

(Mr Jay) I am sorry, I must correct myself because, as Mr Eaton was saying earlier on, those parts of this document which amend the Treaty of Rome will be ratified.

243. Not the whole document?

(Mr Jay) The whole of the document will be ratified, but only those parts which amend the Treaty of Rome will require legislation by the United Kingdom Parliament as part of that ratification process.

244. And I now understand that includes all protocols. What is the status of this Declaration by the 11 on the social policy? It is not a protocol, is it, and, therefore, would it or would it not be part of the ratification process?

(Mr Eaton) There is a protocol and the protocol enables the 11 to, as it were, borrow the Community institutions to, if they so wish, give effect to what they have agreed in their agreement

[**Mr Rowlands** *Contd*]

between themselves. Their agreement itself is not part of the Treaty. It is annexed to the protocol, but that is really for reference. It is not part of the obligation. The obligations are set out in the protocol on the social policy which permits them to use the Community institutions but makes it very clear that the United Kingdom does not participate in that process and is not bound by it nor has to pay for it.

245. When we pass a Bill to incorporate these changes that will be part of it?

(*Mr Eaton*) Yes.

Chairman

246. Just to finally get this clear: the inter-governmental bits of the Maastricht accord, namely the common foreign and security policy and the interior justice agreements, will the House ratify those? They were part of the accord, are they part of the Treaty and will they be ratified by this House of Commons?

(*Mr Eaton*) I think in strict constitutional theory it is the Crown that does the ratifying and the House that passes the legislation that is necessary in order that anything that is ratified can be given effect in the law of this country. Since the parts of the common foreign and security policy and justice and home affairs will not require legislation to give them effect, those will not have legislation.

247. Those are part of this Treaty under Royal prerogative?

(*Mr Eaton*) Exactly.

248. We have to lump it or like it?

(*Mr Eaton*) Yes.

Mr Rowlands

249. What is the position, as is possible in Germany because it is quite a complicated business where they have to get the support of both Houses, the Bundestag and Bundesrat, if that gets halted, or in any of the other countries no ratification process takes place? Do we all just stand still until they do it, or what?

(*Mr Jay*) The Treaty can only come into effect when it has been ratified by all the member states. If any member state is, for whatever reason, unable to ratify the Treaty, then it will not come into effect. The implications of that would have to be considered by the member states if and when the time arose. I might add that it nearly arose in the process of the ratification of the Single European Act, when there was a problem in Ireland which required the Irish to have a referendum which delayed the coming into effect of the Single European Act by some six months or so.

Chairman: Could we pass on to the next aspect of Maastricht which is the question of the budgetary implication.

Mr Rowlands

250. I wondered if we could get some clarification so as to put a price tag on Maastricht. It seems that Mr Delors has done so already. He said, in introducing his EC budget of 87bn ecu, that the Community budget must be increased by 20bn ecu if the commitments made at Maastricht were to be fulfilled. Do we work on a 20bn price tag for Maastricht?

(*Mr Jay*) No, we do not, Mr Rowlands. If I could say a little bit on the background. The Commission was, in any case, obliged to produce reports during the course of this year on the own resources decision and the inter-institutional agreement which were parts of the 1988 review of the Community finances, so a discussion of Community finances during the course of this year was in any case going to happen. The Treaty of Maastricht agreed some policies which will have expenditure implications, notably the agreement on the cohesion fund and the inclusion in competence of some new areas of policy; but there was no agreement at Maastricht about how much should be spent, and no commitment at Maastricht to new resources. We do not see the proposals which the Commission have put forward in the document, to which Mr Rowlands refers, as an automatic consequence of Maastricht, nor as the bill arising from Maastricht. As for the figures, Mr Rowlands is right to say that the Commission is seeking in its proposals to increase the own resources ceiling on the Community's finances from 1.2 per cent of GNP to 1.37 per cent of GNP by 1997 in order to provide sufficient resources to fund an overall real terms increase in expenditure between 1992 and 1997 of about 20bn ecu, that is about £14bn and those are the proposals.

251. He does not pluck these out of the air, presumably, he said £14bn of the Community's money to be provided by 1992, on what basis has he made such an assessment?

(*Mr Jay*) These are calculations based on his assessment of the needs arising from policies, including the common agricultural policy, revisions to the structural funds, the cohesion fund agreed at Maastricht, money for the external resources for the Community to fund, for example aid programmes to Eastern Europe and the former Soviet Union, and he aggregates those to come to a figure of 20bn ecu and concludes that we will need an increase from 1.2 per cent to 1.37 per cent of GNP with a small reserve there as well.

252. If you said that there was no monetary commitment by the Government or any other government to this figure, with what particular aspects do you quarrel of this £14bn? Do you believe it should be half that or that there should be a nil increase amount and Maastricht will not have an expenditure consequence?

(*Mr Jay*) No, we accept that there are some policies which were agreed at Maastricht which do have financial consequences, but the Treasury's calculations suggest that on the assumption of a

[Mr Rowlands *Contd*]

GNP increase of 2.5 per cent, which is the assumption that Mr Delors himself uses in his proposals, it would be possible for some £9bn to be found between now and 1997 without raising the 1.2 per cent GNP ceiling at all. So ministers do not believe that the Commission have demonstrated——

253. You mean there as a result of growth in the European Community's economy?

(Mr Jay) As a result of growth in the European Community's economy, as a result of some programmes which are now operational which will cease to operate over the next few years, and as a result of the headroom which exists even now within the 1.2 per cent ceiling.

254. That would leave us where £9bn of this £14bn could be found by natural growth from savings?

(Mr Jay) Exactly.

255. Do you think the net increase of Maastricht will be of the order of £5bn?

(Mr Jay) I think it is very hard to say what these specific figures would be which stem from Maastricht because that depends on what decisions are taken on the size of the cohesion fund, whether the cohesion fund is in addition to the structural funds, which are in any case due for revision. There are a number of imponderables there which make it hard to come up with any clear figure at all about what the bill for Maastricht might be.

Mr Jopling

256. If the own resources ceiling was to be increased from 1.2 per cent to 1.37 per cent would I be right in saying that that decision remains as it has always been, that it can only be done by unanimity?

(Mr Jay) Yes, Mr Jopling, absolutely right.

257. Are there any movements within the Council or within the Commission or in the Parliament to suggest that the next time the own resources ceiling needs to be altered, steps should be taken to make sure that all member states contribute, rather than having a minority who contribute and a majority who do not contribute on the net balance at all?

(Mr Jay) The proposals which Mr Delors has put forward do involve a small change in the structure of own resources which would be a move towards the principle that member states would contribute on the basis of their proportionate GNP. There is a small element of that already, the so-called fourth resource in the Community, and there is a suggestion that there should be a shift away from the VAT base as the basis for calculating contributions to a GNP resource. That would bring it more into line with relative GNP which would having something of that effect.

258. Will the United Kingdom Government be insisting that there is a greater movement in that direction so that all member states pay something?

(Mr Jay) I think that is a question I wish ministers to answer, and the Treasury in particular to answer. I think ministers would accept that there would always inevitably, in a Community of 12, be some member states who would be net contributors and some who would be net recipients.

Chairman

259. Is our rebate at risk?

(Mr Jay) There have been no proposals so far to change the arrangements for the UK abatement.

Mr Wells

260. Surely you must have had some figure in mind when you signed up to the cohesion facility in the Maastricht Treaty? You indicated that it was complicated because it was muddled with structural funds and I understand that, but surely you must have had some idea which you can give the Committee as to what the cohesion funds would cost.

(Mr Jay) There were no figures mentioned and we did not have particular figures in mind for what the cohesion fund might cost when the negotiations were completed at Maastricht.

261. So we signed a blank cheque?

(Mr Jay) We signed a Treaty which would have probably some financial implications, but it was clear that what those financial implications would be decided in the course of the discussions on the Community's finances which we all knew were going to take place during the course of this year.

262. Presumably there was a Treasury representative there, was there?

(Mr Jay) The Chancellor of the Exchequer was present.

Mr Rowlands

263. Does this mean that we are going to be asked in the next X months to ratify the Treaty and pass a Bill without there being any sort of consensus within the 12 as to the order of expenditure that the Maastricht Treaty is going to create?

(Mr Jay) It will always, I think, be very difficult at the end of the negotiations which we are about to start, which have just started, to say precisely this amount or that amount is a direct result of the Maastricht Treaty. If one takes, for example, the cohesion fund, there will be agreement, I presume, during the course of these negotiations on the size of the cohesion fund, but it will be extremely difficult, or impossible, to tell how much the structural funds would have gone up or down by a different amount as a result of the introduction of the cohesion fund. So putting a bill specifically on Maastricht is, I think, not going to be possible.

264. I agree there has got to be a margin, but at the moment there is a fantastic difference between the Delors view of £14 billion in commitments made to be fulfilled and, I think if we take it globally, the figure of about £5 billion which is the

[**Mr Rowlands** *Contd*]

Treasury's and your evidence here. I do not know what the other 11 have in mind precisely at the moment, but do you not think we are going to have to have some order of magnitude of the expenditure increase as a result of Maastricht?

(Mr Jay) I think that if one looks at the views in other member states, there has been quite a widespread view amongst member states expressed at the discussion which took place at the Foreign Affairs Council earlier this week that it was quite wrong for the Commission's proposals to be seen as the bill for Maastricht, partly for the reasons I have explained and partly because expressing it in those terms may make it more difficult to ensure that the ratification procedure goes forward as most member states would like.

Chairman

265. Did some of the participants at the Maastricht discussions insist on there being expanded European social and cohesion funds as a condition to signing up on EMU?

(Mr Jay) Some member states made it quite clear that their main objective during the Inter-Governmental Conference was to ensure there was greater emphasis placed on cohesion, including a commitment to greater funds, but there was, as so often on these occasions, a powerful debate and a compromise solution. The compromise solution was agreement on a cohesion fund, but no commitment as to what that fund should be. That would be, it was agreed, decided during the course of the financing negotiations which have now just started.

Mr Lester

266. To be fair in terms of the negotiations, an open question is the assistance from the Community to Eastern Europe which surely has nothing whatever to do with the Maastricht agreement, but it is an attitude of high policy and great discussion at the moment with commissioners coming back from those parts of the world saying how desperately we need a Marshal Plan. It is impossible to link all that Monsieur Delors has asked for to Maastricht.

(Mr Jay) Indeed, and that is certainly true of the funds which Mr Delors proposes for the Community's external policies. It is also true for the funds he proposes for the common agricultural policy which again do not depend on the outcome of Maastricht, but will depend on the negotiations on reform of the common agricultural policy which is now in train.

Mr Rowlands

267. May we just briefly turn to what really follows on from this? We are now going to be faced with a 1996 review of Maastricht. When will negotiations begin on this? Have they already started, as it were, and what do you think is going to be on the agenda for those negotiations, aside from the financial issues?

(Mr Jay) One of the agreements at Maastricht was that there should be a further Inter-Governmental Conference in 1996 to consider certain specific points specified in the Maastricht Treaty, including the negative assent procedure, Article 189b, review of the defence article, Article J4 in the common foreign and security policy section, and review of the common foreign and security policy provisions generally. I have no doubt that when the time comes to prepare for the 1996 Inter-Governmental Conference, it will range more widely than that. That has been our experience in the past and I have no reason to suppose it will not be so again. The preparations for 1996 have not yet started. I would think that a review in 1996 would mean, and I am in a sense speculating here, that in 1995 there would be the beginnings of discussions about how the 1996 review should be carried forward and what it should contain.

Mr Shore

268. Back to the budget calculations of Monsieur Delors. Obviously agricultural policy plays a very important part in the forward estimate of expenditure. Do you know whether in his forward projection any allowance was made at all for an agreement with GATT on agricultural policy or has he assumed that no agreement will be made?

(Mr Jay) I think I am right in saying that the assumption behind the agricultural projections in Monsieur Delors' proposals is that the MacSharry proposals as now being discussed in the Community would be accepted.

Mr Jopling

269. But that does not really answer the question, does it, because the MacSharry proposals are distinct really from the GATT negotiations surely?

(Mr Jay) Yes, they are distinct. On the assumption that there is a GATT agreement, then certain further conclusions which will have implications for Community expenditure on agriculture will flow from them, but I think the judgment which the Commission made, as I understand it, was that at this stage in the CAP negotiations and at this stage in the GATT negotiations the only basis on which it was sensible to bring forward proposals for extra expenditure was on the basis of the MacSharry proposals which are on the table.

270. But the Community's approach to the GATT Round was to reduce agricultural subsidies by 30 per cent, as I recall, and the argument is whether or not the Community will agree something larger than that. I think Mr Shore's question was as to what has been written into the assessments or has nothing been written into the assessments as to what might emerge from the GATT Round?

(Mr Jay) I think the answer is that nothing has been written in. It has been done on the basis of the MacSharry proposals. I think that one of the problems which Ministers had with the proposals, Delors' proposals, is that they do envisage an

[*Mr Jopling Contd*]

increase in agricultural expenditure over time, whereas, as the Foreign Secretary made clear in the course of the Foreign Affairs Council earlier this week, most people are assuming that the result of the combination of the agricultural reform and a successful GATT outcome will be a reduction in agricultural expenditure.

Mr Harris

271. Surely the Commission's proposals or assessment is really based on nonsense, is it not, because nobody knows what is going to come out of GATT or MacSharry? It is a huge area of uncertainty here. It seems to me, listening to these exchanges, there is an enormous uncertainty here about the cost implications of Maastricht and deals with the Soviet Union, and I just wonder if ministers are aware of how this Parliament is going to react if ministers come to the House of Commons and say, "In effect we have got assessments but they are pretty meaningless". Do you feel in your contacts with ministers that they are aware of the likely reaction of the House of Commons?

(Mr Jay) I think that the questions you have asked, the doubts you are casting on the nature of the proposals which Mr Delors put forward, are precisely the questions being put and the doubts being cast by the Foreign Secretary in the discussions in Brussels on Monday.

Chairman: I think we must ask ministers about ministers' judgments.

Mr Harris: The fact of the matter is, on what we have heard today unless there is some attempt to find with reasonable precision these extra costs, the House of Commons is going to be asked to buy a pig in a poke.

Chairman: I think we shall hear more of that. Could we then pass on from this section to the nature of the beast. What have we really signed up to at Maastricht?

Mr Shore

272. This is a sort of mystery area. What I would like to explore, first, is what the Government understands by the term "European Union", which, after all, is a Treaty of Union? We have created the European Union, what is it?

(Mr Jay) Perhaps I could give an answer to that, first of all, and then ask Mr Eaton to give a more legal argument. The first point I would like to make is that the Union is *sui generis*; or, I should say, the European Union will be *sui generis*. As I think some expert legal witnesses have made clear to the Committee recently, we believe it would be a mistake to try to fit it into other models, whether the Community or a state or an international organisation like NATO or the United Nations, which itself has its own characteristics. As for those characteristics, I think it can best be characterised as an association of member states which, for certain purposes and in certain ways which are described in the Treaty, act in common; and the Union acts through the instrumentality of

its components, namely, the Community, on the one hand, and the member states acting inter-governmentally under the common foreign and security policy and interior/justice pillars, on the other hand. The Union itself is the concept which links these together as different ways of proceeding. Legally it will be the Community that acts under Community business, and the member states which will act under the other components—the common foreign and security policy and the interior/justice pillar.

273. That is an interesting answer but not an easy one to follow. Let me put this question: will the Union have a legal and internationally recognised legal personality?

(Mr Jay) Could I ask Mr Eaton to answer that question, Chairman.

(Mr Eaton) I would answer that in the negative, and I would point to a number of indicators on that. First of all, there is in the Union Treaty no provision, such as there is in Article 210 of the Treaty of Rome, which expressly says the Community shall have legal personality. There is no similar provision saying that the Union shall have legal personality. Secondly, the various functions that you would expect the Union to exercise if it did have such a legal personality are, in fact, exercised by the Community, which is an entity which undoubtedly does have legal personality. For example, all the provisions on concluding external treaties are actually provisions for the Community to conclude external treaties. They are in the Community parts of the Maastricht agreement and they give the Community that power. Similarly, citizenship, although it is called citizenship of the Union it is actually in the Community section of the treaties and it will be given effect by Community procedures and enforced by Community procedures. Those are some pointers on the actual face of the Treaty which I think bear out what I am saying, that it does not have legal personality in contrast to the Community. Also those indicators bear out what was a very clear intention during the negotiations on the part of the parties not to confer legal personality on the Union. During the negotiations this very question was raised, and the Dutch Presidency said very firmly that the Union would not have legal personality; they were supported clearly by the advice of the Director-General of Council Legal Services, and more recently I have noticed that the Director-General of the Commission Legal Services, Mr Dewost, has in public evidence given to the European Parliament himself also said that in the view of the Commission the Union lacks legal personality.

274. Let us take a practical example that might well illustrate the point. Supposing the Presidency, given its clear and active role in foreign policy, was to sign an agreement of, say, an alliance and friendship with another state, either in Europe or outside Europe. Would the Presidency be able to make such an agreement to begin with? If it was so

[**Mr Shore** *Contd*]

able, surely that would be an act of an internationally legal personality? Can, in fact, the Presidency enter into agreements and treaties?

(*Mr Eaton*) No, I would say it cannot.

275. If it wished to do so—after all, it is perfectly reasonable for a group of nations acting through a Presidency whose role is clearly defined elsewhere in the treaties—if it wished to make an agreement of any kind you are saying it would not be able to do so? Agreement would have to be made by the European Community as such?

(*Mr Eaton*) If we are talking about the kind of agreement you are talking about, which does not sound like an agreement that would be within the Community competence, then I think that would be an agreement between the member states and this third party. At the moment you have mixed agreements for example; you have mixed agreement between the Community and its member states and third countries. Quite a few of the association agreements are of this character. That is because quite a lot of their provisions are concerned with matters that are within Community competence, like trade and so forth, and other bits are not. It is the bits that are not where the member states are there in their own right as parties. That is what we are really talking about.

Mr Wells: Can you explain to us what this citizenship is going to be then?

Mr Shore: I would like to get this legal personality sorted out, first.

Mr Rowlands

276. I would like to make sure I have understood Mr Jay's description. Is it that we had the European Community and then along came a series of activities which are now inter-governmental and are under a separate pillar, and because you have now got this separate set of activities the Union is a description of both activities, the European Community now and inter-government, and the thing that has created the Union is the inter-governmental activity, is that right?

(*Mr Jay*) I think that is right, Mr Rowlands. There was the European Community and there were activities under European political cooperation which have now been extended and grouped together as a common foreign and security policy. There were activities going on in the interior justice field which have now been grouped together as the interior justice pillar; those remain as they always have been, inter-governmental; but the term "European Union" is used to describe the conglomeration of these activities but they have different legal personalities which means, as Mr Eaton was explaining, that they would be signed in different ways.

277. If, for example, in an inter-governmental foreign policy and security meeting and arrangements it is agreed to impose sanctions or take a particular action which requires enforcement of one kind or another, some legal activity, that will be done in the name of the inter-governmental

activity of the Union but then transferred to the Community, would it? With activity that is created under inter-governmental pillars and leads to decisions and possibly enforcement, does the legal personality involved in that stay with the Community, or what?

(*Mr Jay*) If the member states, acting together in common foreign and security policy, decided on an action such as economic sanctions which fell within the Treaty of Rome, then decisions would need to be taken on the basis of the appropriate article of the Treaty of Rome within the Community framework to put that into effect.

278. That is the Community legal personality?

(*Mr Jay*) That is the Community legal personality. That is in effect what happens now. That would not be a new development.

(*Mr Eaton*) It has been codified in Article 228A.

279. But if they took the activity outside the Treaty of Rome, how would that be given legal personality?

(*Mr Jay*) If, say, there was a discussion at the Foreign Affairs Council on relations with a third country which involved the Twelve agreeing to recognise that third country and at the same time to provide it with economic aid, then the economic aid would be given under the terms of the appropriate article of the Treaty of Rome and the recognition would be carried out by each member state taking what acts were necessary to recognise that state.

Mr Shore

280. Is that not a bogus distinction and would it not in fact lead to the merging of the two authorities in order to have or to pursue a consistent policy?

(*Mr Jay*) I do not see why it should. The legal entities are quite separate. There are separate legal procedures. The European Court of Justice has a very powerful role, as we know, within the Treaty of Rome. Acts taken inter-governmentally are not justiciable before the European Court of Justice and that is an important distinction between the two. The role of the Commission is distinct, whether it is within the Treaty of Rome or outside the Treaty of Rome. Mechanisms are now being developed for the common foreign and security policy and the interior and justice pillars which ensure the degree of coherence which is clearly needed, but which respect the different characteristics of the different pillars.

Chairman

281. Just on a practical matter, how distinct is the role of the Commission as between a meeting of the Council of Ministers within the Treaty of Rome and a meeting of the Council of Ministers discussing inter-governmental co-operation? Physically they still sit in the room and they still perform in the same way.

[**Chairman** *Contd*]

(Mr Jay) Physically they sit in the room, but if it is a question which comes within the terms of the Treaty of Rome, then the Commission have the sole right of initiative, the sole right to put forward proposals. If one is discussing, to go back to the analogy we were using just now, the recognition of a third country, then that is a question which will be decided by the member states and the Commission will, if they wish, have the right to speak or to put a proposal, as will all member states, but the decision will be taken by the member states.

Mr Shore

282. Could I turn now to the other aspects of the Union? To the immense surprise of several hundred million people in Western Europe, they are now citizens of a Union. What does this mean? Do they have obligations as citizens of this Union and do they have rights as citizens of this Union?

(Mr Eaton) Indeed the rights, Mr Chairman, are set out in the new Articles 8 to 8e inserted into the Treaty of Rome by the Maastricht agreement. They are a relatively limited series of rights and it is quite clearly stated at the outset that this citizenship of the Union depends on someone having, first, the nationality of a member state and whether that person has the nationality of the member state or not is a matter of the domestic law of that member state and that is made expressly clear in the Declaration. It is not really like a true case of dual nationality because in fact what is happening is that you are adding on to an existing nationality of a member state a certain number of rights which are described as the rights adhering to citizenship of the Union and they are freedom of movement, which is of course already an existing right in the Treaty of Rome, then there is voting in municipal and European elections and then there is consular protection in third countries and there is the possibility of perhaps adding more rights, but, as I am sure you will have noted, that is subject to two fairly high hurdles. One is you have first got to get unanimity and the second is you have got to have ratification on the part of each member state.

283. The freedom of movement which is listed as one of the rights, that includes, does it, is it so stated, the freedom to reside anywhere in the Community?

(Mr Eaton) Yes, that is correct, and that follows on from the three Directives on the rights of residence which were agreed in June of 1990 and it in fact codifies those. You will notice that Article 8a in the first paragraph does say that the right to move and reside freely is expressly made subject to the limitations and conditions in the Treaty, not only in the Treaty, but in the measures adopted to give it effect, and that was an express reference, although it is not spelt out, to these rights of residence Directives which do contain a certain number of conditions, such as adequacy of resources, so that those who come to reside, for example, students or pensioners who did not have the right

before, should not become a burden on the social security systems of the host member state.

Mr Rowlands

284. So if they did not have enough money, that would be a legitimate case for refusing them residency?

(Mr Eaton) Exactly.

Mr Wells

285. So this is a citizenship of a non-legal personality, is it? Have we arrived at that triumphant conclusion?

(Mr Eaton) As I think I tried to explain before, the instrumentality through which the citizenship of the Union is given effect is the Community, so there will be Community enforcement if somebody thinks that he is not being given his rights. If, when the voting rules are all there, somebody from Spain is refused the right to vote in a municipal election in France, then he could go to the Court of Justice and say, "I am not being given my rights". So it is called citizenship of the Union, but it is given effect through the Community.

Mr Lester

286. He also has the right to petition the European Parliament and appeal to the European ombudsman?

(Mr Eaton) That is absolutely correct, but in fact so does anybody who is resident in the Community, so that is not a very substantial change.

Mr Harris

287. So after all is done, what is actually new here? What are the new additional rights confirmed by this section of the Treaty?

(Mr Eaton) The voting one and the consular protection one.

288. Voting in municipal elections?

(Mr Eaton) Voting in municipal elections and elections for the European Parliament.

289. But the right to stand for the European Parliament in another country, of course, presumably already exists because I think a Member of this House actually did it in Italy, did he not, a former leader of the Liberal Party?

(Mr Eaton) That is right. I should have made it clear it is not just voting, but to stand as a candidate. That is absolutely right.

Mr Rowlands

290. Some of the European Community members, Spain, for example, for historic reasons have an open-door policy towards people from Latin America. They feel an historic obligation. Presumably if that population enters Spain under Spanish immigration rules and resides in Spain at any future date, they would inherit the rights of

[Mr Rowlands *Contd*]

residents in the rest of the Community? Is that right?

(*Mr Eaton*) So long as they are Spanish nationals, yes, that is right. The United Kingdom has made a declaration on who are its nationals for Community purposes since we have a somewhat more complicated nationality law than most other member states and that continues to have effect.

Mr Shore

291. Is that declaration one of the protocols of the Treaty?

(*Mr Eaton*) No. We originally made one on accession in 1972 and we revised it in 1983.

Mr Rowlands

292. But if somebody from Bolivia or a large number of people from Bolivia or elsewhere in South America come into Spain under their historic open-door policy and then acquire Spanish nationality, and I do not know what is required to do that, then they would qualify for residency, but not until they had actually acquired Spanish nationality?

(*Mr Eaton*) Absolutely right.

Mr Shore

293. There is an interaction between the two halves of the question brought forward in the last statement. You are entitled to consular protection, what on earth does that mean when the consular protection is afforded by something which is not an internationally recognised legal personality?

(*Mr Eaton*) The consular protection will actually be given by the consulate of a member state. If there is no British Consulate in a particular country but there is a German one and there is a Briton in distress he can go to the German Consulate and say, "Please protect me".

294. The government of the country in which they are dealing would have no particular reason to take any notice of that. They are not dealing with an internationally recognised personality but dealing with a German whose consulate has apparently decided to look after another European national?

(*Mr Eaton*) That is why the relevant article says that member states shall establish the necessary rules among themselves and start the international negotiations necessary to secure this protection. It is quite right, as you say, that the host member state in such a case would not have an obligation to do this, to recognise that somebody else can act as the protector; you have to negotiate it and that is recognised.

Chairman

295. Would that require some new laws?

(*Mr Eaton*) It will certainly require rules among ourselves and negotiations with other countries. Whether it requires legislation here I somehow doubt but we need to think about that.

Chairman: I think we can now move on to common foreign and security policy questions. I want to postpone the security issues, particularly in relation to the WEU, because although I am anxious generally to finish at 12.00 I know that one of our witnesses, Mr Jay, must be released very soon after 12.00. Perhaps we could come back to defence issues specifically a little later and look merely at the foreign policy aspect at the moment.

Mr Lester

296. We have been discussing some joint actions in the common foreign policy, but what I would like to ask you is what other types of joint action in the common foreign policy is Britain hoping to see *vis-a-vis* particular countries or groups of countries? From our experience of Yugoslavia are we satisfied that the mechanisms for agreeing a common foreign policy work quickly enough at times of international crisis?

(*Mr Jay*) It is difficult to be specific about the forms of joint action that we may see because, clearly, they will need to be tailored to the needs of the circumstances. What we expect to happen from now on is that there will be a report to the European Council at Lisbon on the development of common foreign and security policy, including procedures for joint action, which we would envisage would enumerate certain areas which would be susceptible for joint action. These could be quite broad areas which would in theory be susceptible to joint action. Whether or not there would then be joint action would be decided at a later stage—obviously all of this would be after the Treaty comes into effect—by the Foreign Affairs Council acting unanimously. As for what forms of joint action those might be, as I say, I think it is hard to say. I would envisage that to start with the Twelve will tend to decide on joint action in those areas where they already act extremely closely together. Yugoslavia is one example. I think there is one other example of something which is going on now but which could equally well be joint action and that is the representation of the Twelve in the Middle East peace conference, in which a contact group of the Middle Eastern experts in each foreign ministry meet regularly, either in Brussels or in the place where the Middle East conference is taking place, in order to decide the line that the Twelve shall take at the conference, and that line has then to be expressed by the Presidency. The Troika also has a role in this process. That is a rather different example from Yugoslavia but an example of the sort of activity one could expect to see as joint action develops. As for the question of whether or not a joint action can react quickly in a crisis, I think the mechanisms exist for that. There is the COREU system which enables information to be exchanged extremely quickly amongst all member states. The Treaty envisages that ministers should meet within 48 hours when a crisis emerges to decide on action; and the Yugoslav precedent suggests that it is possible to get ministers together extremely quickly when there is a need to do so. We ourselves have suggested that there should be a crisis unit, or an emergency unit, as part of the

[**Mr Lester** *Contd*]

expanded political co-operation secretariat that we want to see set up, again to help the quickness of response to a crisis. The mechanisms, I think, exist and are developing to enable the Twelve to respond quickly to a crisis. That does not guarantee that they will, because that of course will depend on the political will to do so; but that too is developing.

297. What difference will the provision in the Treaty that suggests that "member states shall co-ordinate their action in international organisations and at international conferences. They shall uphold the common positions in such fora" make to our relationship both with the Commonwealth and indeed to the United Nations?

(Mr Jay) I cannot see that that will make any difference to our relations with the Commonwealth. If there were a joint action which was relevant to an issue which came up, say, at a Commonwealth conference, then we would wish to speak in accordance with that; but we would not have agreed to the joint action in the first place unless we were prepared to speak in accordance with it in international fora. As far as the United Nations is concerned, again I would not expect us to agree to a joint action if we were not prepared to speak in accordance with that joint action, but there is a clause, Article J5 of the common foreign and security policy, which makes clear that members of the Union who are members of the UN Security Council will not be obliged to do anything which in any way offends against their obligations under the UN Charter. The position is protected there, which is one of the points which we and the French were keen to see included in the Maastricht Treaty.

298. Have we experience of working so far, before this Treaty, giving different countries the lead in the sense of their historical connection—I mean ourselves with the Commonwealth and the French with their ex-colonies and so on—so that we move around amongst the Twelve giving individual countries the lead in any particular foreign policy initiative and then trying to get agreement from the others who perhaps do not have the depth of knowledge that any one country might have of a specific situation?

(Mr Jay) I think that happens in practice. The formal position is that the Presidency presents the position but if there is a member state which has a particular interest or knowledge of a country that would often make the running and others will do their best to make sure that they support it.

299. It can be seen as a growing influence backing historical connections to the good?

(Mr Jay) Yes, indeed.

Chairman

300. Generally in this area, while obviously the hope would be that matters could be done better by member states working together than apart on certain issues, is there anything in what we are signing up to at Maastricht which will restrain individual member states from pursuing their own foreign policy interests in specific areas as well?

(Mr Jay) There is a stronger obligation in the common foreign and security policy than there was under the political co-operation. For example, for the language of endeavour has been substituted the language of obligation in certain areas, but no positions or actions can be taken on anything of substance except by unanimity. Therefore, if we were not prepared to follow a common position or carry out a joint action it would be open to us or any member state not to accept it in the first place.

301. To use a practical example, and it may be difficult to answer this, if we were drawn into another Falklands campaign this time round would we have to do anything different from the kind of efforts we made back in 1982 when we sought to get the support of Europe but we did it our own way?

(Mr Jay) We would certainly hope, I am sure, that we would get support from our Community partners as we did last time for actions which we took, but there is also a clause in the CFSP articles, for example—Article J6—which provides that in case of imperative need arising from changes in a situation and failing a Council decision, member states may take the necessary actions and measures as a matter of urgency. There are a number of clauses here which enable a member state effectively to safeguard its own activities if there is an urgent need to do so.

Chairman: I would now like to move on to the machinery or the implications of Maastricht for the machinery of the Community itself and indeed the Union.

Mr Wells

302. Mr Jay, could you tell us whether you have been able to make any progress on the membership and staffing of the European Council, the secretariat of the Council for Foreign and Security Policy?

(Mr Jay) Discussions are going on amongst the Twelve at the moment on the machinery which we shall want to see in place both for CFSP and for interior and justice. The consensus is forming in favour of an expanded EPC secretariat which will form part of the Council Secretariat which will be manned mainly by diplomats seconded from member states and which will, therefore, retain its specific character, though forming part of the Council Secretariat to ensure that there is a proper coherence between the activities of the Community and the activities of the CFSP pillar. The same is under discussion and the same consensus being reached on the handling of the new secretariat for the interior and justice pillar.

303. Therefore, by whom will these people be paid and to whom will they be responsible if they are not part of the European Council of Ministers' secretariat?

(Mr Jay) They will be part of the Council Secretariat. They will be seconded from member states, but will form part of the Council Secretariat

[**Mr Wells** *Contd*]

and, although I do not think this has formally been agreed yet, the Secretariat has proposed that they would be financed from the Council Secretariat budget.

Mr Lester

304. For the period of their secondment.

(*Mr Jay*) For the period of their secondment, yes.

Mr Wells

305. How long will these secondments be for? How separate will they be in reality from the general staff of the Council of Ministers?

(*Mr Jay*) They will be there for two or three years. That would have to be decided. They would be diplomats from member states, they would be on secondment to the Council Secretariat and they would be acting as an inter-governmental secretariat within the Council Secretariat.

306. Do you see a danger of them becoming indistinguishable from other servants of the Council of Ministers?

(*Mr Jay*) No, I do not because they will feel different being there on secondment. They will not feel that their whole career lies as being a part of the Council Secretariat. They will also be servicing committees which act in a different way as part of the inter-governmental mechanism from their colleagues in the Council Secretariat who will be serving committees which are part of the Council machinery.

307. Could you explain then the expected future relationship between that part of the Council secretariat responsible for foreign and security policy, the Committee of Permanent Representatives to the Community, which we always refer to by that ugly word "COREPER", and the Political Committee, sometimes called "COPO", and the Commission?

(*Mr Jay*) The discussions are continuing on the precise relationship between COREPER and the Political Committee, but we would envisage—and I think again there is a growing consensus—in favour of the Political Committee remaining responsible for the formulation of the issues of substance in common foreign and security policy, preparing the work for the Foreign Affairs Council insofar as it relates to common foreign and security policy and carrying out decisions made by the Foreign Affairs Council insofar as it covers common foreign and security policy—but we would envisage that in preparing the agenda for a Foreign Affairs Council, COREPER would want to look not just at those issues which fall under Community business, but at the issues which are going to come before Ministers as part of the common foreign and security policy to ensure that there was a proper coherence and that ministerial discussions were properly organised.

Mr Jopling

308. But recalling the British representation in the secretariat of the Commission over the years where we have lost out very seriously because we did not fill the posts which were open to us, which was a major error on our part in the 1970s and afterwards, there is no danger that the numbers of people who have been within the Commission secretariat will be used as a key for this secretariat and there will be a fair sharing out between the member states of posts in the new secretariat, I hope?

(*Mr Jay*) We would certainly envisage that there would be and we would regard it as an extremely important part of certainly the Foreign Office's posting policy to ensure that good people went from the Foreign Office to fill those jobs in that secretariat.

309. And in sufficient quantities too?

(*Mr Jay*) The quantities would depend on the size of the secretariat, and what was agreed about the number of representatives each member state would have, but again we would certainly want to see that we were as fully represented as we could be in that secretariat.

310. There would be a determination that we would not fall into the errors of the past with regards to the Commission?

(*Mr Jay*) There would, Mr Jopling, although I just would like to add that so far as there were errors of the past, I think they have, at least to some extent, been corrected in the last few years through measures such as the arrangements for the European fast stream where we are training young civil servants to be able to take and pass the exams for entrance into the European Community institutions for precisely the reasons Mr Jopling mentioned.

Chairman: Could we now look at the interior and justice matters and how they will work?

Mr Lester

311. We have been very strong on pillars and inter-governmentalism and we have claimed it is a great success as a result of our negotiations in Maastricht, but there are those who have given us evidence who say that this is only a temporary phase and that particularly interior and justice matters will sooner or later come within the competence of the Commission. Do you have any views on that and, more importantly, do we have any reflection of the views of other Member States as to whether they see this as a temporary phase or whether they see this particular area as one which will remain inter-governmental?

(*Mr Jay*) On the first point, I think that the Treaty does distinguish quite clearly in legal terms between the pillars and the Treaty of Rome and the administrative arrangements, which we were discussing just now of separate secretariats with their own characteristics, will apply to the interior and justice as well as to the common foreign and

[*Mr Lester Contd*]

security policy pillar, so there is a clear distinction. Now, the Maastricht Treaty envisages that areas of interior and justice which are now under inter-governmental co-operation could move into Community competence if there were unanimous agreement of all member states to do that and if there were ratification by each parliament to do that. Some member states, to answer your last question, would like to see such a move into Community competence. That is one of the issues which will be discussed certainly in 1996 and in one or two areas probably before that and that would be for decision by Member States nearer the time, but I think that all member states accept that the interior and justice pillar is a distinct pillar with its distinct arrangements and are preparing to operate the pillar on that basis.

312. Particularly considering the debate we had on Monday on immigration and asylum, that must be one of those areas of contention in the sense that it also links into citizenship which is already part of the competence of the Commission.

(*Mr Jay*) There were one or two member states who wanted in the Inter-Governmental Conference to see asylum brought within Community competence, but there was a very large majority against that.

Chairman

313. Could we move on again to what was the most politically prominent aspect of the whole Maastricht meeting and that was the agreement on a very specific timetable to move to economic and monetary union with an opt-in provision arranged for this country. What information do you have, Mr Jay, or your colleagues, about the attitudes of other member states to this timetable? Do you think that they all think it will be achieved as planned in the Treaty, although it is five years ahead, but by 1997 or 1999 we will go into stage 3?

(*Mr Jay*) I am hesitant to comment in any detail, Chairman, on matters of economic and monetary union, which I think are really for ministers and, in particular, for the Treasury. I think all I would want to say in reply to that question is that one must presume it is the clear intention of member states to reach the third stage of economic and monetary union either in 1997 or certainly in 1999, for which there will be an automatic entry into stage three for those member states which are judged to meet the convergence criteria laid down in the Treaty.

314. You must have noticed reports from Bonn that the Bundestag is now laying down conditions before it gives its agreement to going ahead with stage three of monetary union. Does that now somehow imply that what is said to be irrevocable, and what has been locked into a laid down timetable, in fact is going to be conditional upon democratic agreement in legislatures, not just this one here but also in Bonn?

(*Mr Jay*) I would not want to comment. I have seen those reports, and I would not want to comment on the exact state of the debate in Germany. I think it was something of a surprise to some of us that more member states were not concerned about the need for parliaments to have a say before movement towards the final stage of economic and monetary union.

315. Do you get the impression, in trying to make a policy assessment for the future to advise ministers, that this concern is growing and that countries are now beginning to have a debate which perhaps they did not have earlier?

(*Mr Jay*) It would be for my Treasury colleagues to advise ministers on economic and monetary union.

316. Let me broaden it from monetary union to the whole Maastricht *mélange*.

(*Mr Jay*) On the broader question, we do see signs of a debate preceding ratification in member states of the sort of debate that we had before the European Council of Maastricht. There are reports one reads of sentiment in Germany, and one or two other countries as well, in which the attitude towards continuing integration is being questioned perhaps more than it has been in the past. How far that is a lasting phenomenon I think is extremely hard to judge.

317. Just a final question on this. If the Bundestag can now say, "We won't agree to stage three until we have reviewed and debated it further", and that is what this Parliament thinks is its own position, why did we need a protocol at Maastricht to secure this right if the Germans can just take it for themselves as they wish?

(*Mr Jay*) Ministers wanted it to be absolutely clear beyond peradventure that that was the position and that was the right of this Parliament. As I understand the Treaty, there is an automaticity built into the move to stage three in terms of the Treaty for those member states who do not have this right.

Chairman: It does not sound as if the automaticity news has got to the Bundestag, does it!

Mr Rowlands

318. Following very much on your questions and dealing with EMU as an illustration, you told us earlier on that the protocols are a part of the Treaty and in any form of ratification you ratify the protocols as well. The protocol on EMU is very clear, a declared and irreversible character, the Community's move to the third stage and the timetable. There can be no way, can there, that the German Bundestag can ratify this conditionally and say, "We're going to make a condition of our ratification that the protocol on EMU is changed", or "we're not bound by the timetable on this protocol"?

(*Mr Jay*) A member state can only ratify the Treaty which it has signed. The Treaty which all member states have signed has in it the protocol to which you have referred. If any member state, as a result of the actions of its parliament, wished to

[*Mr Rowlands Contd*]

seek some change in these protocols or other parts of the Treaty then that would have to be for discussion amongst all member states. The existing process of ratification and coming into force will be brought into question.

319. The Bundestag in the end has got to be faced with ratifying the Treaty as it stands and cannot place any reasonably worded conditions upon its ratification?

(*Mr Jay*) I would not want to comment on what the Bundestag could or should do, only about the consequences of what it might do. If the Treaty, as signed by the German government, were not ratified by the Bundestag and the Bundesrat with the majorities that were required, then the question of whether or not the German government could ratify the Treaty would be one they wish to consider.

Chairman: Subsidiarity—another aspect about which we have heard a great deal.

Mr Rowlands

320. This Committee has followed the issue of subsidiarity from its earliest days and, with the introduction into the Treaty of Article 3b, we wonder how it is going to affect the United Kingdom's approach to the development of Community policies. How will the UK Government set about making sure the article works? Has it got some plans and thoughts on how to turn this article into a series of specific policy measures, issues or mechanisms?

(*Mr Jay*) I think that the aim must be to ensure that the climate of opinion in the Commission and the Council changes so that respect for subsidiarity becomes a habit of mind amongst the Community institutions. That is what we hope will happen. The aim of the subsidiarity clause, as the Committee knows, is to make sure a decision should only be taken by the Community when it cannot be taken effectively at the level of the member states. That downward pressure on decision-making can happen in a number of different ways. It can happen by the deterrent effect on the Commission in coming forward with appropriate proposals. That, I think is where what one is already seeing and hearing is encouraging. Certainly from our own private conversations with the Commission, and perhaps from some of the conversations that the Committee has had too, we gain the impression that the concept of subsidiarity is being taken seriously within the Commission, and greater attention is being given to this concept in deciding whether or not to put forward proposals. To that extent I think it is already working. If an inappropriate proposal comes forward then it would be for member states in the Council to argue against a proposal on the grounds that it infringed subsidiarity. If it still went forward then, ultimately, there is the prospect of a case before the European Court. I think that the main area in which we would hope to work would be on persuading the members of the Commission, staff of the Commission cand other member states of the

importance of ensuring that subsidiarity is taken into account at the earliest possible stage of formulating legislation.

321. I appreciate what you are saying. You are trying to create an environment to policy-making and decision-making which has subsidiarity built into it and those are very good general words, but when it comes down to it what is going to happen? For example, in the presidency in the next six months are we going to try to make something of subsidiarity in that six months? We have heard suggestions that we could draw up a list of things to repatriate back to nation states, as it were. Do you think there is an initiative on that side which you could do?

(*Mr Jay*) I think it is going to be harder to roll back the *acquis communautaire* than it is to ensure that we do not, in the future, have proposals coming forward which offend against subsidiarity. As for the position in our presidency, I should stress that although it is very encouraging that the Commission at the moment seems to be respecting the principle of subsidiarity it will not actually have legal force until the Treaty comes into effect in 1993.

322. Are you envisaging, as an adminstration that supports subsidiarity, preparing a guideline on subsidiarity which you will try to negotiate through the Community, so you have a further clarification of how subsidiarity can apply and work?

(*Mr Jay*) I think I would like to reflect on that suggestion. For the moment what we have got to try to do is to persuade the Commission to take the concepts seriously.

323. We were told last week by one of our witnesses that, in the end, it will be the European Court of Justice that is the only real effective backstop in this matter. A number of us were pointing out, indeed the witness himself pointed out, that in fact the ECJ has tended to have an expansive view about Community powers and responsibilities rather than a restrictive one in many regards. We were rather worried that we were going to be very dependent upon a Court of Justice that may not exactly be buying subsidiarity in philosophical or decision-making terms.

(*Mr Jay*) The European Court of Justice certainly would be a backstop. Mr Eaton may want to comment a little more on that, but I do think that the success or failure of the clause on subsidiarity will be seen not by whether it goes to the European Court of Justice and what the European Court of Justice decides, but by changing the climate of opinion so that proposals do not come forward which would have to be challenged before the European Court of Justice at the end of the day.

Chairman: Could we move on to the Conference of the Parliaments which gets an honourable mention in the Maastricht Treaty?

Mr Wells

324. What steps have been taken since the signature on Maastricht to work out how the Conference of Parliaments might work, what its role would be and how it would relate to the other Community institutions?

(Mr Jay) I think we regard this as primarily a matter for the Parliament and the parliaments themselves rather than for governments or for civil servants to involve themselves in. Could I ask Mr Arthur to say a little bit more about where we stand on the Conference of Parliaments?

(Mr Arthur) Thank you, Chairman. What I think is clear from the face of the Declaration itself, which of course does not come into force until after the Treaty is in force anyway, but it is clear from the face of that that the initiative for convening any conference would lie with the parliaments concerned, which is 13 parliaments, the European Parliament plus the Twelve. As I understand it, there have been some contacts on a parliamentary basis already about the possibility of having such a conference during this year. But I am not sure those have got very far advanced yet and they are still preliminary soundings.

325. Was it envisaged that the European Parliament would be included in every meeting of this Conference of Parliaments or would it be possible for the national parliaments to meet separately from the European Parliament?

(Mr Arthur) As I understand it, the actual beast called the "Conference of Parliaments" would indeed always involve the European Parliament as well as the 12 national parliaments, but there have been in the past arrangements between, for example, the scrutiny committees in the different parliaments who do not, I think, necessarily meet with the European Parliament present. But that is a slightly separate procedural arrangement to the Conference of Parliaments as set out in the Declaration attached to the Maastricht Treaty.

326. Well, such a meeting obviously needs a secretariat, just as your common foreign and security policy meetings require a secretariat as you have just outlined. What arrangements have been made for a secretariat to convene this Conference of Parliaments or are we relying on the European Parliament to do that?

(Mr Arthur) So far no arrangements have been made. There is only one precedent, and it is not a direct precedent, which was the Assizes in Rome a year and a half ago where in fact, as I recall, most of the hosting was done by the Italian Parliament and they provided some of the support for that, but I think the European Parliament was also brought in to provide some facilities like translation facilities and so on. No new arrangements have been made for the next round of this conference.

Chairman

327. Am I not right that qualified majority voting as a procedure is in fact in the Maastricht Treaty proposed to be extended into some aspects of the implementation of common foreign policy and is it the intention or is it the view of the Government or of you, as advisers to the Government, that the European Parliament will, therefore, have some defined role of calling those decisions to account or is it your thought that the European Parliament should focus entirely on the Rome Treaty, the supranational aspects of European affairs, and it is this Conference of Parliaments which should focus on the inter-governmental side?

(Mr Jay) Perhaps I could answer that, Chairman. Of course there is a provision for qualified majority voting in the common foreign and security policy, a provision that there could be unanimous decision that certain decisions are to be taken by qualified majority voting. The understanding is that those would be quite narrowly-defined implementing measures, not matters of policy. On the question of the European Parliament, the common foreign and security policy envisages that there would be, I think, consultation with the European Parliament, informing and consulting the European Parliament, but there is no suggestion in the relevant article of the common foreign and security policy that the European Parliament should have the sort of role in decision-making in CFSP as it has under the cooperation procedure or the negative assent procedure for decisions taken by qualified majority voting within the Treaty of Rome.

Mr Wells

328. But, therefore, this Conference of Parliaments would not be able to intervene or interpose itself between the European Parliament on matters for which it has got power under the Treaty of Rome and its amendments, so they could not discuss those kind of matters, could they, but what could they discuss? Presumably they would be confined to the issues of the pillars.

(Mr Arthur) As I understand it, I think the Conference could discuss and debate whatever it chose to discuss and debate. Indeed the Declaration says that the President of the Commission and the President of the Council will report to it on the state of the Union, as it were, but your words were, I think, to "interpose itself" between the European Parliament and the Council on Community business and it is certainly my understanding of the case that it might very well debate issues, say, relating to the co-operation procedure, but it would not have a formal role under the Treaty of Rome in that area. But there would be nothing to preclude it debating that if the Conference so chose.

Mr Lester

329. When we were in Germany we got the distinct impression that the German Lander had a

[Mr Lester Contd]

very big influence on the setting up of a Committee of the Regions and I wondered if you could tell us whether any other countries had an equal say in the desire to establish this body. What areas of policy would you imagine this Committee would actually advise on and have we got anywhere near sorting out our own regions and how we would appoint the 24 members we are entitled to on to this Committee?

(Mr Arthur) Chairman, if I may, the Treaty itself specifies that the Committee will have an advisory role. In certain areas of policy it is to be consulted. For example, in education, culture, health, networks and cohesion it shall be consulted. It may be consulted on other areas if the Council wishes that to happen and indeed it may volunteer opinions itself, but I emphasise the word "opinions" because the Committee does have an advisory capacity rather than a formal legislative role. As to the establishment of it, thinking is beginning within the British Government about how our 24 members should be appointed, but no decisions have been taken and of course there is quite a long time ahead because it does not begin to operate until next January at the earliest, which is a long time.

330. It is actually quite a sensitive issue whether we regard our regions as Scotland, Ireland, Wales and England or whether we think of county councils, district councils, town councils or all the bally lot.

(Mr Arthur) It is for the member states themselves to decide who and how they appoint their 24 members and so it will be decisions to be taken by the United Kingdom, but I am afraid those decisions have not yet been taken.

Mr Lester: Knowing how coherent they are in terms of domestic policy, it will be quite interesting to see whom they ally with in any Committee of the Regions when they are trying to comment on European policy.

Mr Rowlands

331. Are you saying that the article involved does not at least define the general terms of who should turn up?

(Mr Arthur) No. As I understand it, it is for the member states themselves to come forward with their list which will be formally appointed by the Council in the way it happens for the Economic and Social Committee. Member states themselves will decide who it is they put forward.

332. It is the national governments who will appoint their delegation, as it were?

(Mr Arthur) In effect.

333. Therefore it would be possible to send 24 civil servants to this Committee?

(Mr Arthur) I think, subject to what Mr Eaton says, that would legally be one possibility, yes.

334. I thought it was supposed to be representative. Is the word "representative" interpreted not in any democratic way but purely people chosen by the government of the day?

(Mr Arthur) To be representatives of regional and local bodies, that is the phrase used in the Treaty.

335. It would have to have be representative of some unit of local government in Britain?

(Mr Arthur) Of regional or local bodies.

Chairman

336. Does it knock out the Economic and Social Council?

(Mr Arthur) No, that Committee will continue in parallel and they will share some facilities. That is the plan for the future, but the details of that have yet to be resolved.

337. Do you envisage it being run in the same sort of ambience as the Economic and Social Council, with the same kind of set-up, the same kind of semi-parliamentary chamber they have in Brussels and that sort of thing?

(Mr Arthur) There are certain differences, even on the face of the Treaty. The Committee of the Regions will be consulted on the areas that I mentioned and, of course, under the Treaty itself the Economic and Social Committee is divided into three different blocks of representatives. Its function is to have those three different ones, so that may in itself affect the nature of the debates and how they operate in producing their opinions, because they will be structured slightly differently. Of course it will be for the Committee itself, I think, to define how it organises its work as and when it is appointed.

Mr Jopling

338. Which Minister within, let us say, the British Cabinet do you envisage would have an overall responsibility for this new Committee?

(Mr Arthur) I am not sure I have a clear answer to that. It is probably something you ought to ask ministers rather than us.

339. There is no thought that the Foreign Office should have responsibility for it?

(Mr Arthur) In all the memoranda we put to Parliament we say that the Secretary of State for Foreign and Commonwealth Affairs has overall responsibility for policy towards the Community, but individual areas of policy obviously fall to different ministers as appropriate.

340. In that the Minister of Agriculture looks after the Common Agricultural Policy and so on, do you imagine the Secretary of State for Trade and Industry would be responsible for this particular one?

(Mr Arthur) A range of ministers will have direct interests.

Mr Lester

341. The Scottish Office, Welsh Office and Northern Ireland?

(Mr Arthur) Yes, the Scottish Office, Welsh Office and Northern Ireland Office. There will be a range of ministries which will have a direct interest in this.

Mr Jopling

342. I am wondering which one will be the lead?

(Mr Arthur) It is not a question I find very easy to answer.

Mr Lester

343. From what we have seen in other parts of Europe regional government is far more powerful in both its elected representatives, the role that it plays, and in Germany and France the role it plays in actually appointing national parliamentarians to the Bundesrat and the French Sénat, and I just wonder whether you feel, in terms of looking at the future of this body that element will be infinitely more powerful than the sort of structures that we have in this country which tend to be, dependent on which way we go, purely local government without any of the overriding powers involved in national policies?

(Mr Arthur) The role of this Committee is relatively limited as defined in the Maastricht Treaty. It seems to me quite possible that some Member States will want to review that in the 1996 IGC. I think you yourself mentioned earlier, the German Government have taken a strong interest in this Committee. It seems quite likely that it will be looked at again next time round. As I said at the beginning, it has a relatively limited function as of now.

Mr Rowlands

344. Just to get it absolutely clear, it would therefore be possible within the terms of the articles of the Treaty for the Secretary of State for Wales to appoint one of his own civil servants to be a representative on the Committee. It regards the Welsh Office as a regional body and it does not specify that the person concerned ought to have any democratic credentials at all, is that right?

(Mr Arthur) The Treaty says that members of the Committee shall be representatives of regional and local bodies, whatever that phrase may mean. It goes on to say that they shall be independent in the performance of their duties, which is a clear injunction on anybody appointed.

345. That last caveat might rule out a person in the Welsh Office, who could not be seen to be independent of the Government?

(Mr Arthur) That is a hypothetical question.

Chairman: Unless being represented by the Secretary of State for Wales. Could we finally turn to our defence issues and utilise the presence of Mr Goulden, who I am afraid has been waiting in the wings this morning. I hope he does not think we have wasted too much of his valuable time. We do want him to share his views on some of the defence aspects that have come up.

Mr Jopling

346. What we would like to ask is about the future role for WEU. I wonder if we could be told what progress has been made over evolving that new role; what has been happening; what are likely to be the next stages; how soon is WEU likely to move to Brussels; and, also, whether you could tell us what the attitude of the United States has been, which is crucial, to the emerging new role for WEU?

(Mr Goulden) Thank you, Mr Jopling. I think the action in the WEU really falls under three main headings: one is how to organise the transfer to Brussels and the new relationship which the WEU, with its extra activities, will have with the two bodies to which it will have to relate—the Community on the one hand and the Alliance on the other. A lot of issues are being thrashed out at the moment about the feasibility of moving before the end of the year. I would guess the end of the year looks like the most likely target for getting to Brussels. Who will make up the Council in Brussels? In London it is made up of bilateral ambassadors. The thought is that in Brussels it would be done in a different way. The Council would be made up either of NATO permanent representatives, double-hatted, or Community representatives, double-hatted, or some other alternative. As you can imagine, there is a lot of theology involved in these issues, and about how the WEU itself will relate to the Secretariat and the presidencies of the Community and the Alliance. One issue which is perhaps for the longer term but is a very interesting one, is what should be the WEU's relationship in the future with the other European bodies that have analogous functions—the Euro Group and the Independent European Programme Group which does defence procurement. There is a lot of talk about perhaps brigading those more closely with the WEU. The second big issue is enlargement of the WEU's membership following the declaration of Maastricht, which said that Community members could become full members or observers and that other NATO European allies could become associate members. That is a pretty difficult subject, not made any easier by the fact that the WEU Treaty itself is not entirely up-to-date; and some articles of it are more relevant to today's world than others. The key problems are, firstly what happens to Article 5, the WEU Treaty Defence guarantee, who would benefit from that and who would not, and how would Article 5, relate between members and associate members? Secondly, in what circumstances can associates participate? Maastricht said they would be able to participate fully in the activities of the WEU, and it is very much the view of our Government that they should be able to do so. Clearly, they will not necessarily participate in every activity. There will be occasions when one

[Mr Jopling *Contd*]

can imagine the WEU Council full members might want to meet by themselves. Deciding the circumstance in which that can happen is actually a rather sensitive one for the prospective new members and new associate members. The third issue, which is in concrete terms perhaps the most important, is what do we mean by making forces available to the WEU, which is an important part of the Maastricht Declaration. There is a lot of discussion about which forces will be "declared" to the WEU, how they will be organised, how they might be commanded and mobilised in the event of an activity run by the WEU. Our view is that it would make sense for a very wide range of forces to be available, but those forces should all participate on the basis of equality and with absolute transparency between them. They should all come under the same planning cell in Brussels and most of them, we assume, will be double-hatted with forces in NATO. There would obviously be close co-ordination between the WEU planning cell and the NATO planning authorities. Those are the three broad areas. You asked about the United States attitude. The United States attitude has in principle been benign and encouraging to the development of the WEU, although the United States officials and ministers recognise that there will be interface problems between the WEU and NATO. We shall have to make sure we handle those in a sensible way. The Americans do not want, for example, to be confronted by WEU positions on a take-it-or-leave-it basis. They do not want the Europeans to get involved in scraps which might then involve NATO without NATO having been consulted. Those are problems we are all well aware of and I think they can be handled perfectly satisfactorily. In general the United States attitude is encouraging.

Chairman

347. Does the Government have a view on the future of the WEU Parliamentary Assembly?

(Mr Goulden) No, and it was not referred to in the WEU Declaration. I think that is very much a matter for the Assembly to decide for itself.

Mr Rowlands

348. As I have listened to the evidence, I wonder if in fact during the whole of 1993 we find that in various parliaments and various constitutions of the Twelve the Maastricht Treaty is being held up, failing to be ratified at least in the timescale envisaged that it will come into operation in 1993, what are the operational consequences of a delay of 12 months or more in implementation of the Treaty? Will most of the governments assume, "Well, the Treaty is in place" and behave so but obviously stick to the legal niceties of it, or will it in fact have quite a disruptive effect on European affairs in the next year or so? How many of the Maastricht teeth need to bite quickly as opposed to gradually evolving over the next five or six years?

(Mr Eaton) Mr Chairman, I think it would be very difficult to give some form of what amounts to a provisional application or a *de facto* application of much of the Maastricht Treaty because that part which involves amendments to the Treaty of Rome you cannot really do differently from the Treaty that you are bound by at the time because if you do it differently, then the Court will say, "You should not have done that". This is a Community of law, it is based upon a constitution and it has to operate on the constitution which is in force *pro tem*. There are other aspects of it, I would have thought the common foreign and security policy, co-operation on home affairs and justice, where you could effectively give what is in this agreement effect, yes, you could. You could move to stronger commitments to common policies and joint action and you could move to consulting one another on more matters of home affairs. It is really in the area of the Community treaties themselves where I think you are right, it is either there or it is not.

349. Can you identify any policy issues that really would cause strains and serious problems if, for example, this Treaty is not ratified by the end of 1993, and there is at least a 12 month delay?

(Mr Arthur) The one area where policy decisions are expected during this year which flow from Maastricht is the area we touched on at the beginning of this evidence, which is the *paquet* Delors II on the future financing decisions. We do not actually require the Maastricht Treaty to be in place in legal terms in order for the decisions to be taken. There are Treaty Articles on which such decisions could be taken, for example, the cohesion fund where it was agreed this would be established by the end of 1993 so you would expect a decision to be taken during this year for that. In other policy areas the Treaty of Rome would carry on as before and action would flow from that.

Chairman: Gentlemen, I think we must leave it there with the perennially difficult question for policy-makers which is, what happens if things do not turn out as planned? On that, we would like to thank you all very much for illuminating some aspects of what is a very big canvas indeed. Clearly, much more will need to be elucidated and much more understood before we get to the stage of ratifying or, indeed, approving new laws in this Parliament or in the next Parliament. In the meantime, thank you very much indeed for coming.

Printed in the United Kingdom for HMSO.
Dd.0507480, 3/92, C6, 3382/5B, 5673, 190393.

ISBN 0-10-291592-X

9 780102 915921

HMSO publications are available from:

HMSO Publications Centre
(Mail, fax and telephone orders only)
PO Box 276, London, SW8 5DT
Telephone orders 071-873 9090
General enquiries 071-873 0011
(queuing system in operation for both numbers)
Fax orders 071-873 8200

HMSO Bookshops
49 High Holborn, London, WC1V 6HB
071-873 0011 Fax 071-873 8200 (counter service only)
258 Broad Street, Birmingham, B1 2HE
021-643 3740 Fax 021-643 6510
Southey House, 33 Wine Street, Bristol, BS1 2BQ
0272 264306 Fax 0272 294515
9-21 Princess Street, Manchester, M60 8AS
061-834 7201 Fax 061-833 0634
16 Arthur Street, Belfast, BT1 4GD
0232 238451 Fax 0232 235401
71 Lothian Road, Edinburgh, EH3 9AZ
031-228 4181 Fax 031-229 2734

HMSO's Accredited Agents
(see Yellow Pages)

and through good booksellers

ISBN 0 10 291592 X